IMAGES
of America

CHATTOOGA COUNTY

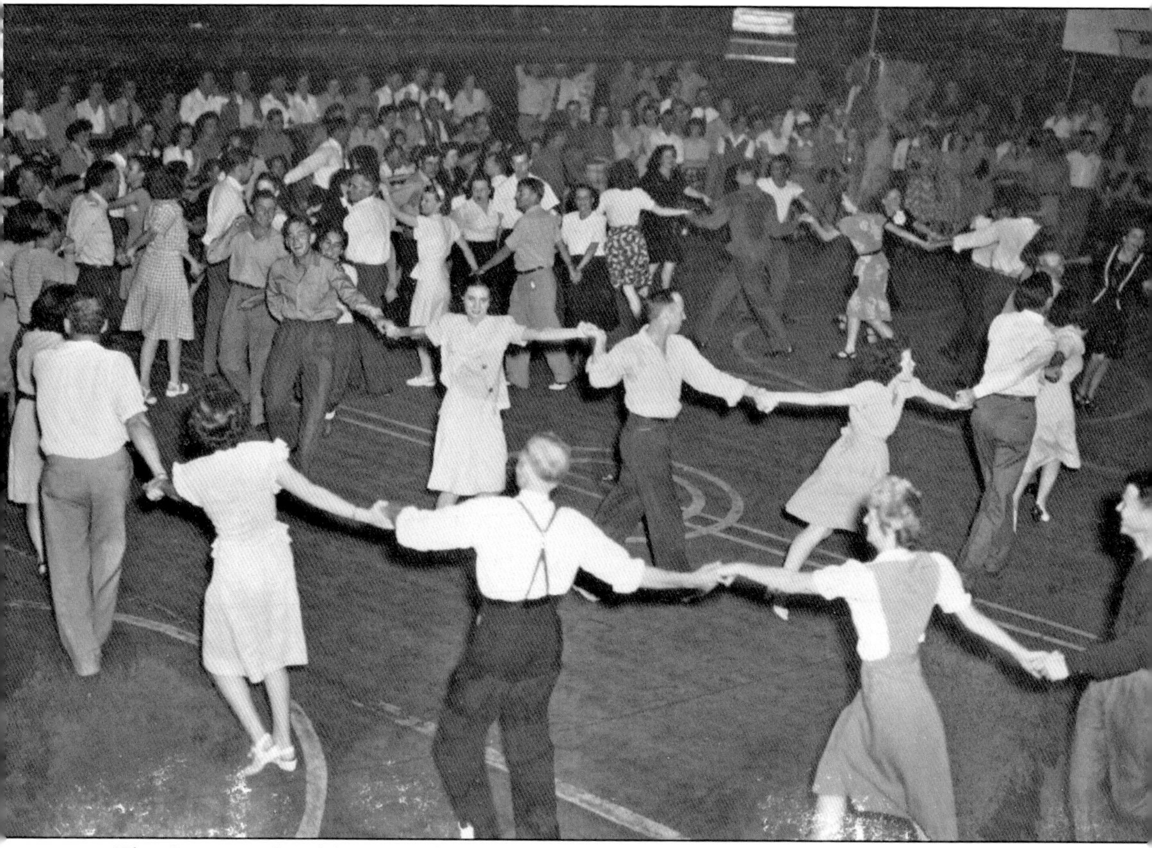

The Centennial Celebration of the Trion Company began on Saturday evening, September 29, 1945, with a barbecue supper, a fireworks display at the company golf course, and an old-fashioned square dance at the community gymnasium. This photograph shows the dancers celebrating their employer's longevity and perhaps the recent end of World War II. (Courtesy of Chattooga County Library.)

On the Cover: On Saturday, May 31, 1958, photographer Sheeny White climbed atop the Montgomery Knitting Mill building in Summerville and shot this image of the Rodeo Festival Days parade. Another of his photographs covering the event appeared in the *Summerville News* the following week. (Courtesy of the *Summerville News*.)

IMAGES
of America

CHATTOOGA COUNTY

Greg McCollum

ARCADIA
PUBLISHING

ISBN 978-0-7385-9164-3

Published by Arcadia Publishing
Charleston, South Carolina

Printed in the United States of America

Library of Congress Control Number: 2011941251

For all general information, please contact Arcadia Publishing:
Telephone 843-853-2070
Fax 843-853-0044
E-mail sales@arcadiapublishing.com
For customer service and orders:
Toll-Free 1-888-313-2665

Visit us on the Internet at www.arcadiapublishing.com

This book is dedicated to the memory of my parents,
Harvey and Hazel McCollum, who moved to Chattooga County
and made their dreams come true.

Contents

ACKNOWLEDGMENTS

This book presents photographs from dozens of contributors, too many to list here individually but credited at the end of each photograph's caption. They allowed me to take their cherished photographs to copy and trusted me to return them unblemished.

Brenda and Mike Lanier spent many hours with me in the Georgia Room of the Chattooga County Library reviewing images and suggesting contacts for others. Librarian Susan Stephens and her staff were always willing to help locate an article, book, or photograph. Gene McGinnis was an early and enthusiastic supporter and contributed many photographs and suggestions.

Nobody knows more about Chattooga County's history than Steve Strickland, who was kind enough to review an early draft and made many helpful suggestions. Gene Espy, editor of the *Summerville News*, contributed several priceless images in addition to publicizing the book in his newspaper. Susan and Mike King knew how to contact just about anyone in Chattooga County and were my "detectives on the case."

Jennifer Cox at Mount Vernon Mills granted me access to the company's photographs. Many members of the Chattooga County Historical Society were ardent supporters and contributed images.

A click of the shutter goes posthumously to T. Emmett Nunn and Earl McConnell, two of the area's most prolific photographers. Much of the county's visual history exists because of their work.

Writing captions for many of this book's images would have been impossible without two important sources: Robert S. Baker's *Chattooga: The Story of a County and Its People*, considered to be the definitive history of the area; and *The Heritage of Chattooga County*, a voluminous collection of local family histories.

And finally, I want to thank my wife, Barbara, forever a Menlo girl at heart, who tolerated my many hours away from home and hearth while searching for photographs for this book.

INTRODUCTION

Chattooga County is located in northwest Georgia and shares its western boundary with Alabama. Walker and Floyd Counties are adjacent to the north and south, respectively. The original settlers were members of the Creek Confederacy, one of several Indian tribes living in the southeastern United States. In the 1700s, the Creeks were pushed southward by Cherokees from Tennessee reacting to a wave of settlers moving into their own territory.

By the early 1800s, six Cherokee settlements were inside the future boundary of Chattooga County, and some became the current cities and towns. However, pressure by Georgia to disenfranchise all Native Americans in the area became law in 1828. In 1830, Congress passed the Indian Removal Act, giving legal authority to remove the Cherokee, and two years later, the Georgia Land Lottery gave much of the Cherokee land to whites.

Before 1838, people living in what would become Chattooga County had to travel to LaFayette or Rome, the seats of Walker and Floyd Counties respectively, to file deeds, pay taxes, serve on a jury, or carry out any number of tasks associated with land ownership or citizenship. Due to poor road conditions, going to these towns to conduct business was an arduous task, so in 1838, the Georgia legislature created Chattooga County from the southern part of Walker County and the northern part of Floyd County. The county was named after the river that flowed through it, a name originally derived from several Cherokee settlements scattered about the region.

Two of the Georgia Land Lottery winners were relatives of John Fluker Beavers. In 1834, Beavers and his family moved to what was then part of southern Walker County. The legislation creating Chattooga County also gave legal authority to purchase land, divide it into lots, and sell the lots to raise money for a county courthouse and jail. In 1839, the county purchased 90 acres from John Beavers on which to locate the new county seat, Summerville. The property had one key characteristic: a spring producing enough water to meet the needs of the town for years to come. Robert Baker notes in his book *Chattooga: The Story of a County and Its People* that the county seat was originally named Selma according to federal Post Office Department records.

In 1845, a cotton mill was organized on the site of a former Cherokee village called Island Town located along the Chattooga River. The three mill owners, Judge Spencer Marsh, A.P. Allgood, and Col. W.K. Briers, chose to call the location Trion. Their first mill was a small two-story structure that manufactured yarn to be sold locally. By 1850, the operation had 10 looms and 45 workers.

In 1861, delegates from all across Georgia gathered at the state capitol in Milledgeville to vote on secession from the Union. Chattooga County was an area of small farms and few slaves, and its representatives to the convention—Wesley Shropshire and Lowry Williams—voted the will of their constituents by opposing secession. Despite their votes, the majority of state delegates voted in favor of an ordinance of secession.

During the Civil War, the Trion Factory supplied the Confederacy with woolen cloth. The factory managed to escape destruction by Union soldiers, especially the 100,000 Union troops under the command of Gen. William Tecumseh Sherman who pursued Confederate general John Bell Hood and his 30,000 soldiers through Chattooga County. Despite the enormity of the forces, the two armies made no significant contact.

After the war and Reconstruction, the county soon faced another invading force, this time bellowing steam. In 1888, the first railroad into the county was completed and made its inaugural run. This new transportation made shipment of more goods to and from the area possible, resulting, for example, in an expansion of Trion Mill. By 1898, the mill had switched to electricity for its power and had over 600 workers on its payroll.

About the same time, the Raccoon Manufacturing Company was established in what would later be called Berryton. It went through bankruptcy and was reorganized in 1910 as the Berryton Mills with a workforce of over 200. The Summerville Cotton Mill began production in 1907 and became a major employer for decades. Montgomery Knitting Mill opened in 1927, expanding over the years to include 300 workers.

During World War II, the Trion Mill was manufacturing over a million yards of cloth a week to be used for Army uniforms, tents, and other needs. After the war ended, new industry, schools, churches, stores, houses, and civic buildings began appearing. New industries like Georgia Rug Mill and Best Manufacturing Company began operations in the county.

In recent years, Chattooga County has suffered along with the rest of the nation through an economic malaise. Local industry has been impacted by trade agreements and a national trend of outsourcing manufacturing jobs to foreign factories.

The 2010 census recorded 26,015 inhabitants, an increase of 6,121 in 50 years. With about 5,000 people, Summerville continues to be the largest city in the county, while Trion, with around 2,000 inhabitants, remains the second-largest incorporated community. The towns of Lyerly and Menlo each have about 500 people. A quick calculation shows that the majority of people living in the county live outside of its incorporated areas. Chattooga County still maintains its rural character, and many of its citizens work at least part-time in farming and agriculture. The county's slow growth and rural lifestyle appeal to many newcomers who have moved from more populated areas just to "get away from it all."

In Images of America: *Chattooga County*, the author has gathered over 200 photographs from more than 60 sources documenting the people, places, buildings, homes, churches, and schools throughout the county over the past 100 years. Many more photographs were digitally copied than space allows for display in this book, but more images may be viewed at the Chattooga Photo History website, www.chattoogaphotohistory.com. The author regrets the exclusion of some contributors' images in this volume due to space limitations and hopes to include everyone's photographs on the website at some point.

One

People and Places

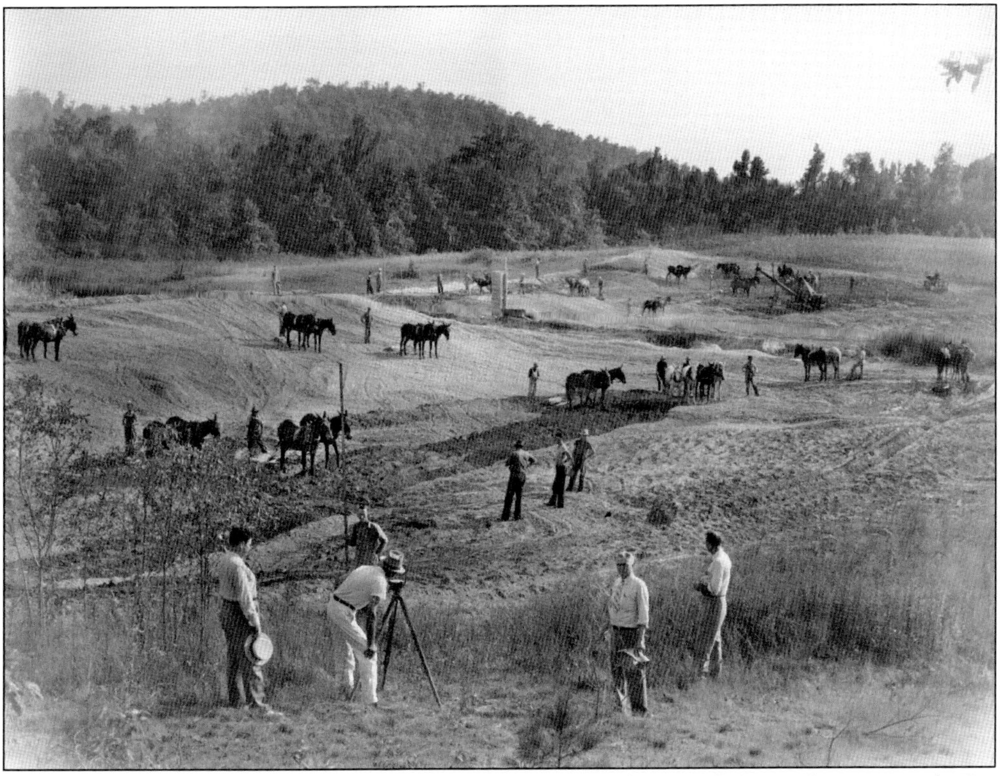

Dr. William B. Hair (second from right, facing camera) used over a dozen mule teams to dredge what would become Hair Lake in 1939. Originally built for Dr. Hair's cattle, the 17-acre lake became a popular swimming place with two diving boards and separate bathhouses for men and women. Admission was 15¢, and there was always a crowd on summer weekends. (Courtesy of Will and Judy Hair.)

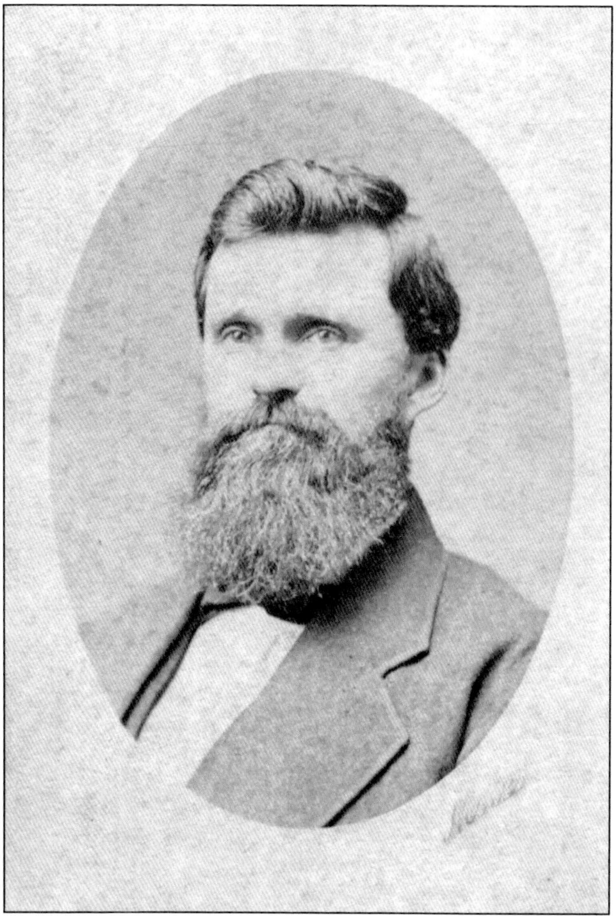

William Ham Penn was born in 1839 on his father's 2,700-acre farm, Penn Place, south of Trion. In 1846, his grandfather William Penn sold the land on which Trion Factory was founded. The farm and the community to the south are known to this day as Pennville. (Courtesy of Bill and Pat Selman.)

The town of Menlo owes much of its early existence to a railway that bypassed its more populous neighbor to the south, the Alpine community. The Menlo Baptist Church is visible in the middle background in this c. 1900 photograph. (Courtesy of Gene McGinnis.)

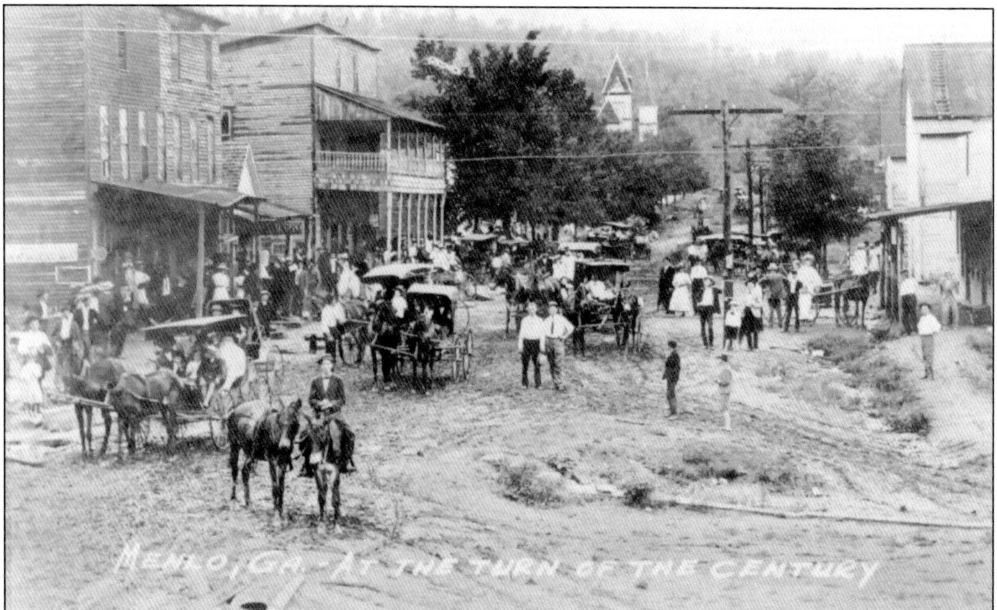

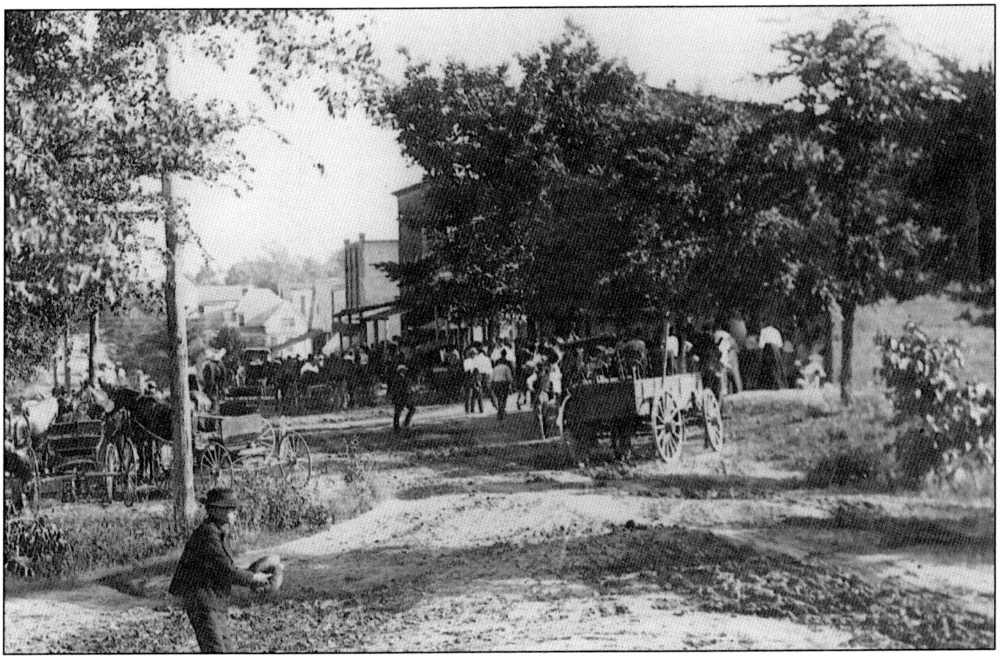

The first train rode through Menlo in 1891. By the time this photograph was taken, Menlo was a thriving little town with a post office, churches, stores, a livery stable, a fruit-packing company, and several sawmills. In 1913, Menlo could boast of having more than 400 residents. (Courtesy of Gene McGinnis.)

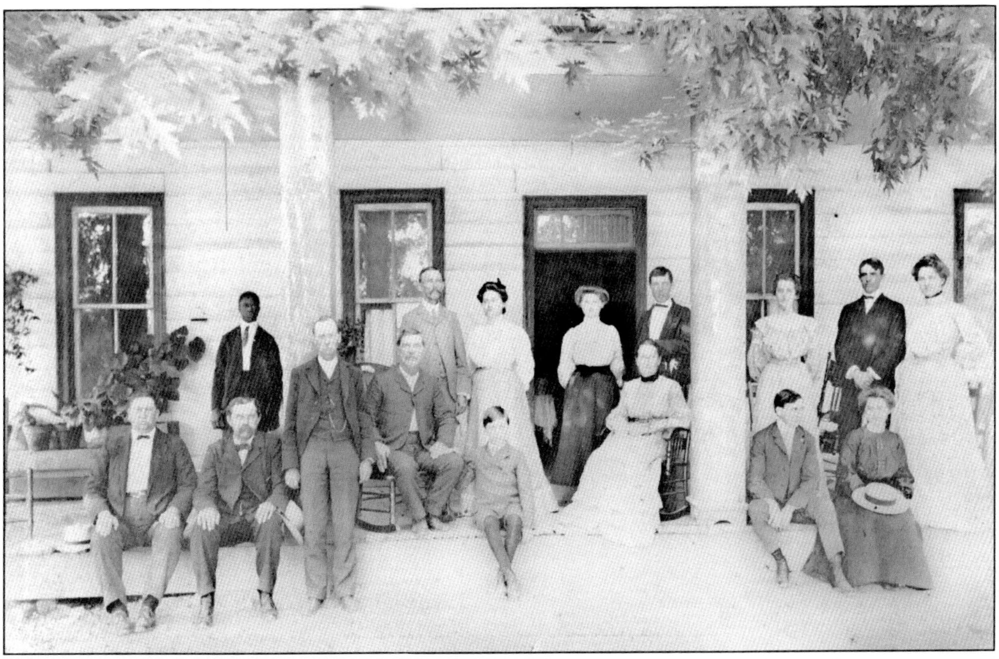

In 1901, Mr. and Mrs. Henry Clay Gilbert leased a hotel that stood on the southwest corner of Washington and Union Streets in Summerville. The building, considered by some to be the first hotel in the county, was destroyed by fire in 1912. This photograph shows the couple standing in the middle, surrounded by family and staff. (Courtesy of Joe and Jan Pullen.)

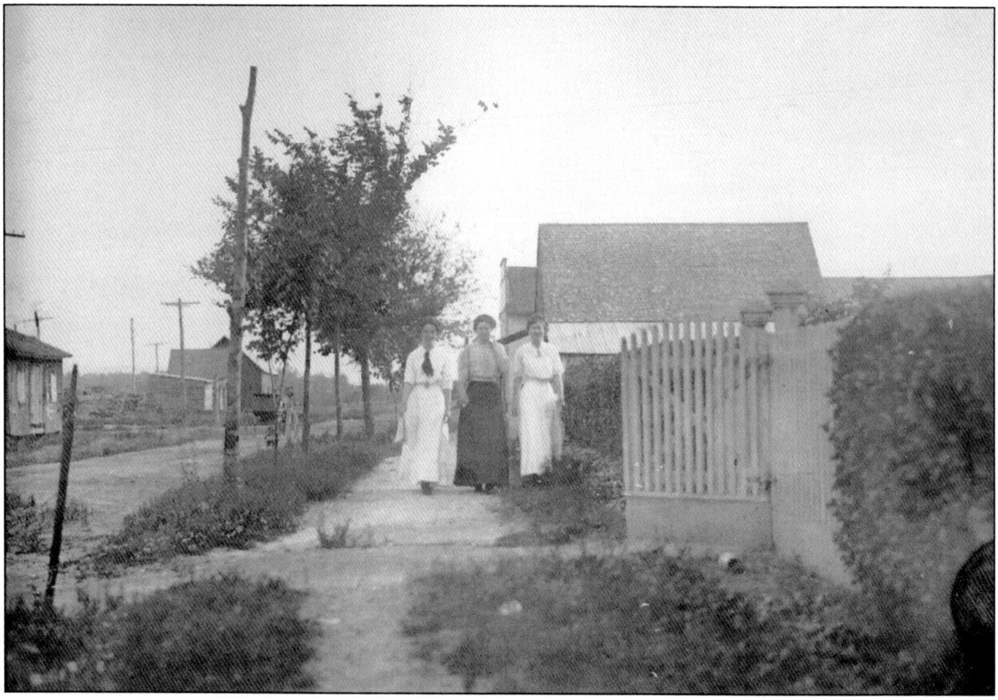

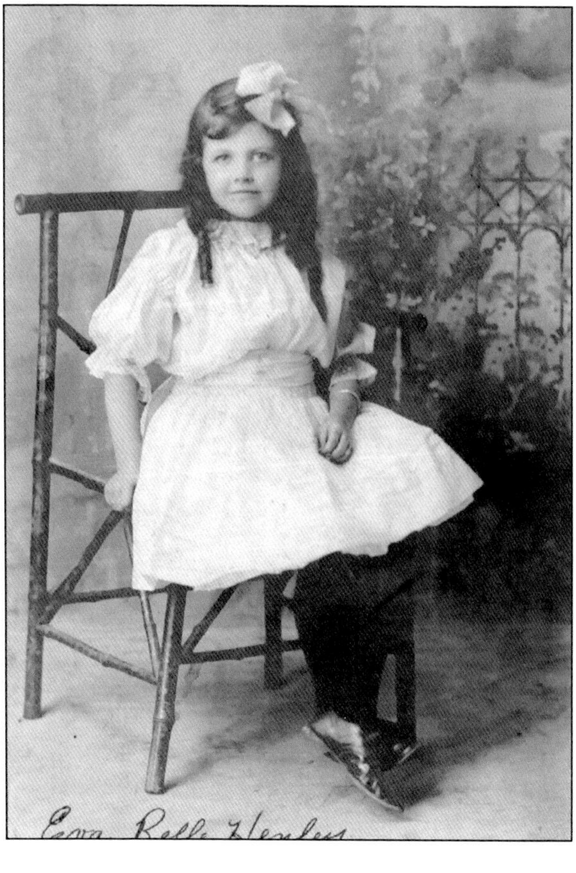

Three ladies strolling along the Lyerly sidewalk are visible in this c. 1905 photograph. On the left is Annie Belle Lee, born in 1878 to the affluent Lee family of Lyerly. She married Winfield Desota Martin in 1901, and they became parents of eight children. (Courtesy of Nena Martin Colbert.)

Eva Belle Henley was born in 1901, the daughter of David P. Henley Sr. and his wife, the former Venice Clemmons. In 1909, Eva Belle moved with her parents into a new house, which still stands on East Washington Street in Summerville. The Henley farm once extended from the family home all the way to the Chattooga River. (Courtesy of Norris Gamble.)

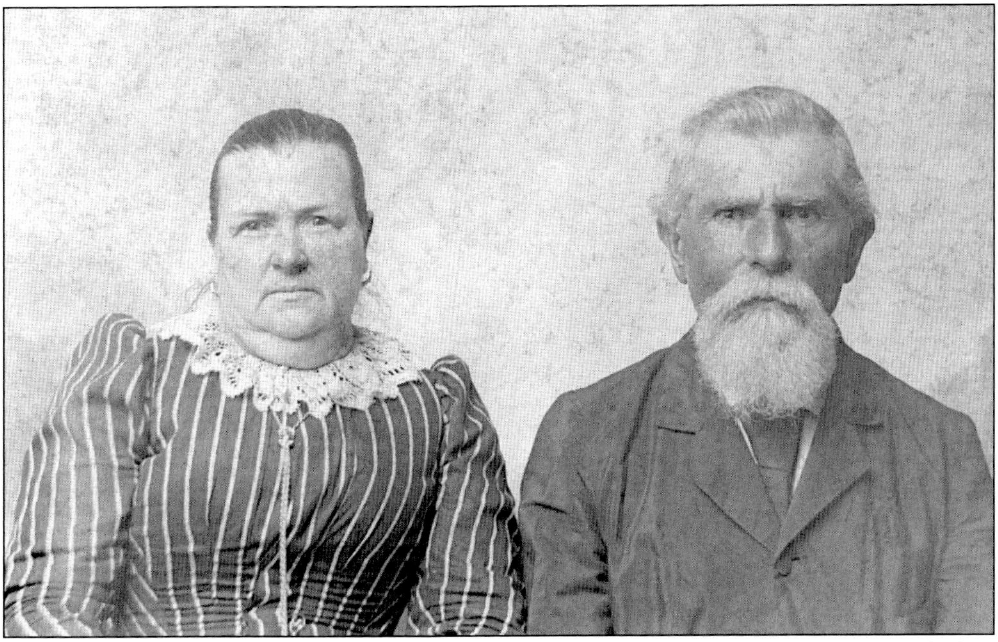

William Harvey Strain is pictured with his second wife, the former Nannie Malinda Burkhalter, in a photograph made in 1890. Strain was born in 1841 and served four years in the Civil War. Strain's first wife was Sarah Fluker Beavers, who died eight years earlier. (Courtesy of Nancy Smith McDaniel.)

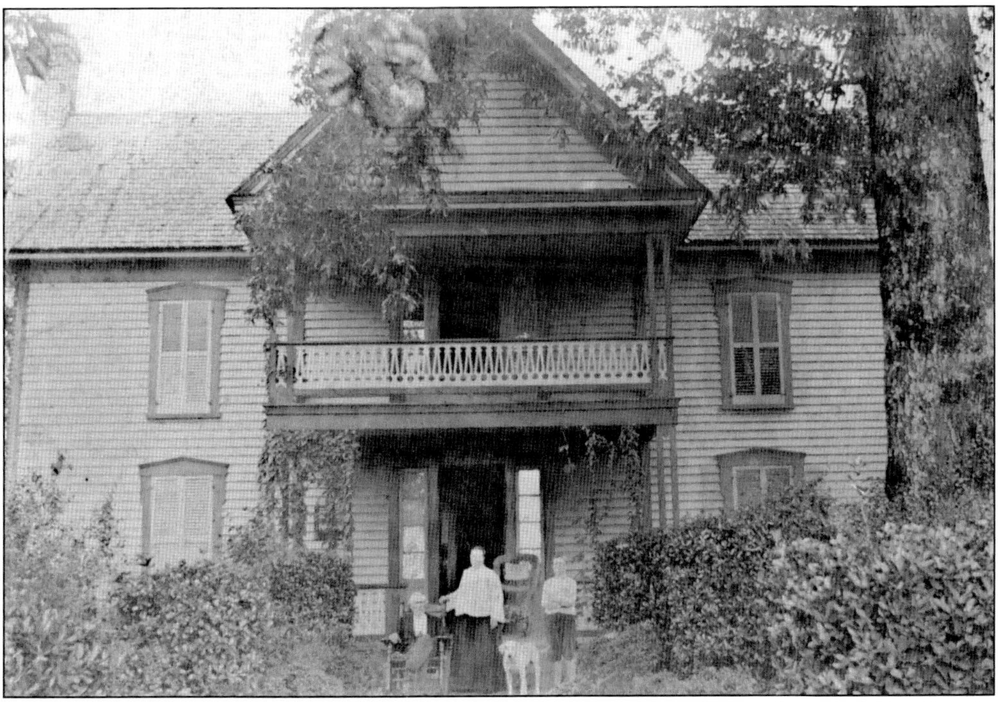

In this 1910 photograph, William and Nannie Strain are pictured at their home north of Lyerly with grandson Charles Dover. This house is now owned by Larry Weesner. (Courtesy of Nancy Smith McDaniel.)

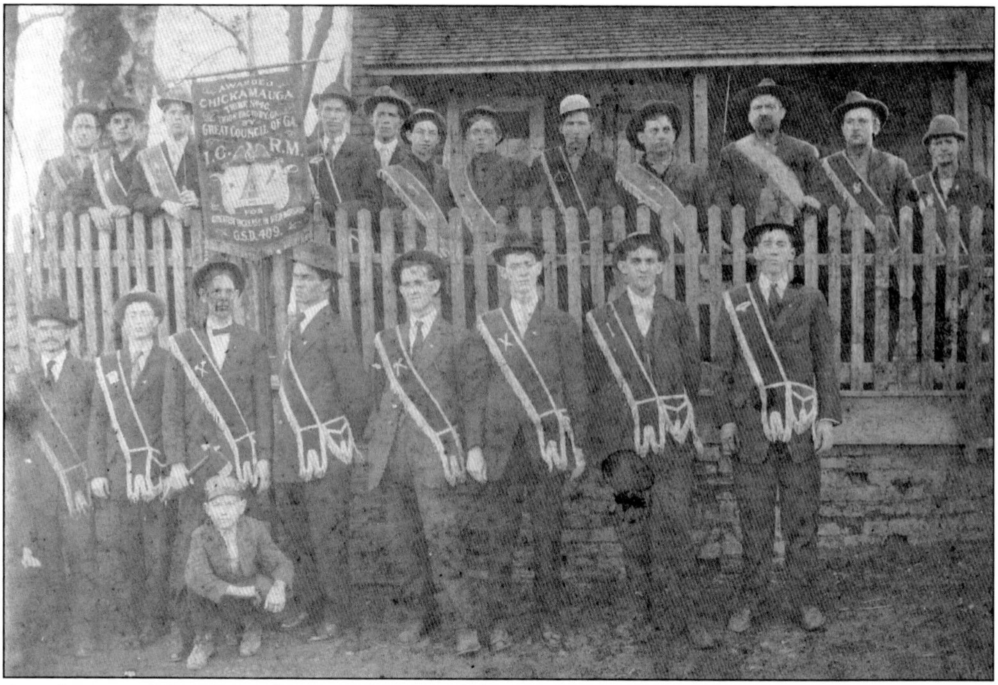

A gathering of the Haymakers, a subgroup of the Improved Order of Red Men, one of the oldest fraternal organizations in the United States, is shown in a photograph made around 1910. The banner reads, "Awarded Chickamauga Tribe No. 40, Trion Factory, Ga., by the Great Council of Ga. For Greatest Increase in Membership." Photographer Emmanuel Griffitt is second from left in front. (Courtesy of Darlene Norton Mallonee.)

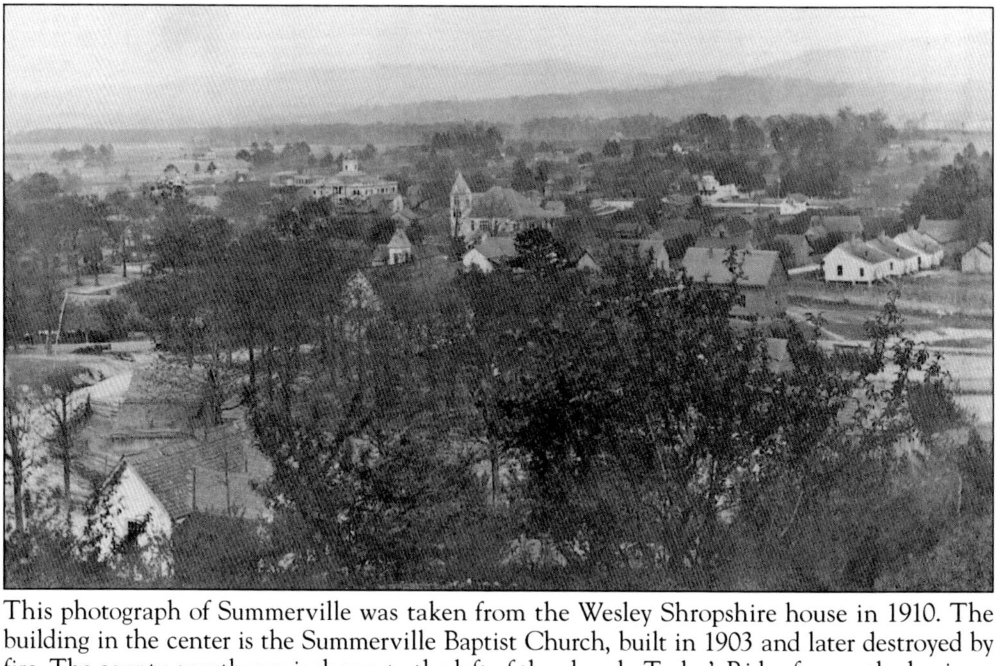

This photograph of Summerville was taken from the Wesley Shropshire house in 1910. The building in the center is the Summerville Baptist Church, built in 1903 and later destroyed by fire. The county courthouse is shown to the left of the church. Taylor's Ridge frames the horizon. (Courtesy of Gene McGinnis.)

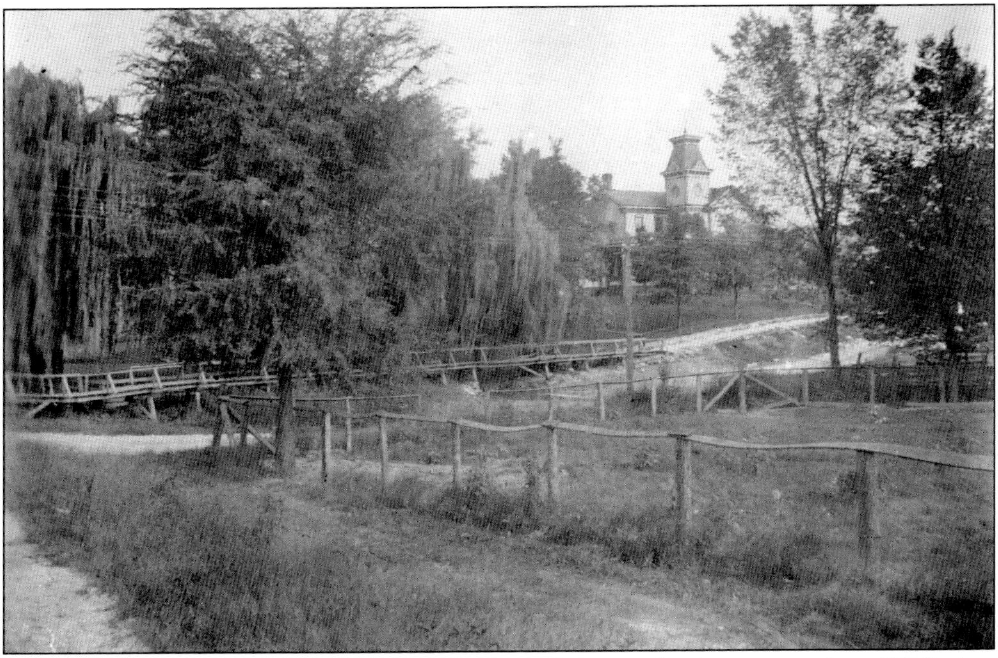

In 1883, John Storey Cleghorn built a large house in Summerville that sat just above Big Spring, later called Willow Springs by the family and Cleghorn's Spring by the community. Cleghorn and his wife planted trees along the footbridge that crossed the spring. In 1961, the property was sold by his heirs. The next year, the house was destroyed by fire. (Courtesy of Gene McGinnis.)

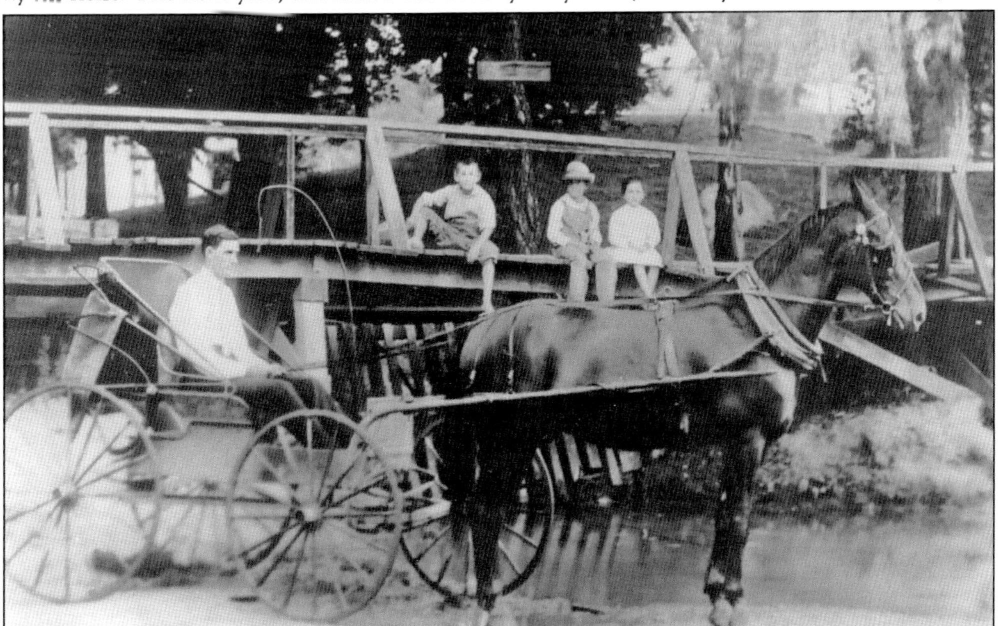

Big Spring was located at what is now the intersection of Commerce Street and First Avenue in Summerville. It was considered a favorite place for young couples to court. When this photograph was made, there was only a footbridge; wagons and buggies forded the creek. Frank Echols sits in the buggy. (Courtesy of Gene McGinnis.)

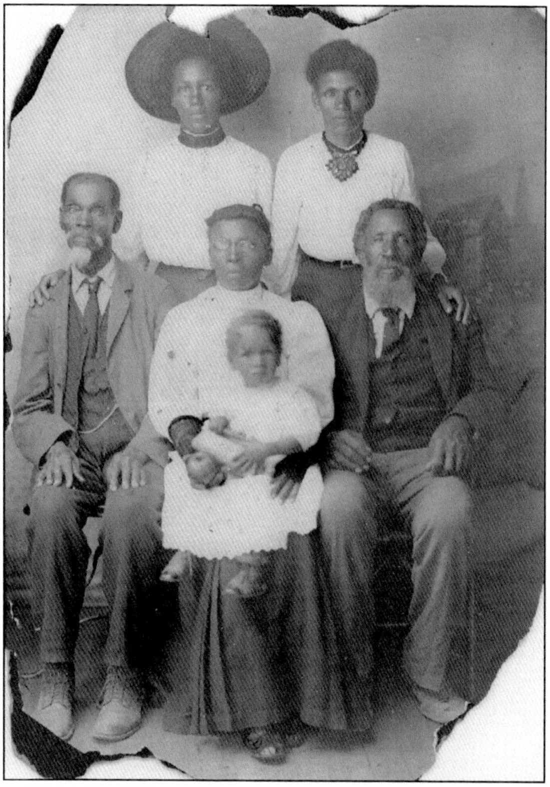

Augustus Finley (seated left) was born a slave in Chattoogaville. As a young man, he bought his future wife, Mary, from his master. In this 1906 photograph, he sits next to his daughter Elizabeth (or Betsy) and her husband, John Ware. The Wares' son Alton Powell is seated on his mother's lap. Standing in back are Finley's other children, Mary Thompson Moore and Margaret Thompson. (Courtesy of Clemmie Adams Black.)

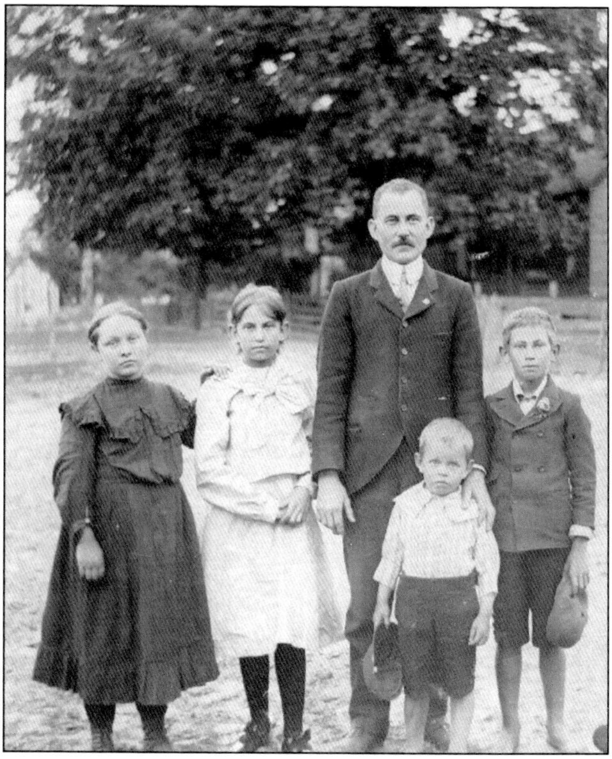

The Anson Griffitt family includes, from left to right, Minnie Ethel, Mary Alice, father William Anson, John Lester, and (in front) William Henry. In 1913, Anson's father, William Emmanuel Griffitt, became one of the first photographers in Trion following a back injury at the mill. (Courtesy of Darlene Norton Mallonee.)

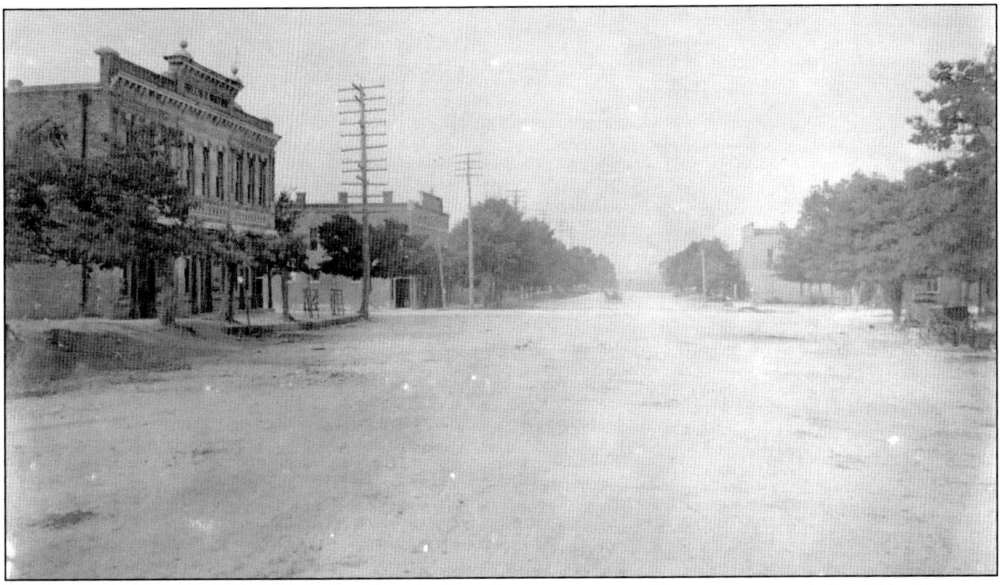

The building on the left was located at the northeast corner of Commerce and East Washington Streets in Summerville and housed Hollis & Hinton, "dealers in staple and fancy dry goods, dress goods, notions, boots and shoes, groceries, hardware, etc., etc." The store became Taylor Mercantile Company around 1919 and added a funeral parlor to its growing list of goods and services. (Courtesy of Gene McGinnis.)

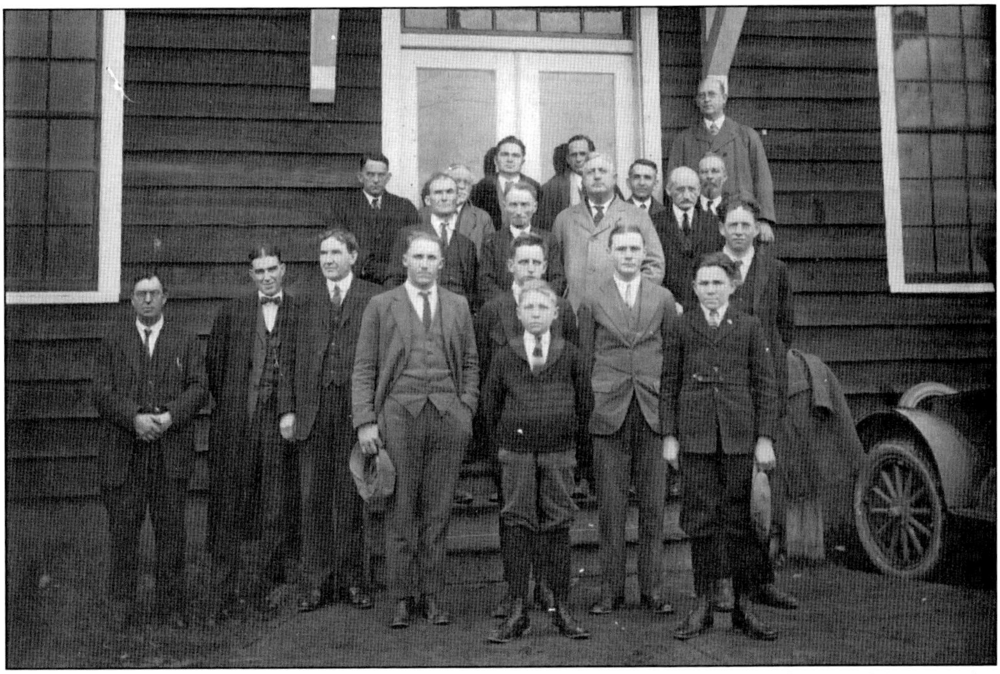

The short-lived Summerville Civitan Club started in 1923 and met at the YMCA near the Summerville Cotton Mill. Some of the members included James McGinnis (third from left on ground); Middleton Miles Allen, Dr. Oscar A. Selman, unidentified, and John D. Taylor Sr. (the first row on the steps, from left to right); Dr. William B. Hair (behind Selman); and Baker Farrar (top right). (Courtesy of Gene McGinnis.)

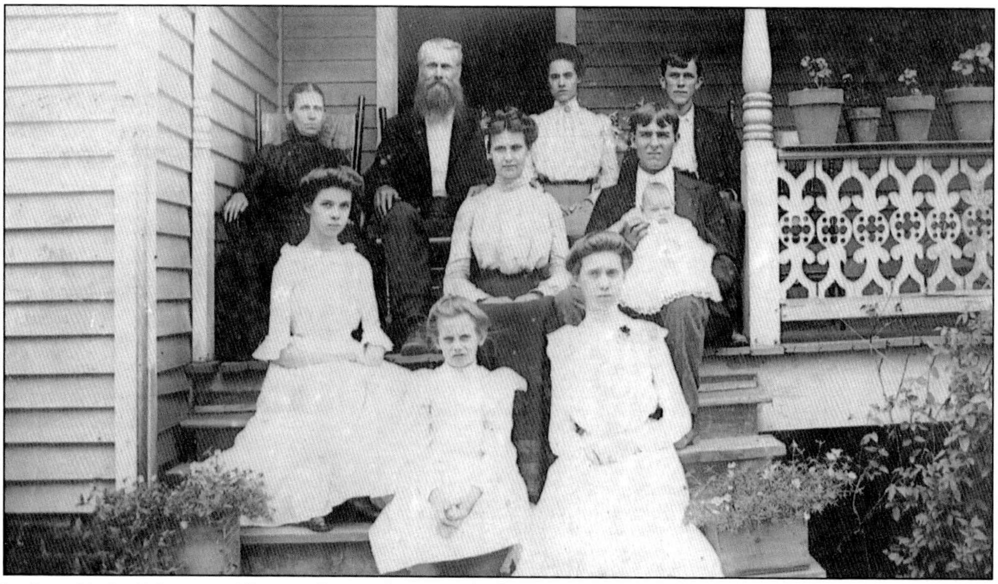

Joshua Parks Johnston II served as ordinary of Chattooga County for 28 years. This photograph, taken on the steps of the Johnston home in Summerville around 1920, includes, from left to right, (first row) daughters Georgia and Jennie; (second row) daughters Frances Majors and Alice Orr and son-in-law Charles Orr holding a grandson; (third row) wife Emline, J.P. Johnston II, daughter Maggie Thomason, and her husband, Clark. (Courtesy of Jeanette Parham.)

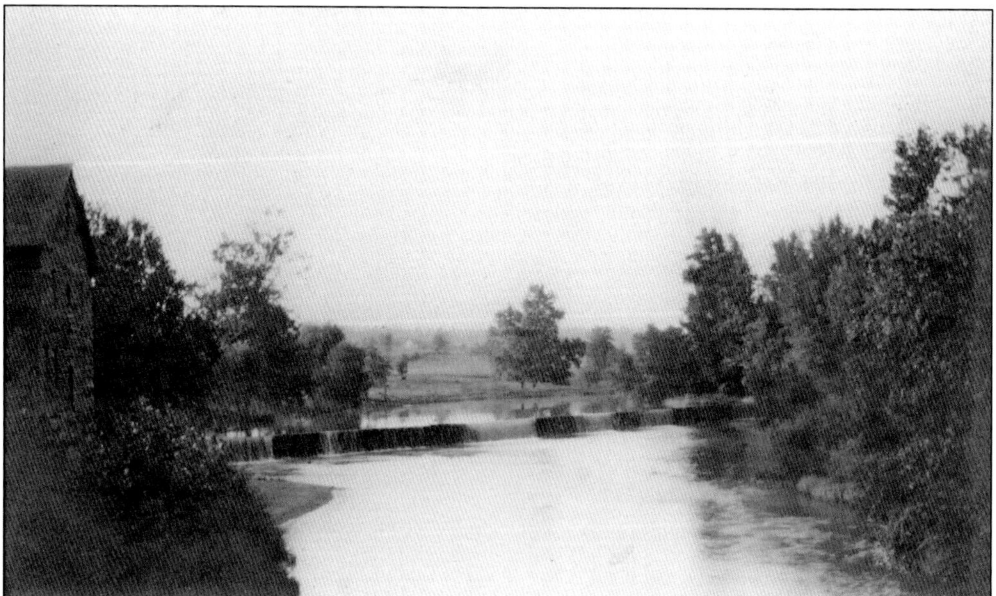

John S. Owings was born in Mississippi in 1871 but later moved to Lyerly, where he built a hydroelectric plant on the Chattooga River. In 1920, Owings donated 12 streetlights to the city of Lyerly and provided electric power for their use. (Courtesy of Nena Martin Colbert.)

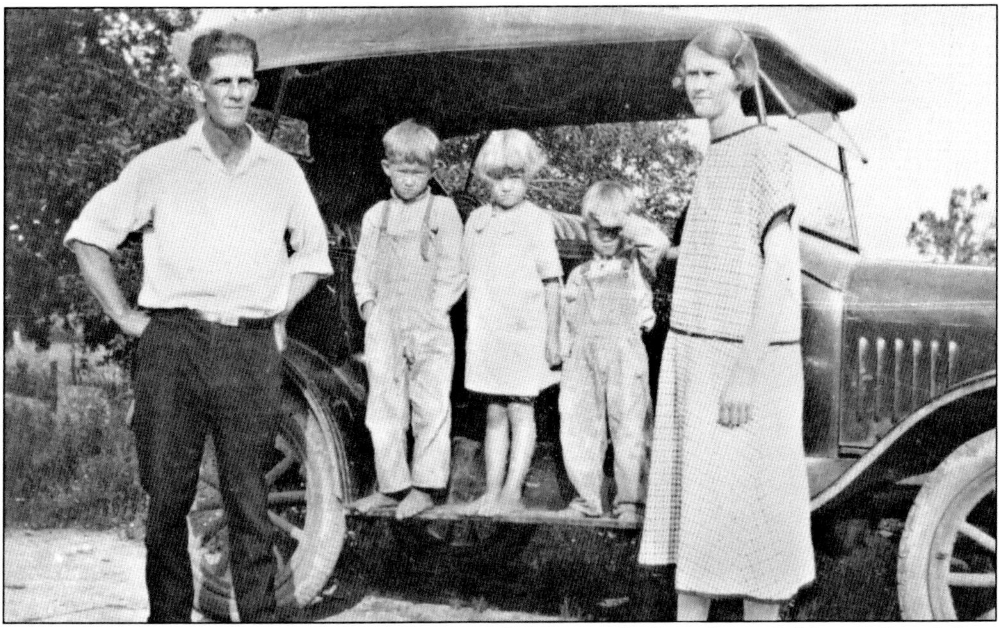

Tim Pickle and his wife, the former Emma Brady, pose with their three children—from left to right, Wilburn, Maurene, and Harold—in a photograph made in early 1926 near Oak Hill. Twin daughters Haynie and Waynie were born to the couple later that year. (Courtesy of Waynie Pickle Edge.)

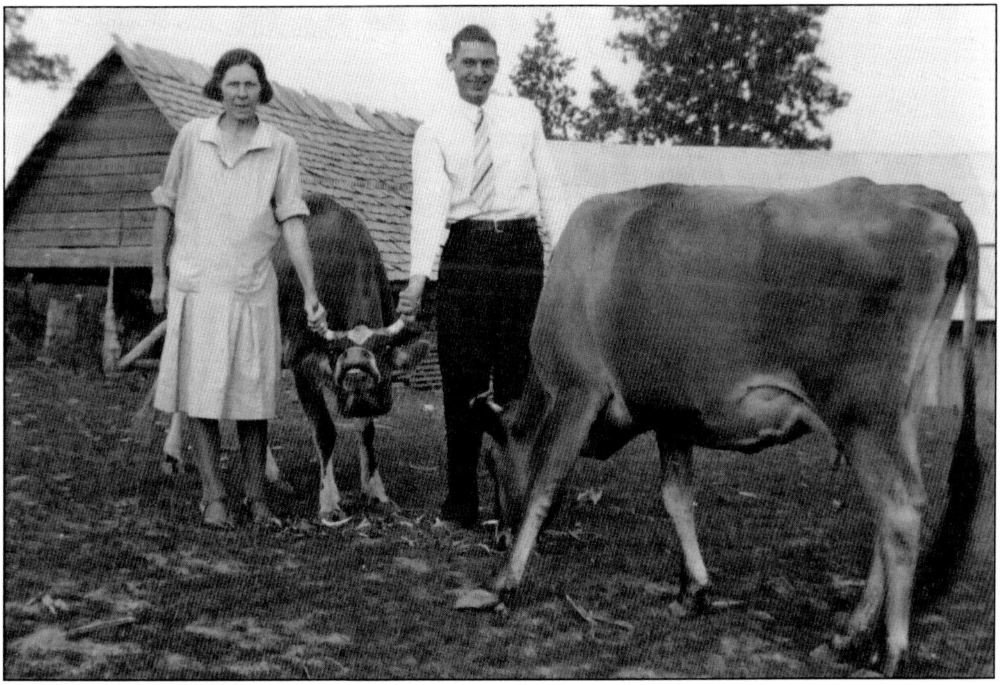

Bessie White Rosser and her son Ballenger Wright Rosser are pictured at the family farm on Little Sand Mountain in this photograph taken around 1930. The son was named for the two doctors who helped deliver him in 1910. During a trip out west at the age of 30, Ballenger Wright Rosser was killed by a train. (Courtesy of Ben T. Bridges.)

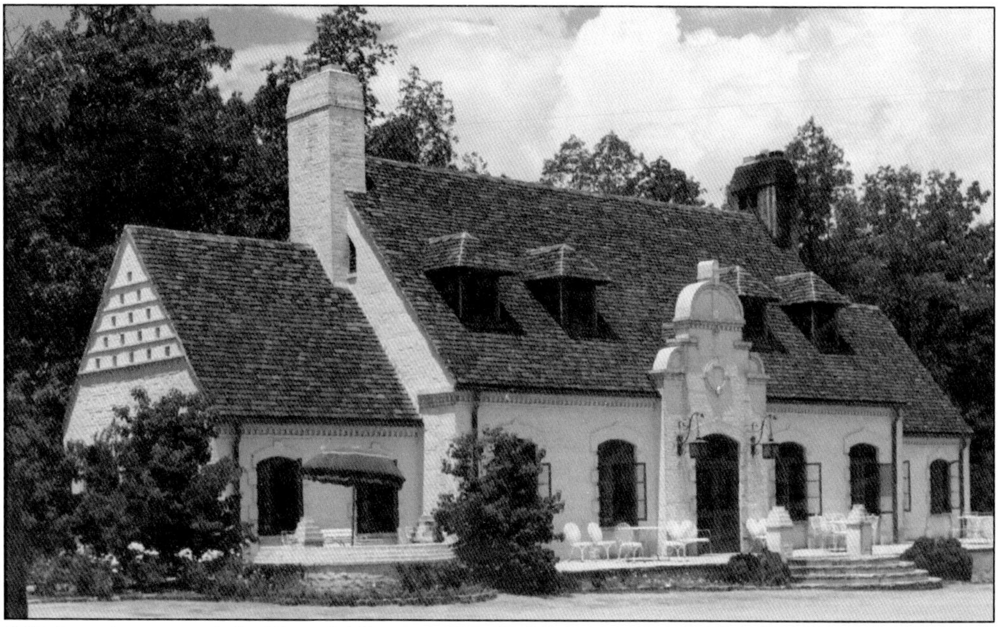

B.D. Riegel, owner of the Trion Mill, wanted to build a restaurant and store across the road from his dairy to sell milk products to tourists on US Highway 27. The architect's plans were given to L.C. "Sadd" Dalton, the mill construction engineer, with orders to finish it in six weeks. Working night and day, a crew completed the Riegeldale Tavern in the summer of 1936. (Courtesy of Mount Vernon Mills.)

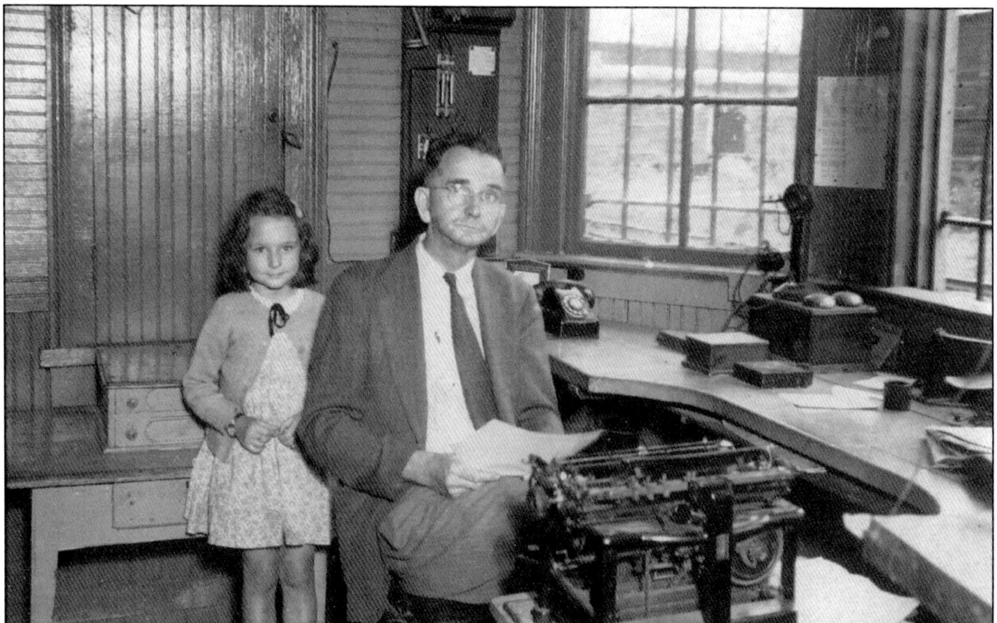

For many years, Horace L. Abrams was the depot agent for the Central of Georgia Railway in Lyerly. He is pictured with his daughter Martha Katherine in a photograph taken around 1942. Rail service began in the 1880s in Chattooga County. Regularly scheduled passenger service was discontinued in 1950. (Courtesy of Brenda Hogg Lanier.)

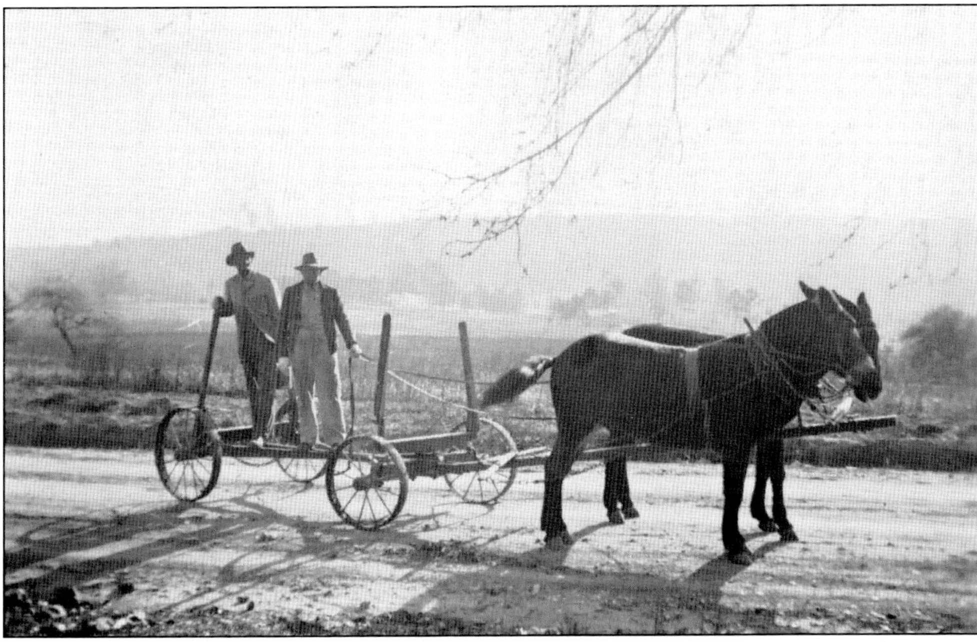

Mack Hogg (left) and Basil Lewis are on their way to haul hay at Hogg's farm near Berryton in this 1944 photograph. The mules are named Zigg and Sam. (Courtesy of Brenda Hogg Lanier.)

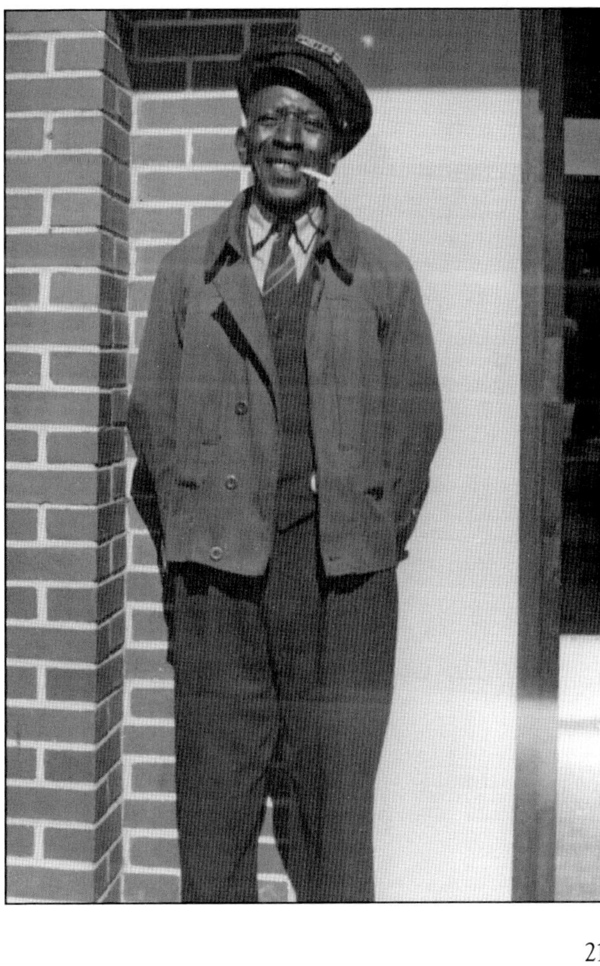

Eddie Brown moved to Trion around 1930 and was a beloved presence in the community for many years. During World War II, however, he was considered by many Trion residents to be the scariest man alive. Brown rode a bicycle delivering telegrams, and anyone who saw him approaching a house knew it could be devastating news. He died in 1958. (Courtesy of Charles Logan.)

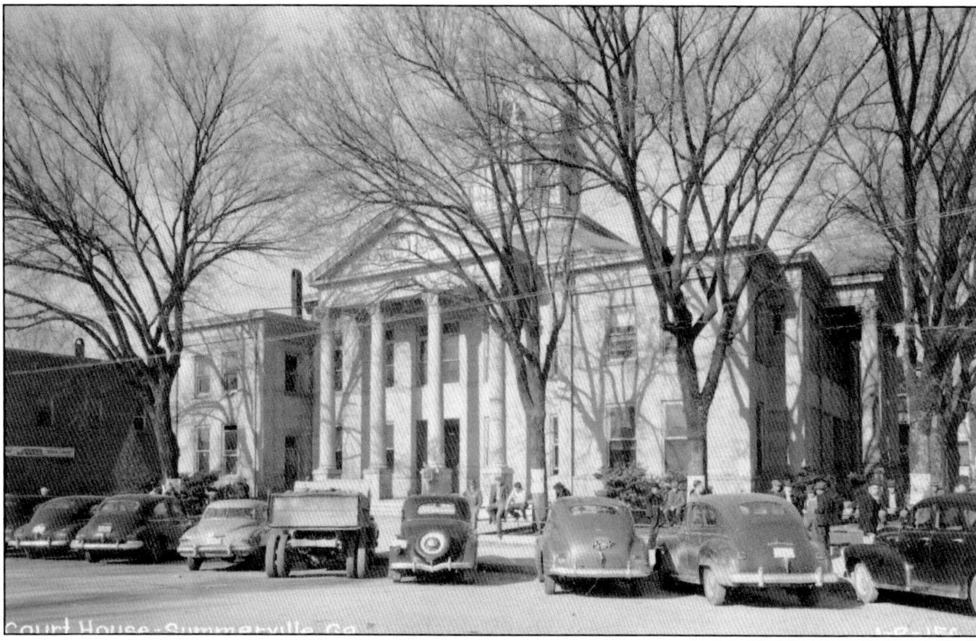

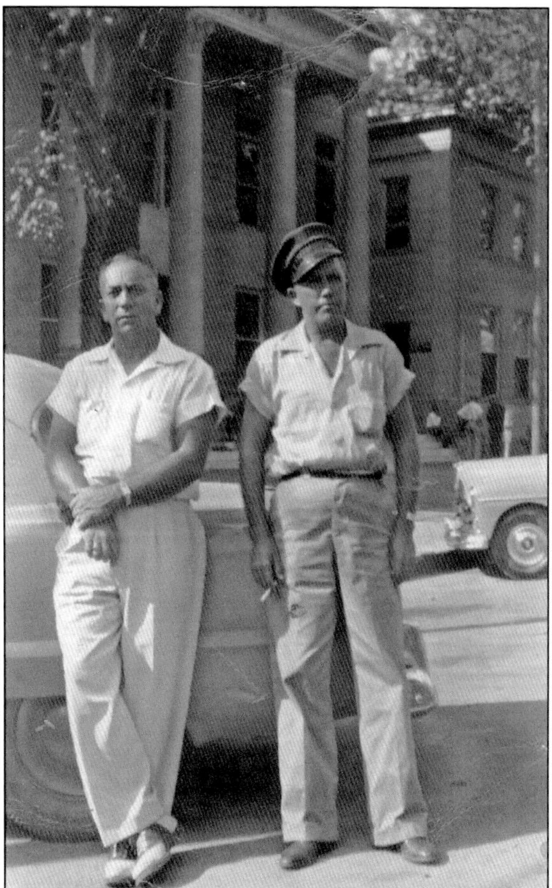

The Chattooga County Courthouse is shown in this photograph from the early 1950s. It was built in 1909 of concrete and modeled on an earlier one built in Appling County. In addition to a hall of justice, the courthouse for many years served as a community center, hosting county fairs, cakewalks, beauty contests, revivals, and singings. (Courtesy of Darlene Norton Mallonee.)

Will Stephenson (left) and Frank Hamby are shown standing in front of the courthouse in a photograph made in the 1950s. Stephenson was a well-known Summerville businessman and civic volunteer. In 1960, he managed the Summerville Little League All-Stars. (Courtesy of Darlene Norton Mallonee.)

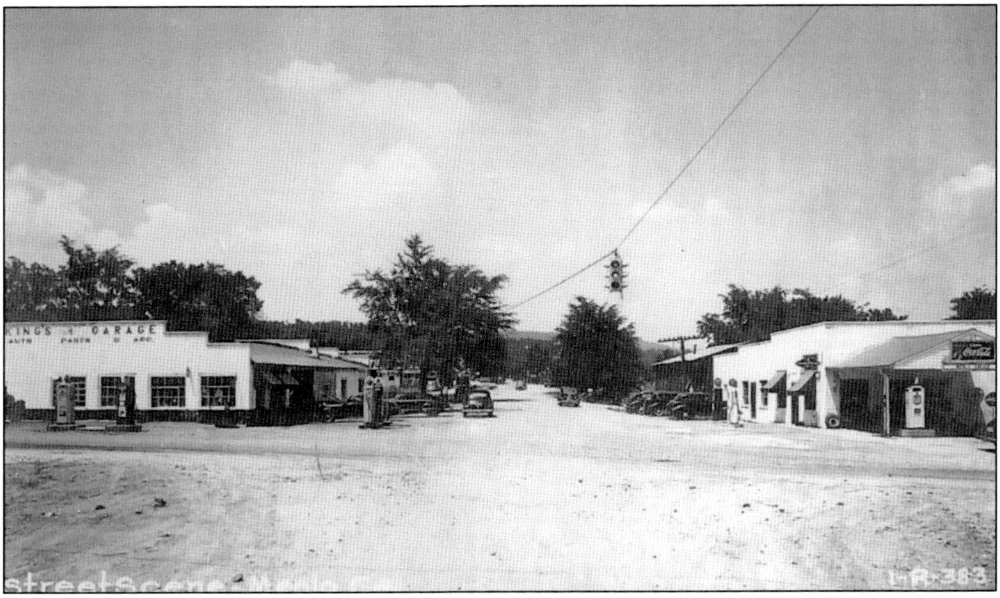

Menlo is shown in a c. 1950 view looking north across Highway 48. Best Manufacturing Company would soon add a large presence to the little town. (Courtesy of Menlo City Hall.)

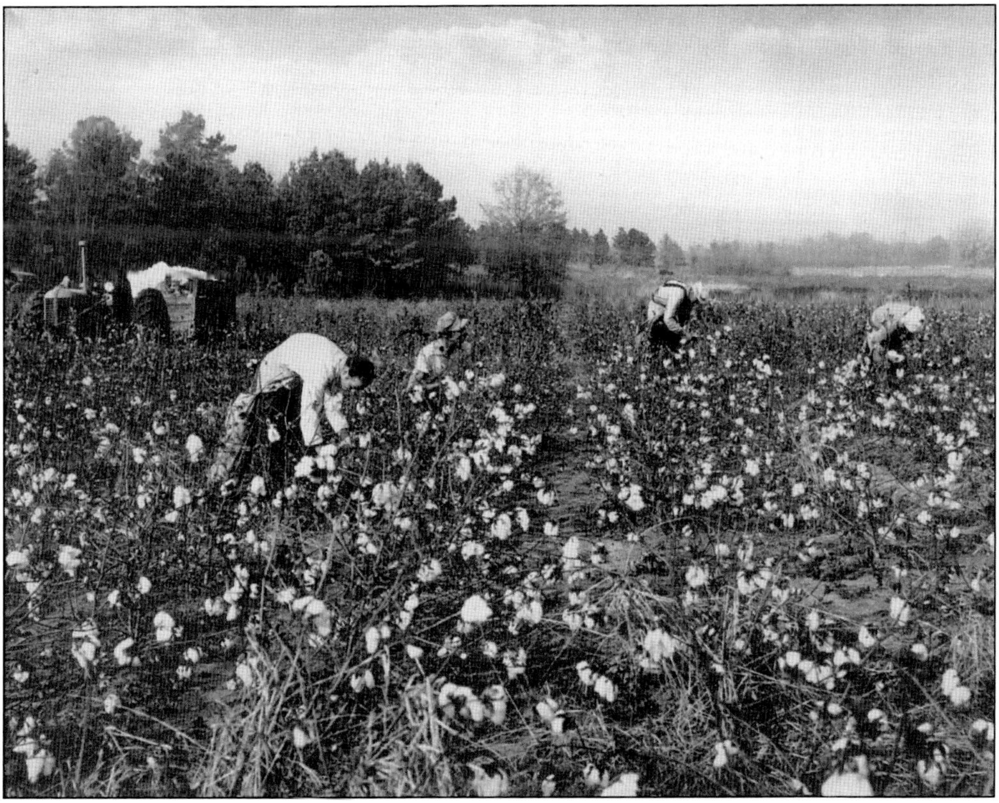

The backbreaking work of picking cotton was an annual ritual for farmers and their families. This 1952 photograph shows, from left to right, Martha Jo Chisolm, Buddy Chisolm, Carl Chisolm, and unidentified. (Courtesy of Bobby Chisolm.)

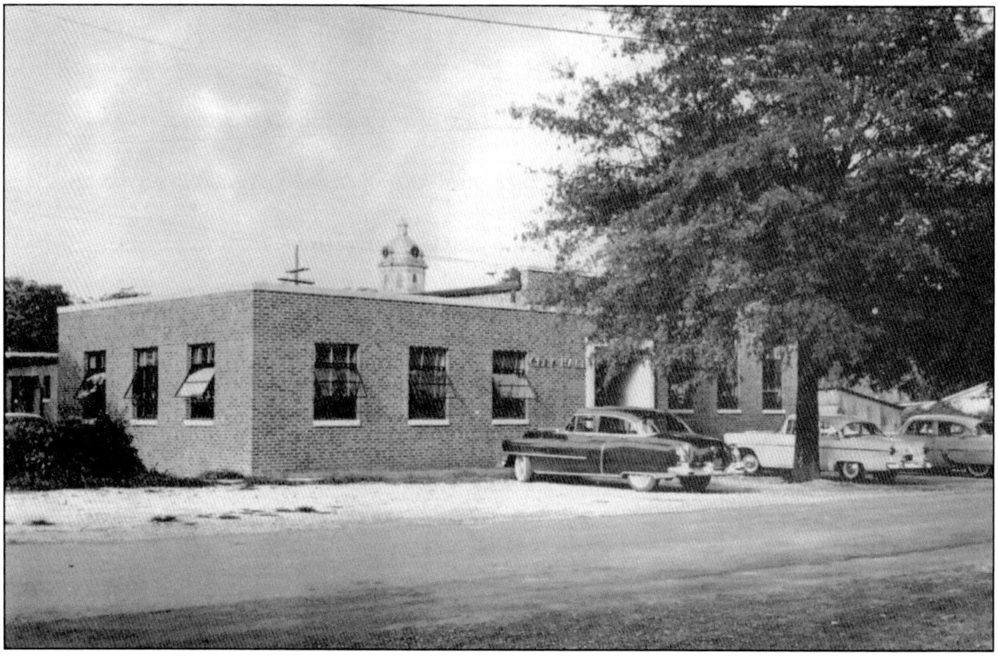

In 1955, the City of Summerville erected a new $75,000 city hall at the corner of Georgia Avenue and Cox Street. The building housed all municipal operations, the city engineer's office, and the library. At the time, Summerville had a population of 4,700. (Courtesy of Chattooga County Chamber of Commerce.)

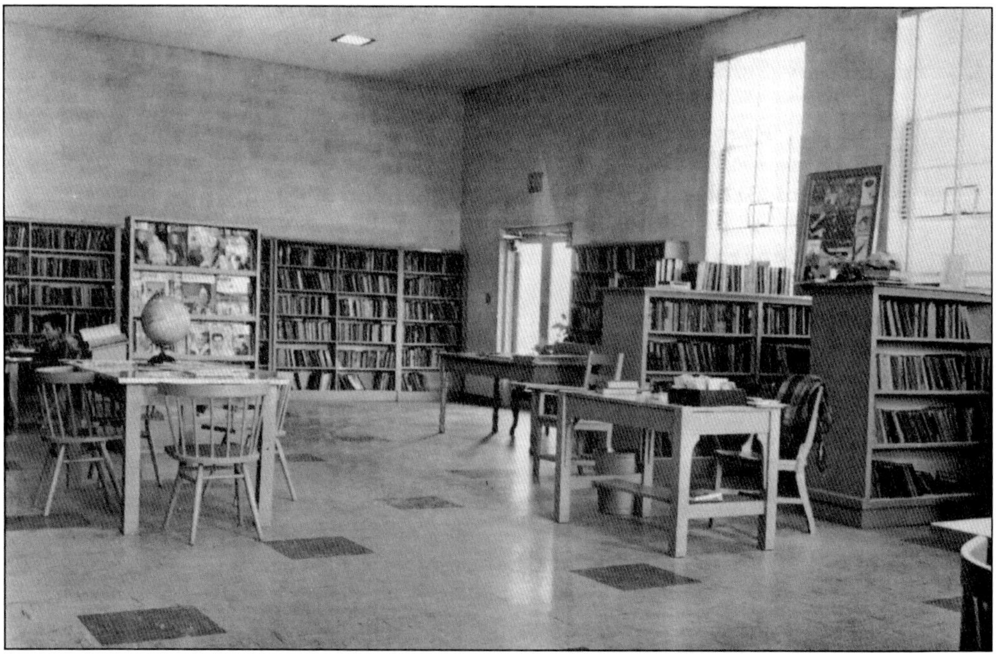

The Chattooga County Library was headquartered inside Summerville City Hall with an entrance off Cox Street. Patrons could choose from over 45,000 books. This 1956 photograph shows a view looking from the circulation desk to the main entrance. (Courtesy of Chattooga County Chamber of Commerce.)

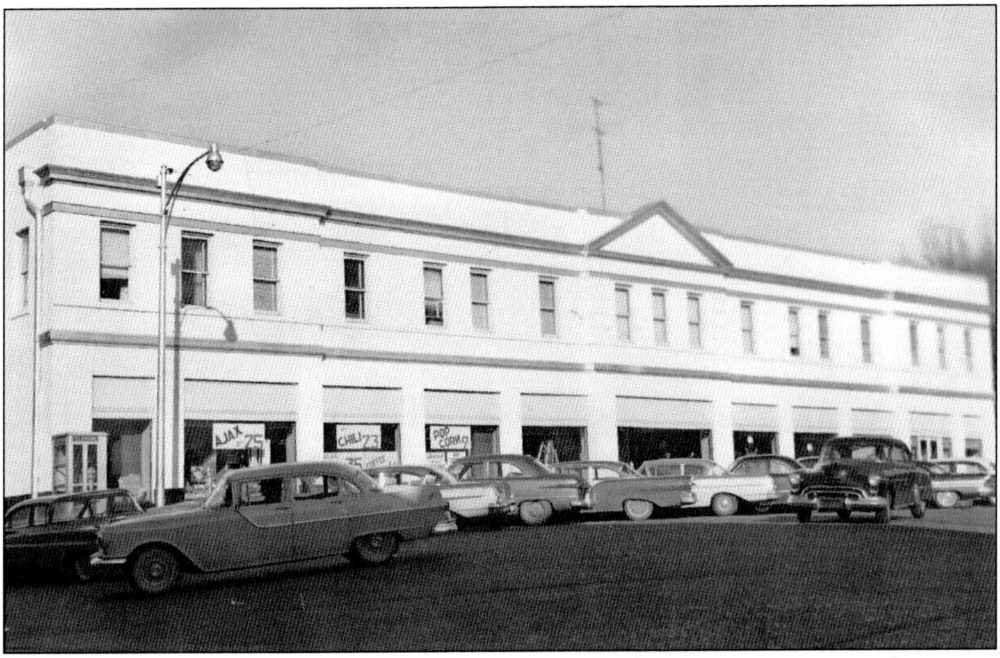

This 1960 photograph shows the Trion Department Store, also known as the "Big Friendly." Under one roof, a buyer would find groceries, shoes, hardware, furniture, clothing, a pharmacy, a café, a bank, and a beauty parlor. The store was owned by the Trion Mill and was located on mill property. (Courtesy of Charles Logan.)

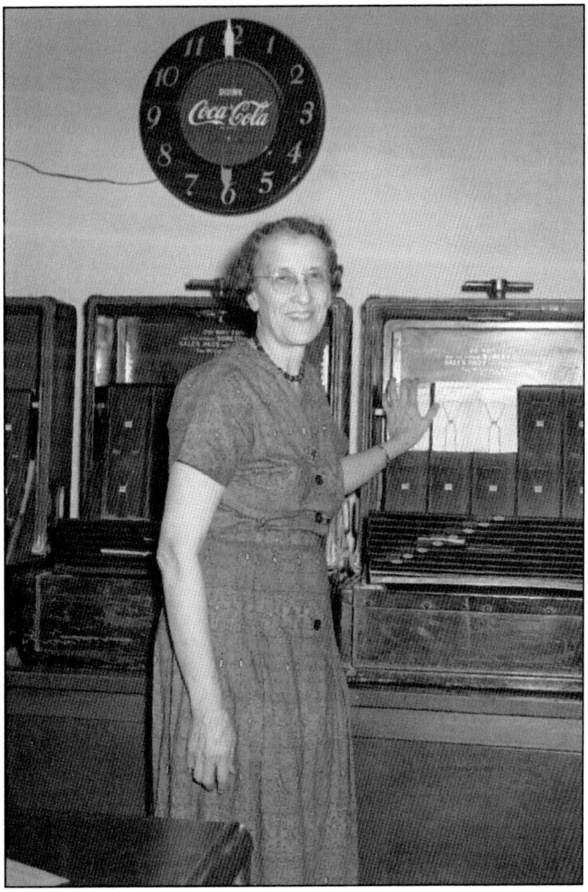

Dolly Bohannon was the head cashier of the Big Friendly for many years. Anyone needing store credit had to first get her approval. (Courtesy of Charles Logan.)

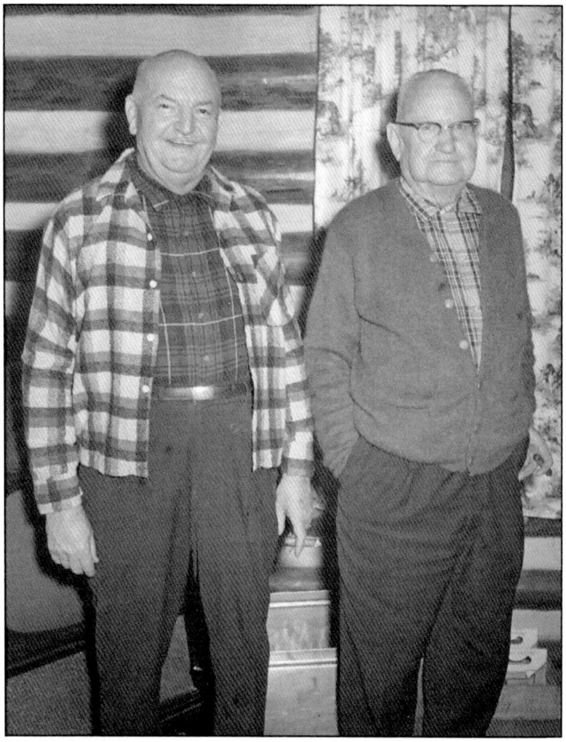

Born in 1902, L.C. "Sadd" Dalton (left) succeeded his brother-in-law, Chum Gray, as master mechanic, plant engineer, and construction superintendent of the Trion Mill, a job he held for 47 years. He supervised the construction of the Trion Community Center, the hospital, Leila Riegel Hall, the Riegeldale Tavern, and Trion High School. (Courtesy of Bill Barker.)

This c. 1957 photograph of downtown Summerville shows Farmers & Merchants Bank sitting across Commerce Street from the tree-lined courthouse. Next to the courthouse stands the old county jail building, and across Cox Street sits Wilson Motors, destroyed by fire in 1960. The train depot on East Washington Street is visible in the lower-left corner. (Courtesy of the *Summerville News*.)

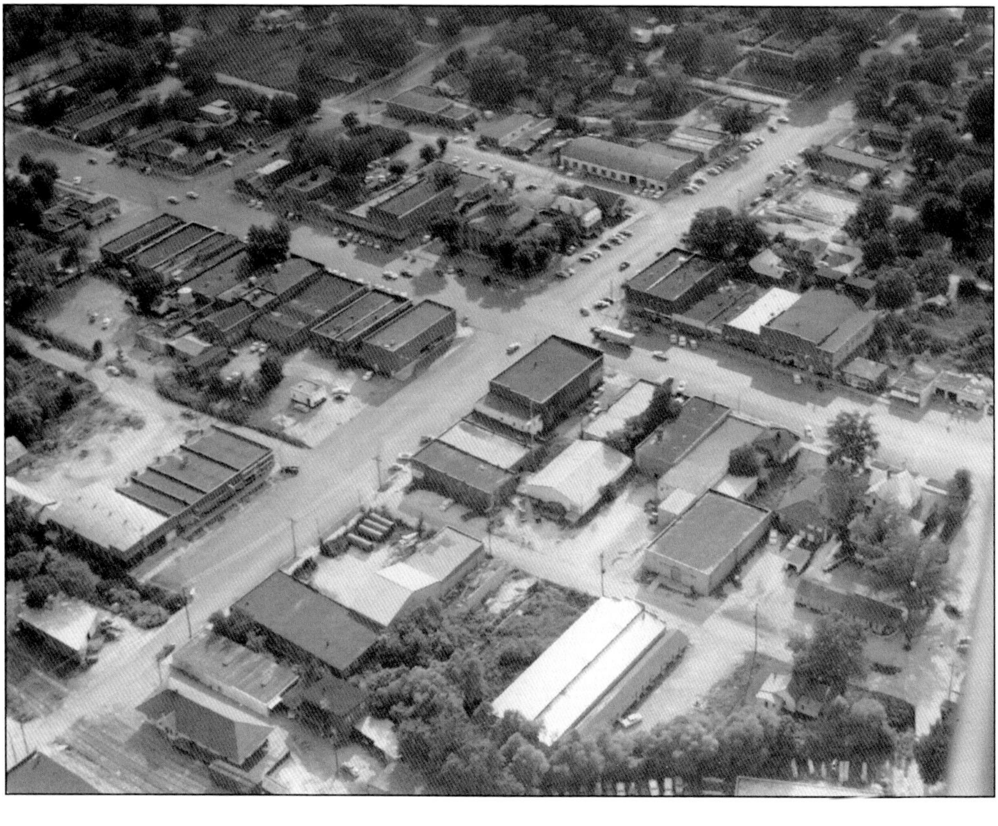

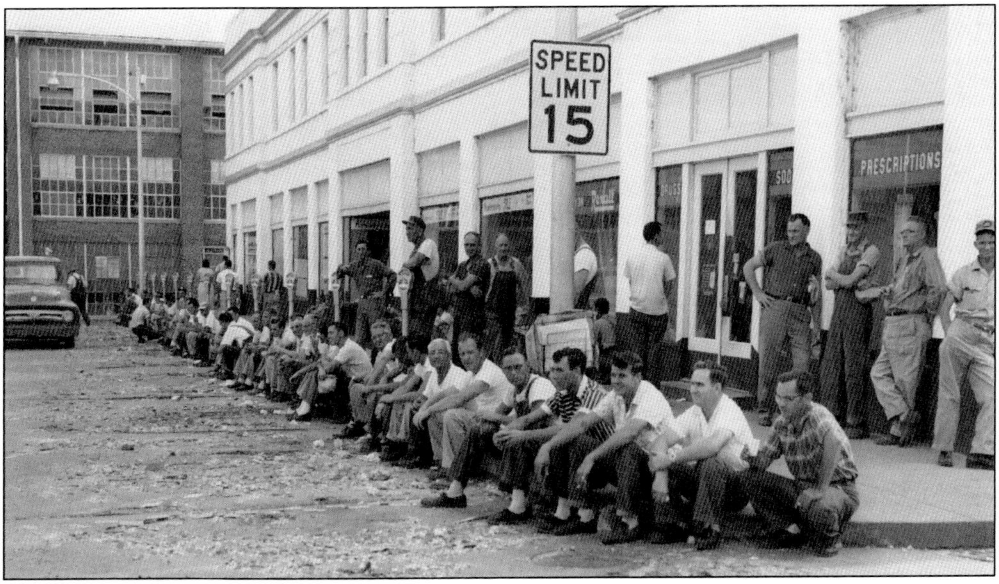

Employees of Trion Mill await the start of the second shift in this photograph taken in June 1961 in front of the Big Friendly store. Due to a shortage of parking and the mill's need to grow, the store became expendable. Demolition of the parking lot was already underway, a prelude to the store's closing and the opening of the nearby Triangle Shopping Center in November 1961. (Courtesy of Charles Logan.)

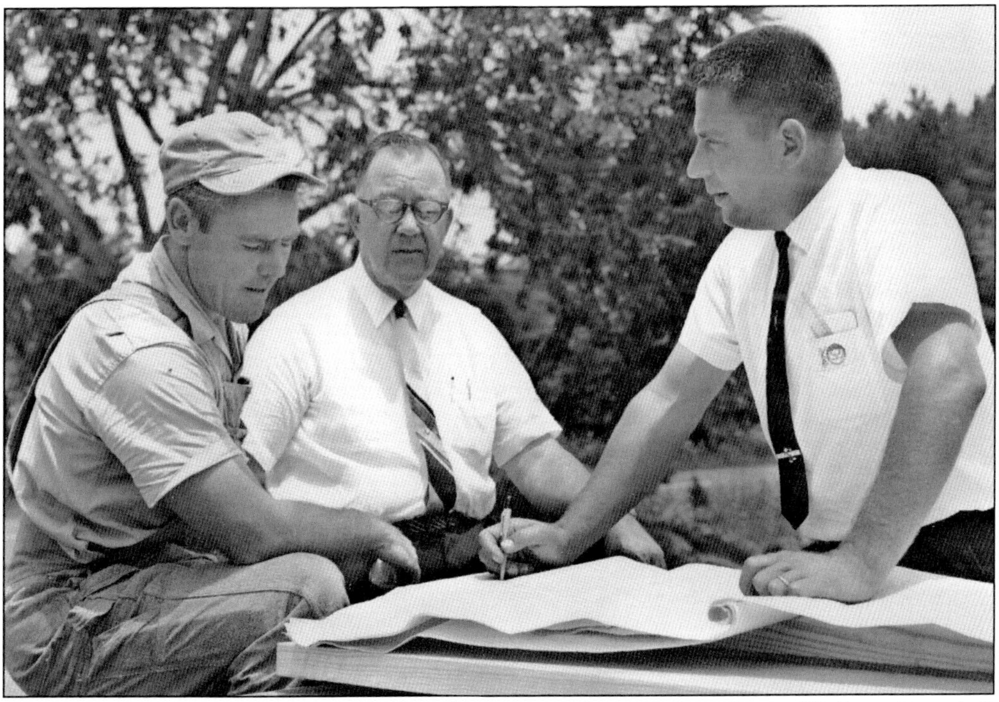

Building contractor Brice Evans (left) is shown consulting with architect Wallace Campbell and Georgia Power representative Jess Lee in a photograph taken around 1962. Evans began his construction business in the 1950s and was a respected home builder in the Chattooga County area for many years. He retired in 1982. (Courtesy of Rex Evans.)

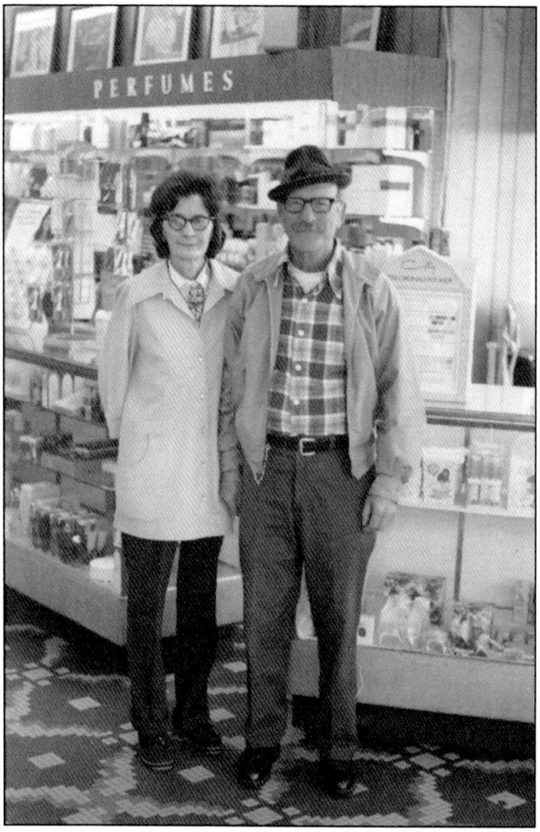

Thelma Eason helmed the lunch counter at McGinnis Drug Store for years and trained many high school girls to serve afternoon customers such popular fare as chicken salad sandwiches, fried pies with ice cream, and cherry smashes. Eason is shown with her husband, Cecil, in a c. 1969 photograph. (Courtesy of Gene McGinnis.)

Mary Scoggins and her husband, Evans, are shown at the Summerville home they shared for 56 years in a photograph made in 1973. Evans Scoggins was scoutmaster for Boy Scout Troop No. 7 for 30 years and was a positive influence on hundreds of boys. He was chosen to carry the torch during the relay for the 1996 Atlanta Olympics at the age of 80. (Photograph by the author.)

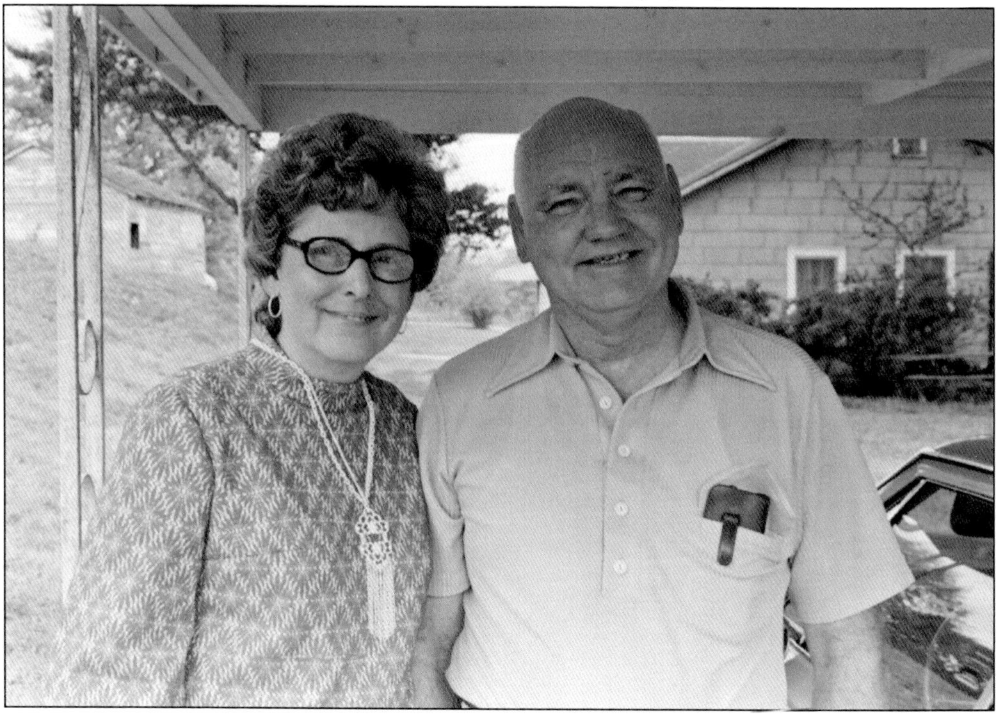

Two

Business and Industry

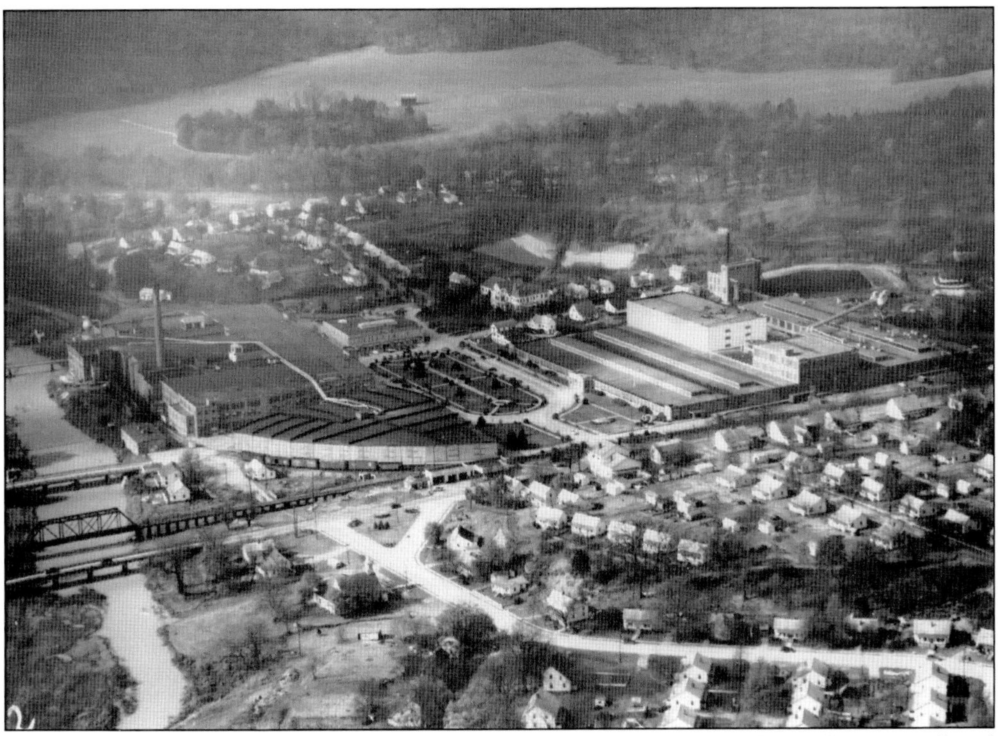

This photograph of the Trion Mill, made some time during the 1940s, shows the grey mill and cotton warehouse on the left, the Big Friendly company store at the end of the plaza, the old Trion Inn, and the Round Pond in the field at top. The Chattooga River flows along the left side. (Courtesy of Bill Barker.)

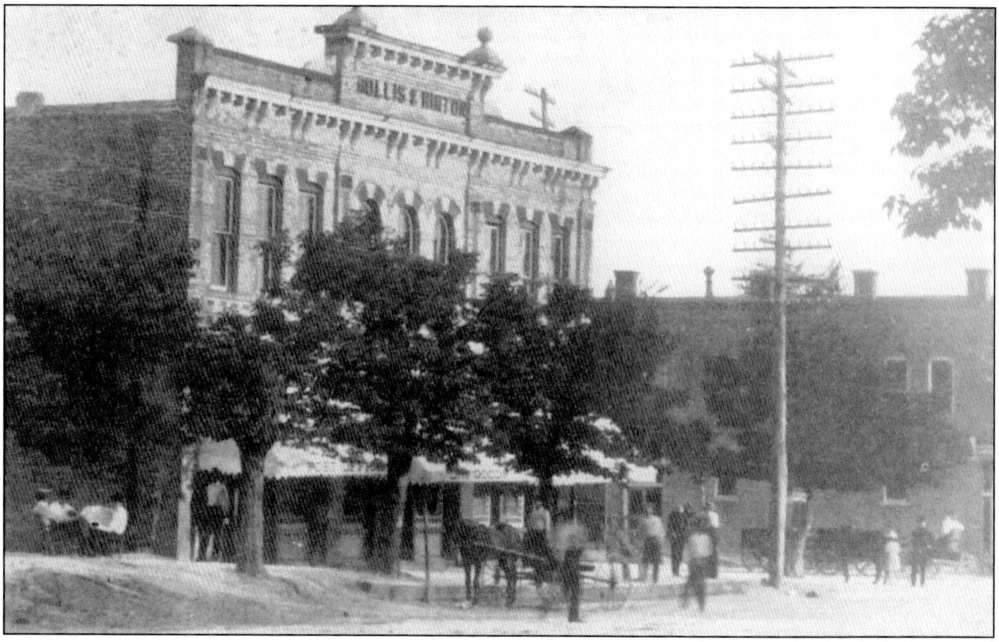

Hollis & Hinton was the name of a general store located on the northeast corner of Commerce and Washington Streets in Summerville. In 1919, John D. Taylor and his partners purchased the building and started Taylor Mercantile Company. The new business included the county's first ambulance service as well as a funeral home on the second floor. The store became insolvent during the late 1930s and closed. (Courtesy of Dave Henley.)

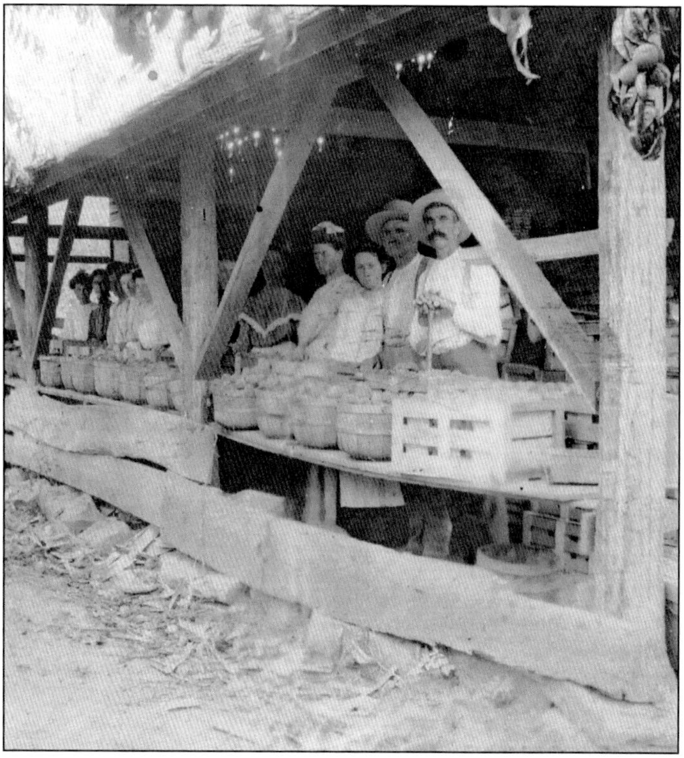

In 1895, Chattooga farmers and businessmen jumped on the peach orchard bandwagon, and by 1903, there were an estimated one million peach trees in the county. This image shows Menlo packers preparing the fruit for shipment. The second man from the right is Alfred Day, born around 1845. He served as a sergeant in the Civil War and died on Christmas Day, 1917. (Courtesy of Tim Day.)

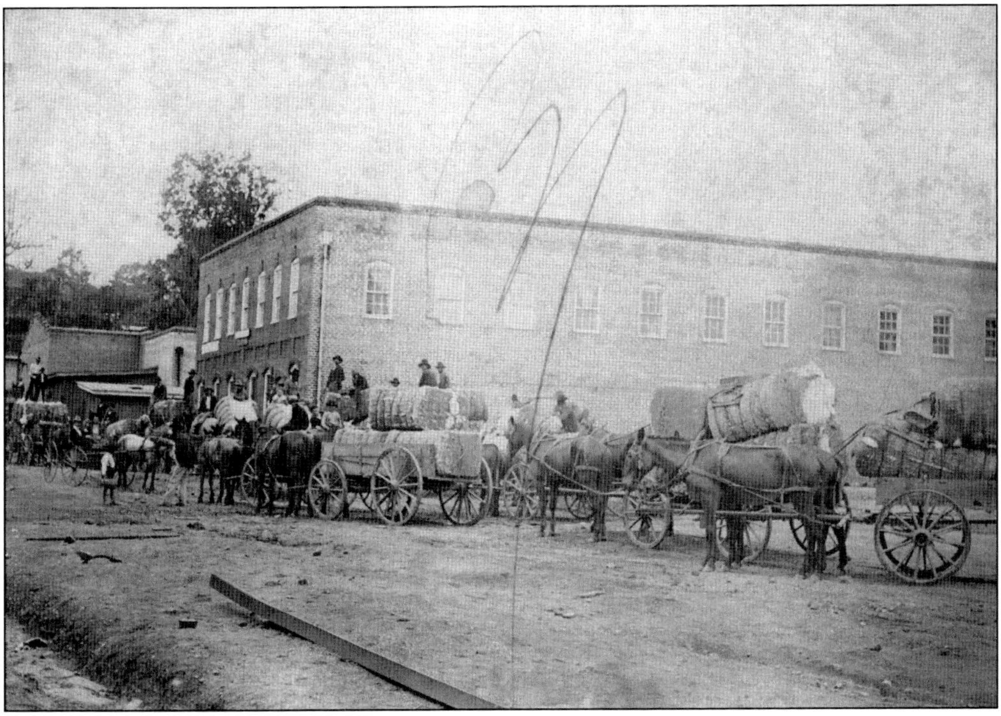

Cotton arrived at the Trion Mill via the Allgood wagons, as shown in this 1907 photograph. Before 1888, when rail transportation became available in Chattooga County, the team of wagons hauled finished fabric to Rome, Georgia, to be sold or distributed. The wagons would be loaded with cotton and other necessities for the return trip to Trion. (Courtesy of Bill Barker.)

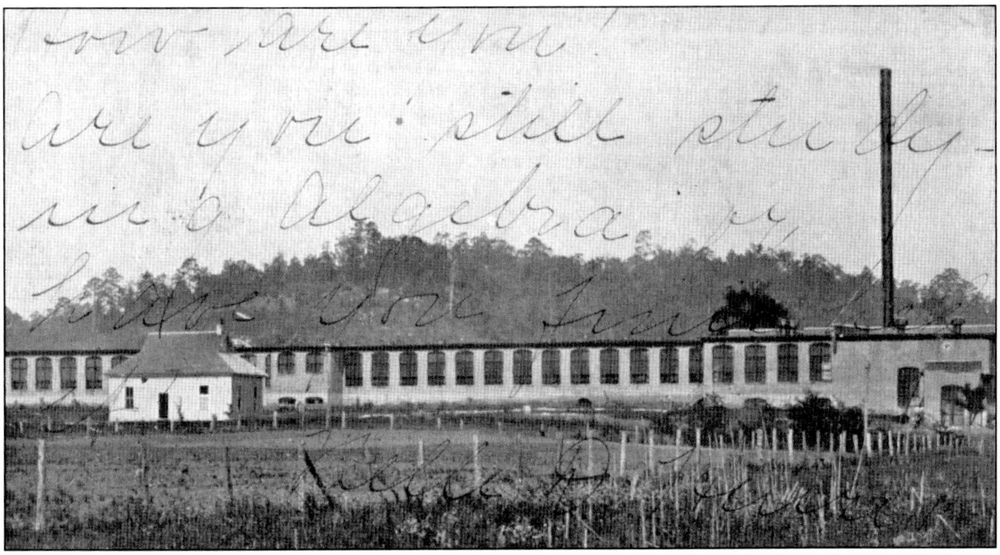

This 1908 photograph shows the Summerville Cotton Mill a year after it began manufacturing fabric. By 1923, the mill had been enlarged several times and was producing almost three times its initial capacity, but a county-wide strike of all textile mills in 1934 helped push it into bankruptcy. (Courtesy of Chattooga County Library.)

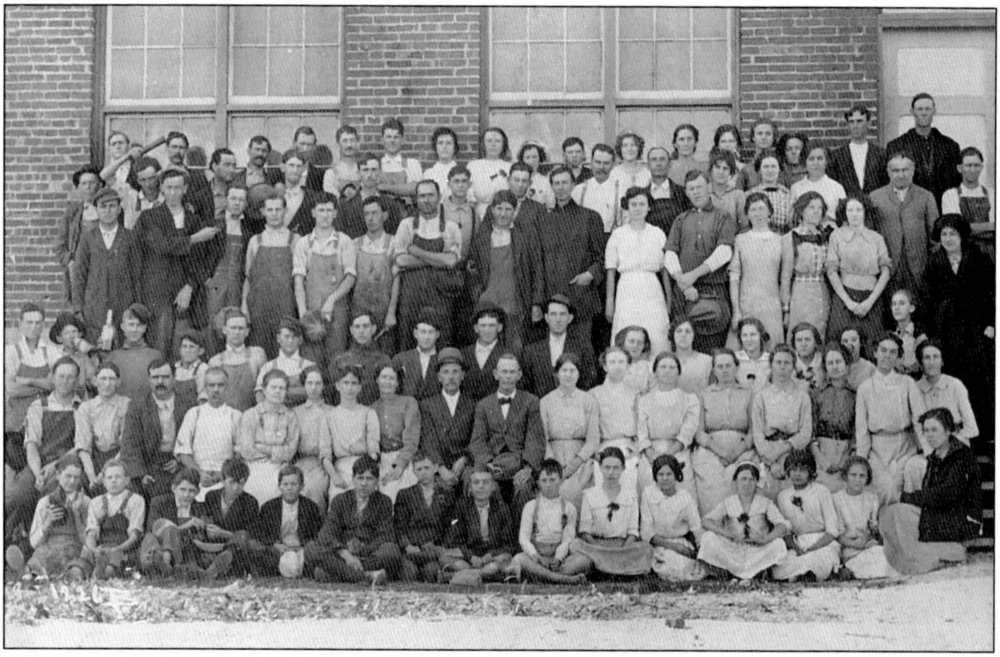

This c. 1917 photograph shows the workforce of the Summerville Cotton Mill. The first superintendent of the mill, Ernest Montgomery, is seen in the center wearing a bow tie. He resigned in 1925 and became the first general manager of Montgomery Knitting Mill two years later. (Courtesy of Thelma C. Sprayberry.)

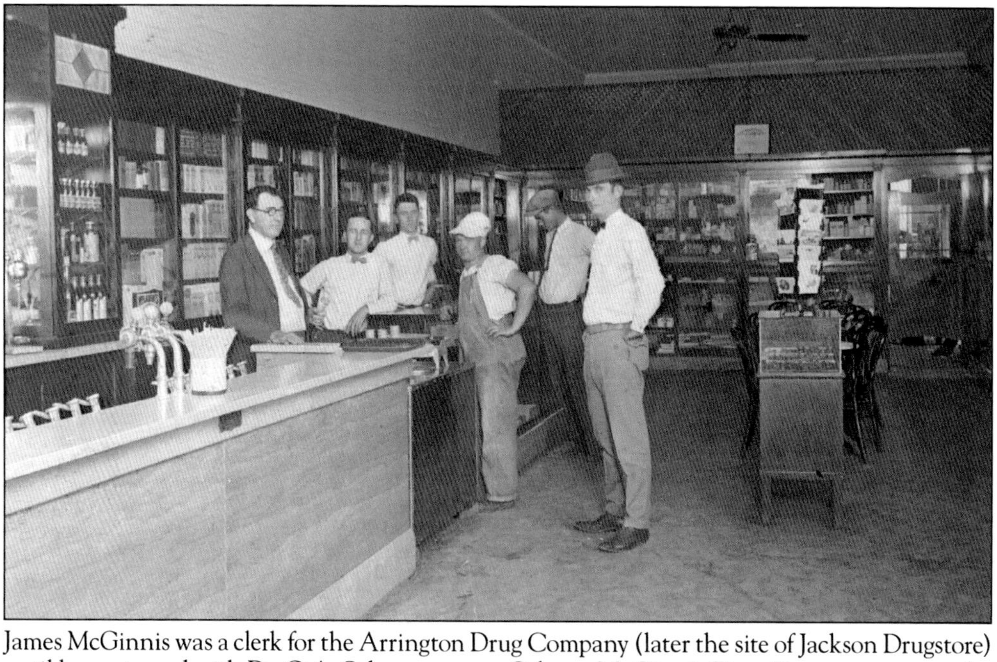

James McGinnis was a clerk for the Arrington Drug Company (later the site of Jackson Drugstore) until he partnered with Dr. O.A. Selman to open Selman-McGinnis Drug Company next to the courthouse in Summerville. This photograph, taken to commemorate opening day in 1920, shows, from left to right, James McGinnis, Penn Selman, Ellis Echols, Grady Newsome, unidentified, and W.E. Turner. (Courtesy of Gene McGinnis.)

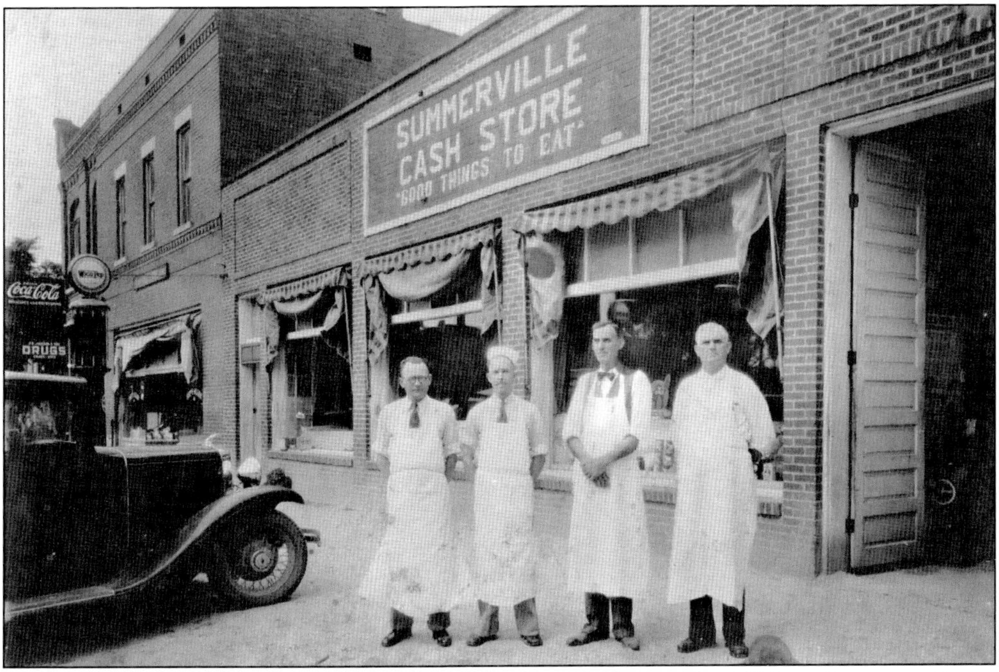

The Summerville Cash Store, featuring "good things to eat," opened in 1932 on Commerce Street next to Espy-Allen Hardware in a building that previously housed Citizens Auto Company. A gravity-operated gas pump for dispensing Woco Pep gasoline is seen in this photograph. The grocery store later moved just south of McGinnis Drug Company. (Courtesy of the *Summerville News*.)

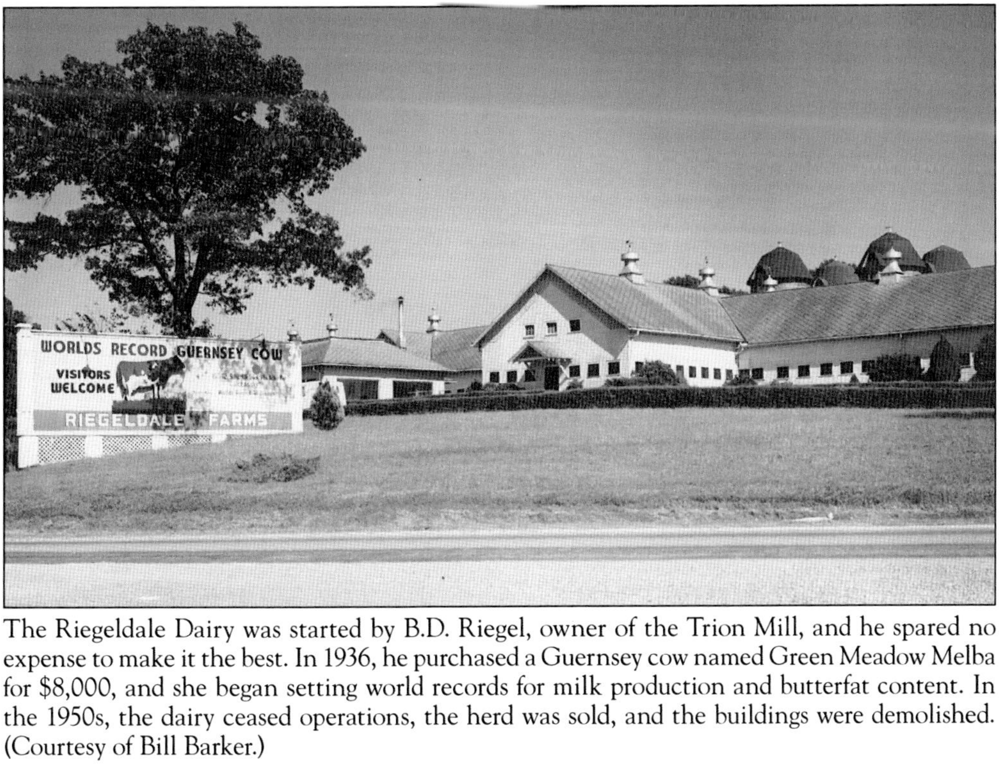

The Riegeldale Dairy was started by B.D. Riegel, owner of the Trion Mill, and he spared no expense to make it the best. In 1936, he purchased a Guernsey cow named Green Meadow Melba for $8,000, and she began setting world records for milk production and butterfat content. In the 1950s, the dairy ceased operations, the herd was sold, and the buildings were demolished. (Courtesy of Bill Barker.)

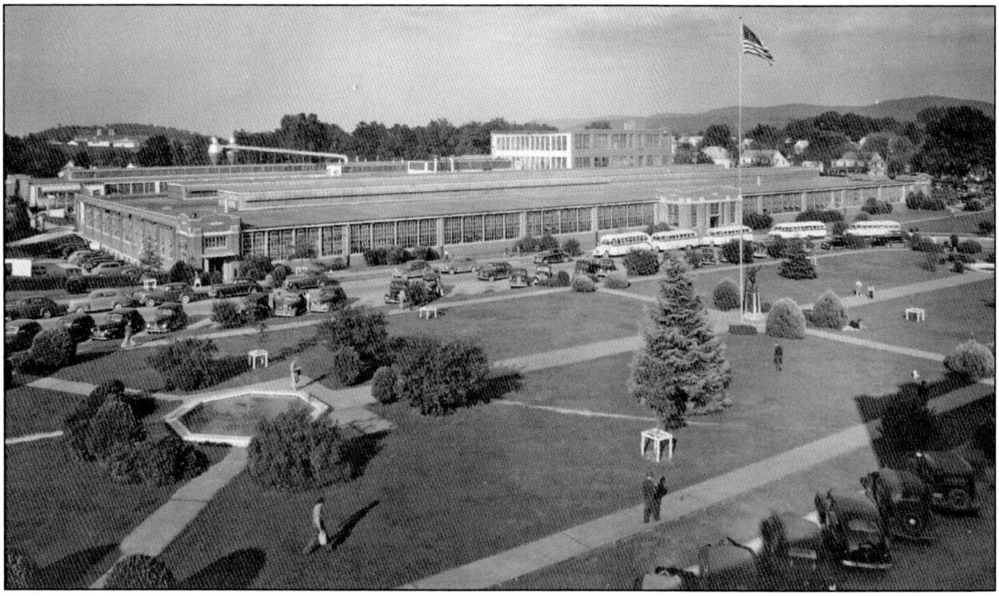

The "victory buses" parked in front of the glove mill at Trion provided transportation for mill workers during World War II, when gasoline and tire rationing made personal transportation difficult. The bus service soon grew to 14 buses operating around the clock. The victory buses hauled up to 2,000 passengers a day, primarily within an 18-mile radius of Trion. (Courtesy of Bill Barker.)

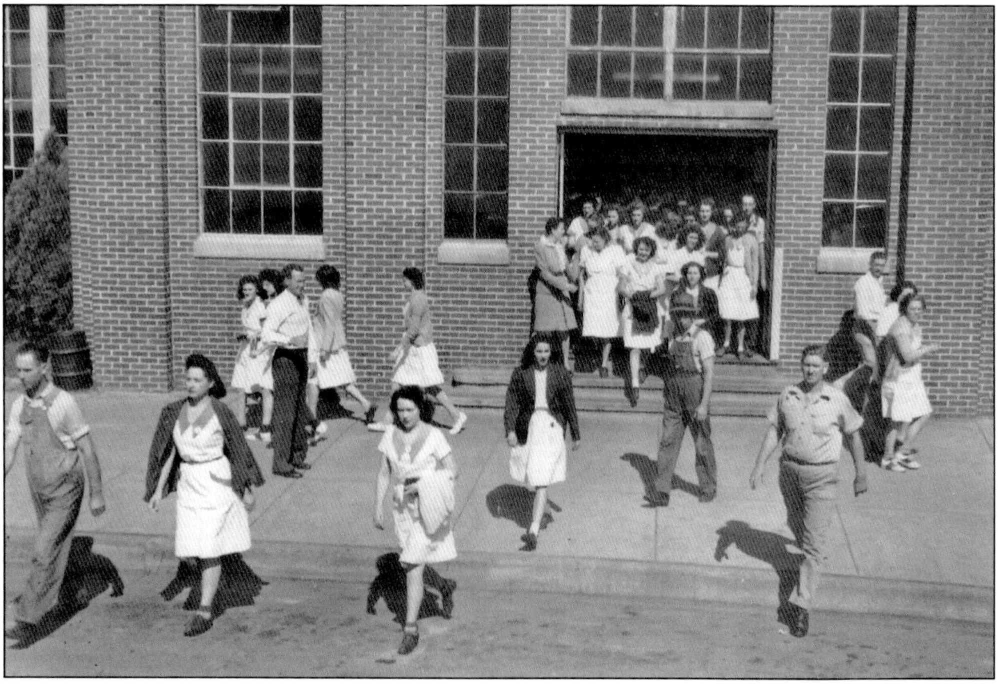

Workers at the Trion Mill are seen leaving the glove mill in this 1940s photograph. B.D. Riegel spent $1 million during the depths of the Great Depression to open the glove factory in 1932. After 20 years of operation, it was closed and the equipment moved to another Riegel facility located outside the county. (Courtesy of Mount Vernon Mills.)

Elizabeth Swafford Strange (back) and Vera Greene were telephone switchboard operators in Trion in the 1940s. The office was located above Glenn Hendrix's barbershop, in a house across from the Big Friendly store. When this office closed, Elizabeth Strange became an operator at the Summerville Telephone Company until her job became obsolete in 1960 with the arrival of direct dialing for local calls. (Courtesy of Ben T. Bridges.)

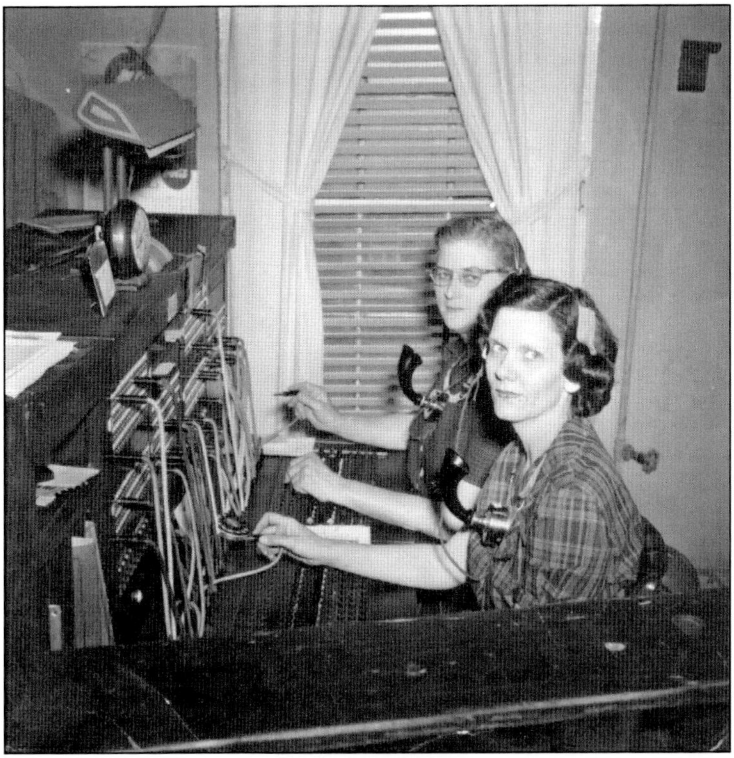

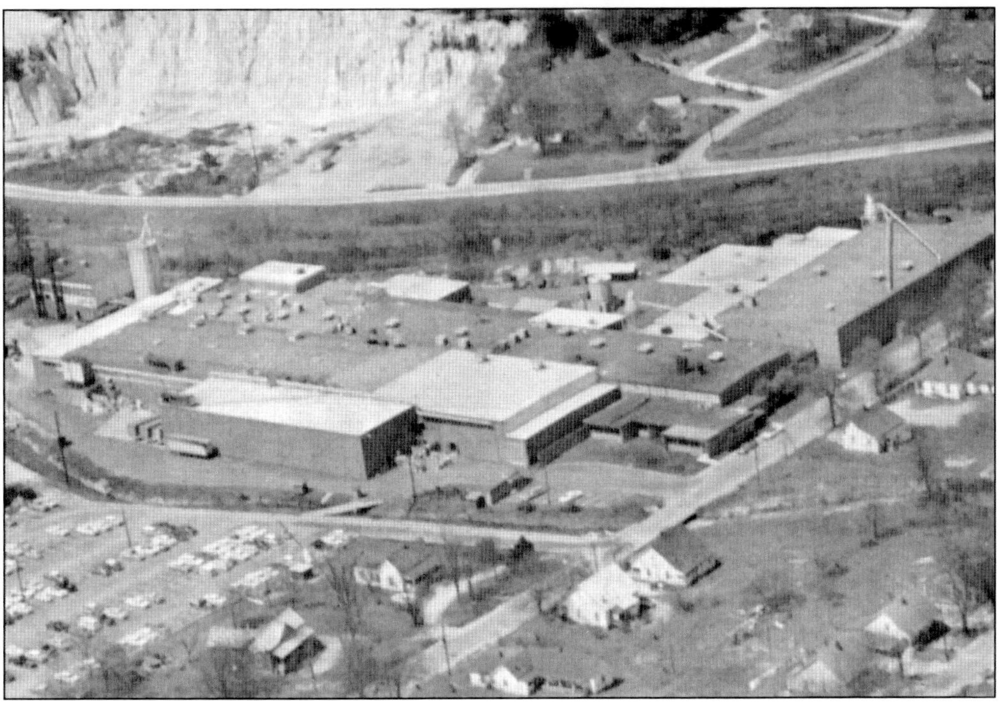

Georgia Rug Mill began making small rugs and bath mats at its Summerville plant, located near the cotton mill. In 1951, it was purchased by Bigelow-Sanford Carpet Company and became one of the largest plants for tufted carpets in the nation. (Courtesy of Robert Floyd.)

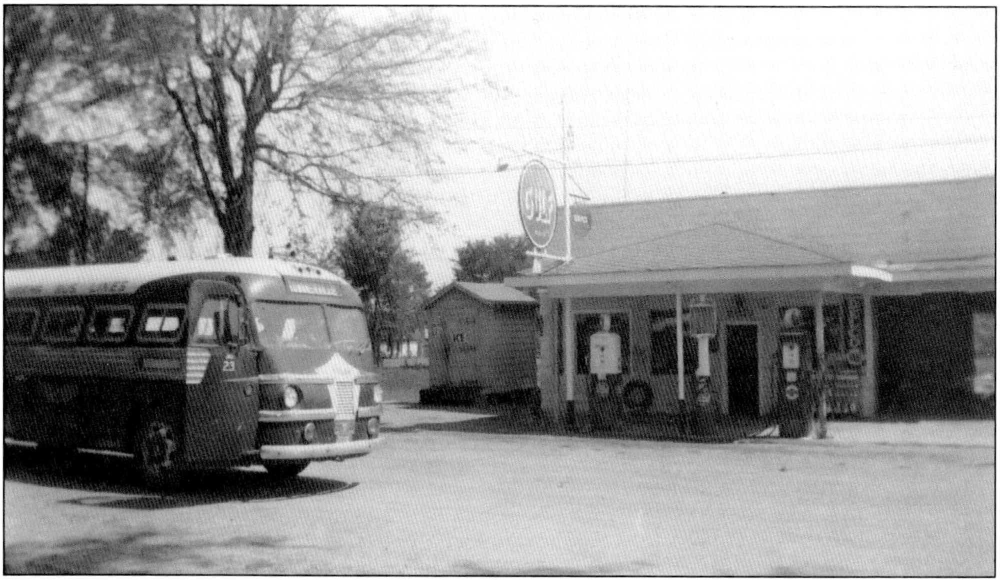

A bus from Alabama destined for Summerville makes a stop at Menlo in front of the Gulf service station in this photograph made around 1951. (Courtesy of Menlo City Hall.)

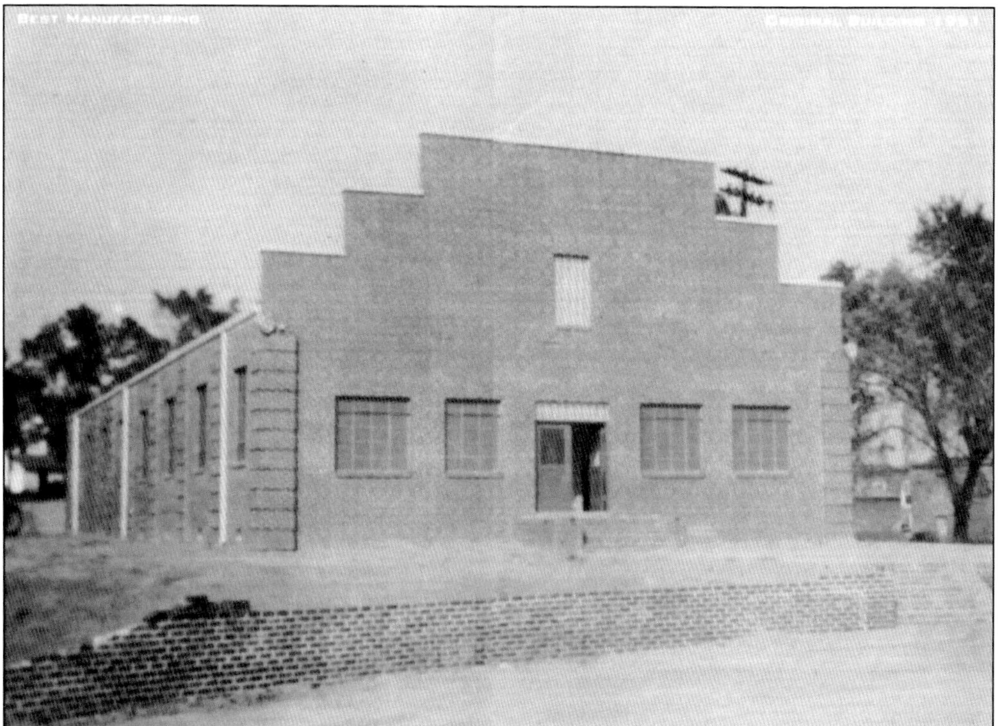

Best Manufacturing Corporation hired almost 50 employees when it started producing gloves in 1951 at its new plant. By 1960, the Menlo facility had 300 workers on the payroll. Roy Mann was president of the new company. (Courtesy of Carol Mitchell and Best Manufacturing.)

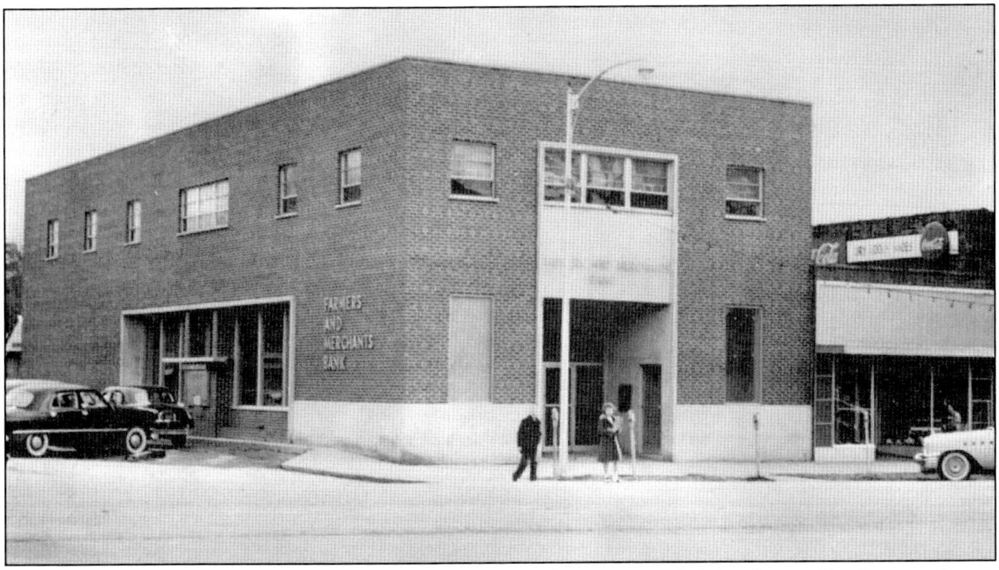

Opened in 1926 by a group of county businessmen, the Farmers & Merchants Bank moved into a new building in Summerville on the southeast corner of Washington and Commerce Streets in 1954, two years before this photograph was taken. The structure cost $125,000 to build and remained in use by the bank until a 1974 move to a larger building at the south end of Commerce Street. (Courtesy of Chattooga County Chamber of Commerce.)

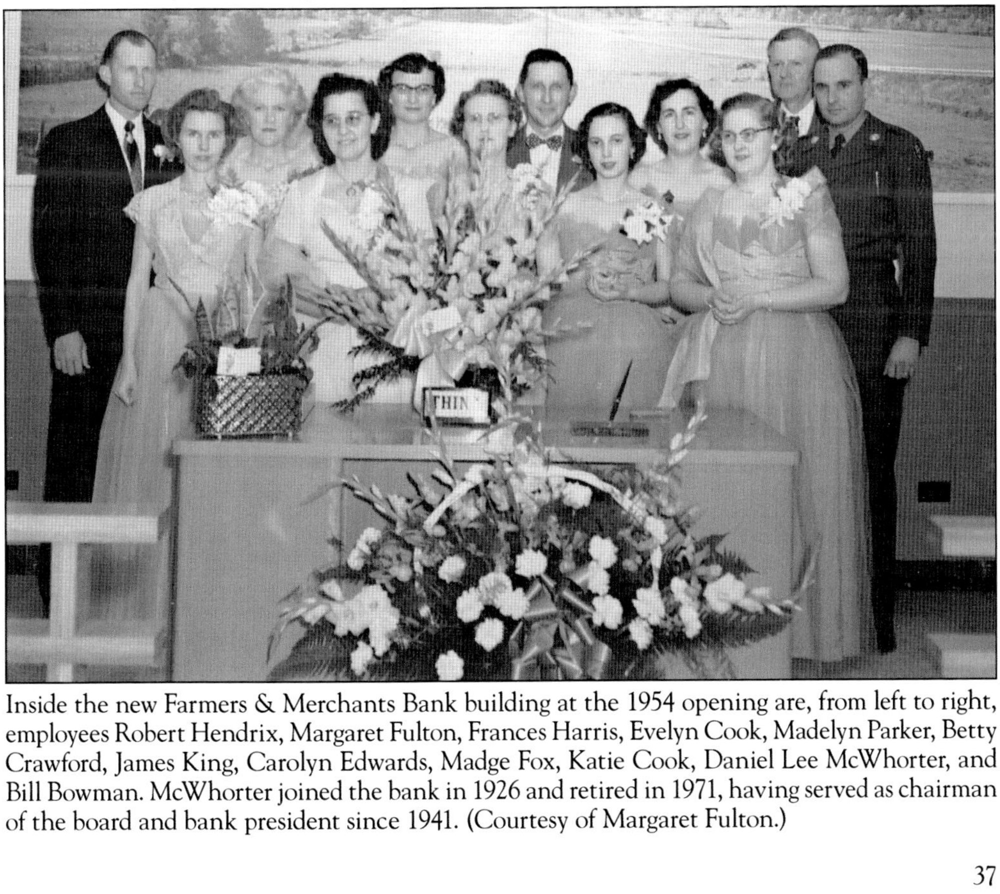

Inside the new Farmers & Merchants Bank building at the 1954 opening are, from left to right, employees Robert Hendrix, Margaret Fulton, Frances Harris, Evelyn Cook, Madelyn Parker, Betty Crawford, James King, Carolyn Edwards, Madge Fox, Katie Cook, Daniel Lee McWhorter, and Bill Bowman. McWhorter joined the bank in 1926 and retired in 1971, having served as chairman of the board and bank president since 1941. (Courtesy of Margaret Fulton.)

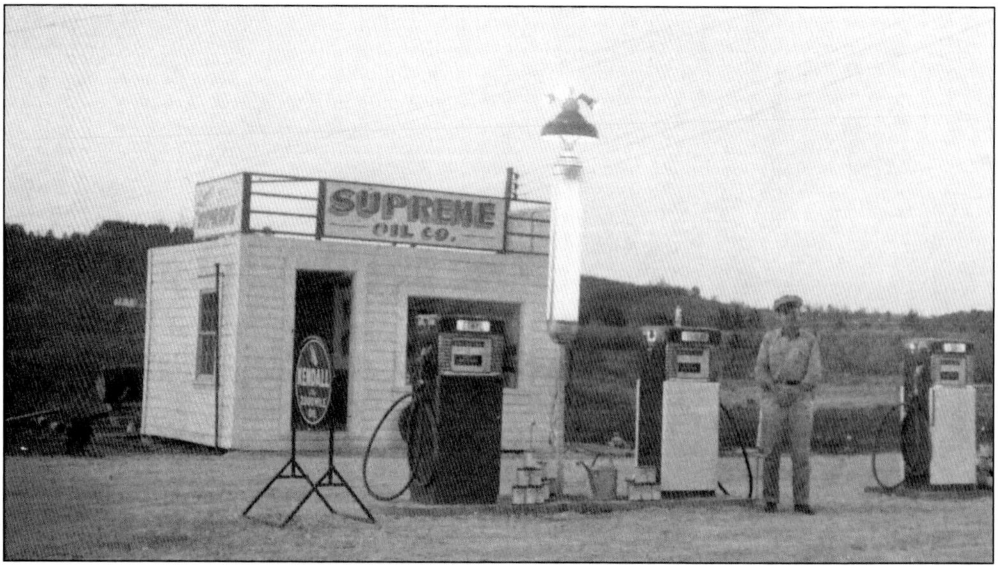

The author's father, Harvey McCollum, stands between gasoline pumps at his station on North Commerce Street in Summerville in this 1954 photograph. The Bittings Avenue area is in the background. Supreme Oil Company eventually grew to 15 gas stations across North Georgia. (From the author's collection.)

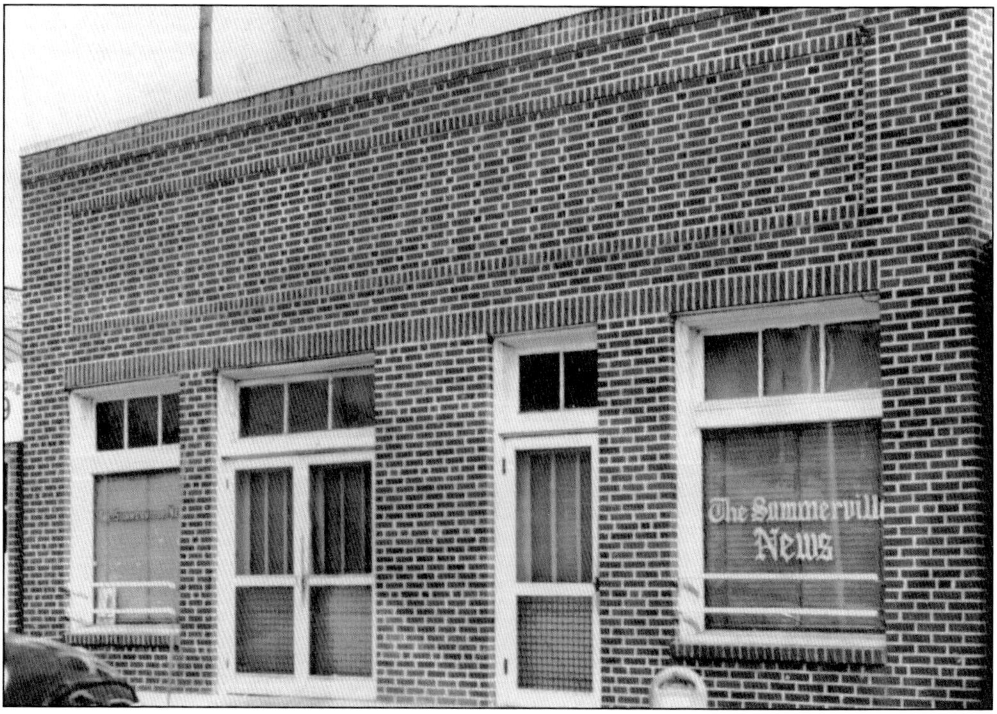

The *Summerville News* started publishing as the *Chattooga News* in 1886, making it the second-oldest business still operating in Chattooga County after the Trion Mill. The current owners of the weekly newspaper, the Espy family, have been associated with it since 1900. This 1956 photograph shows the publication's home on Commerce Street before it moved to its present location in 1973. (Courtesy of Chattooga County Chamber of Commerce.)

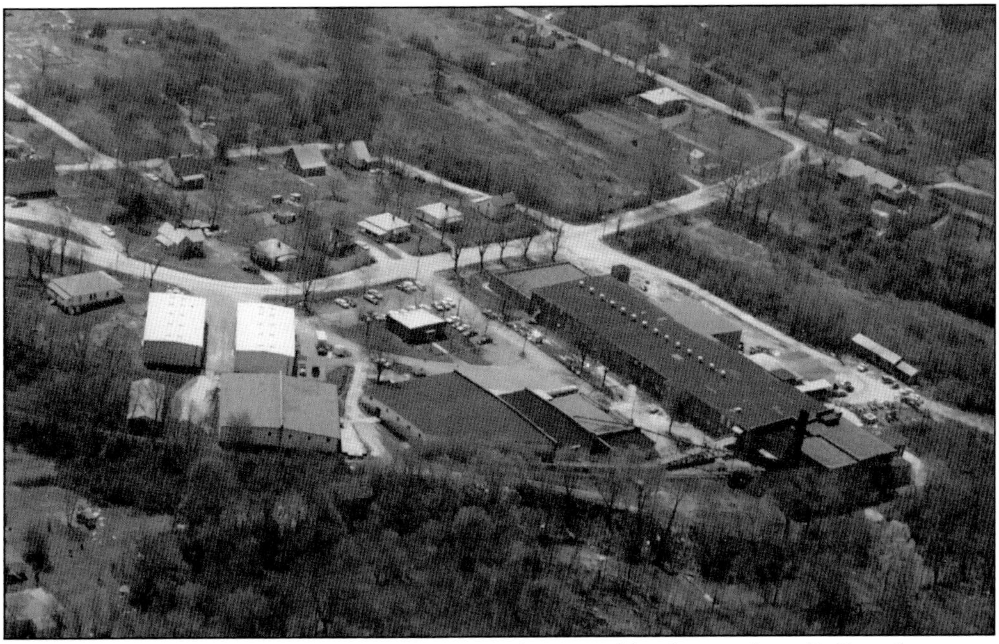

This 1960 view shows the Berryton community, dominated by the textile mill. Once known as Raccoon Mill due to its location along Raccoon Creek, the factory had its origins in the 1880s but was inactive for many years until John M. Berry of Rome took control in 1910. Afterward, the area became known as Berryton. (Courtesy of Tony Evett.)

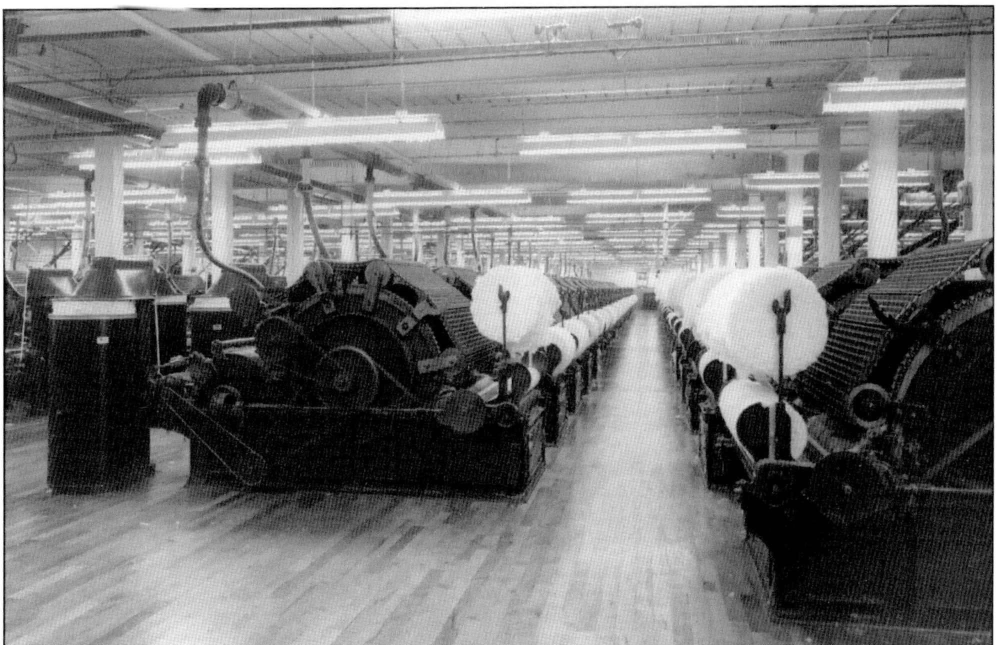

Following a strike in 1951 and the death of John M. Berry in 1952, the mill was sold to a North Carolina company, Harriett & Henderson, in 1958. The new company operated the mill until 2000, when it was closed and operations moved outside the county. This 1960 photograph of the card room shows some of the machinery used to turn cotton into yarn. (Courtesy of Tony Evett.)

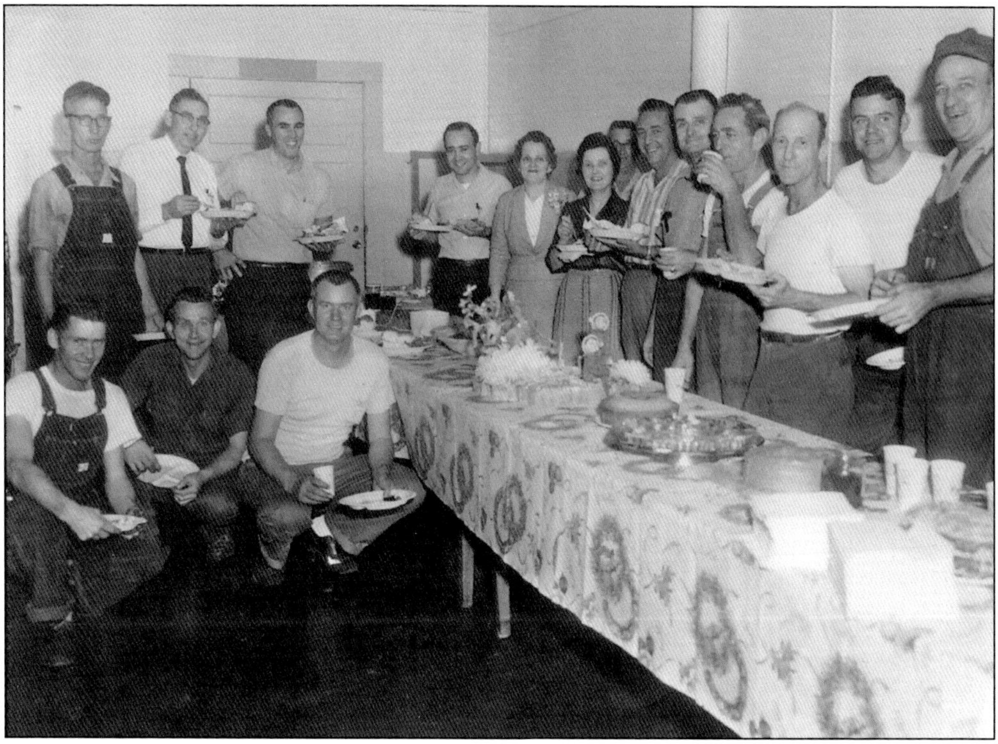

These first-shift card room employees at the Trion Mill enjoy a Christmas dinner together in 1960. They are, from left to right, (kneeling) unidentified, Harold Crider, and James Barfield; (standing) Robert Duckett, Robert Allen, Charles Freeman, Roland Nunn, Betty Crane, Mildred Speer Allen, Ed Bryant (partially hidden), Paul Gardner, R.W. Williams, Paul Ward, Homer Eason, Rudolph Crane, and Howard Williams. (Courtesy of Mount Vernon Mills.)

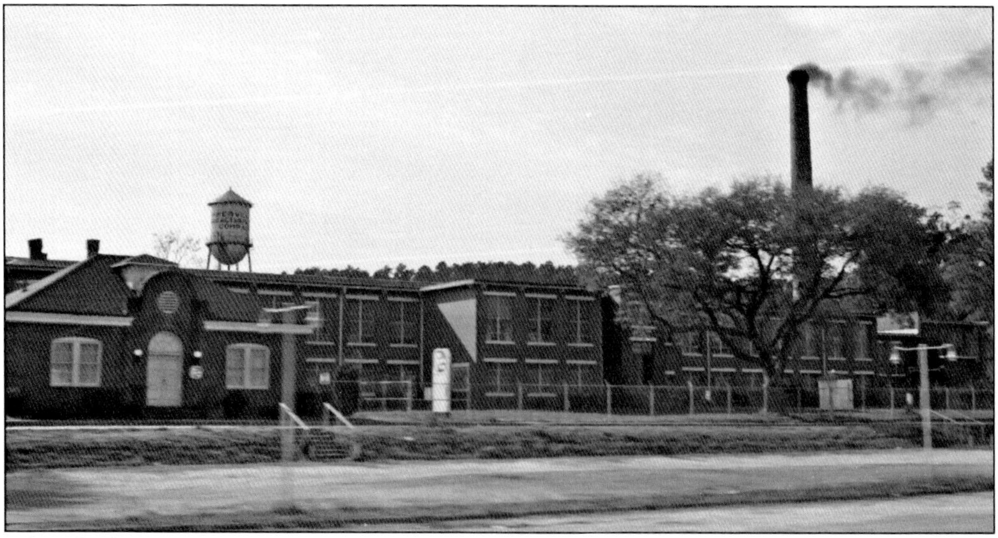

After the bankruptcy of the Summerville Cotton Mill in 1935, the factory changed ownership several times and was often shuttered. World War II brought the mill back into production, and it remained operational as a major county employer for many years. By the 1980s, the mill had ceased production, and most of the buildings were demolished. (Photograph by the author.)

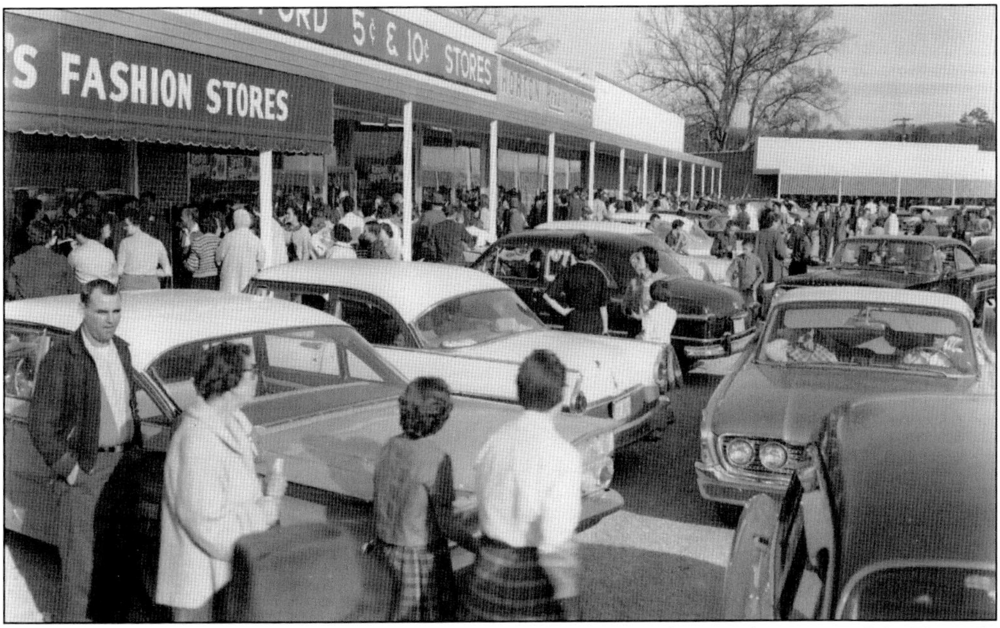

A drawing for a $500 cash prize drew hundreds of local citizens to the grand opening of the Triangle Shopping Center in Trion. The shopping center opened in November 1961 and succeeded the Big Friendly store as a center of retail activity in Trion. (Courtesy of Charles Logan.)

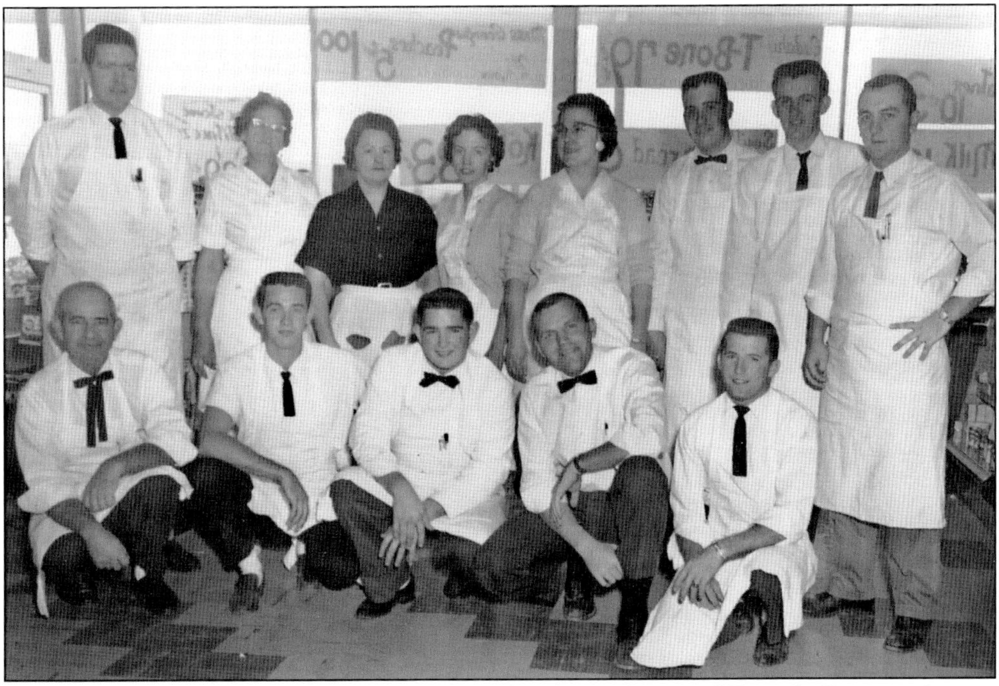

Hurley's Food Center was one of the stores located at the newly opened Triangle Shopping Center. Shown in this photograph are, from left to right, (first row) Dixie Strayhorn, Robert Lee Smith, Mike Dodd, Charles Harris, and Dave Crowe; (second row) Billy Wayne Duke, Leila Woods, Dot Adams, Shelba Hammonds, Esther Styles, Franklin Jackson, Charles Loggins, and owner Fay Hurley. (Courtesy of Charles Logan.)

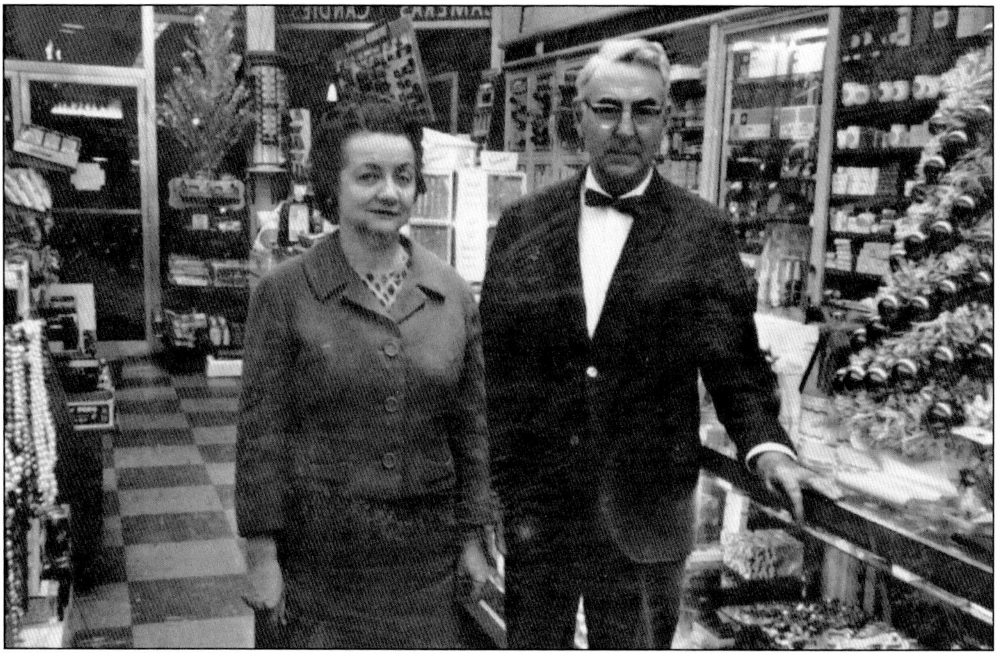

J.R. "Jimmy" Jackson Jr., shown here with his wife, Eleanor, was the second of three generations to own and operate Jackson Drug Company on the northwest corner of Commerce and Washington Streets in Summerville. The store, which opened in 1894 under the ownership of H.H. Arrington, maintained a soda fountain until 1967 and was a popular gathering place for many years. Jackson Drug Company closed its doors in 2008. (Courtesy of Gene McGinnis.)

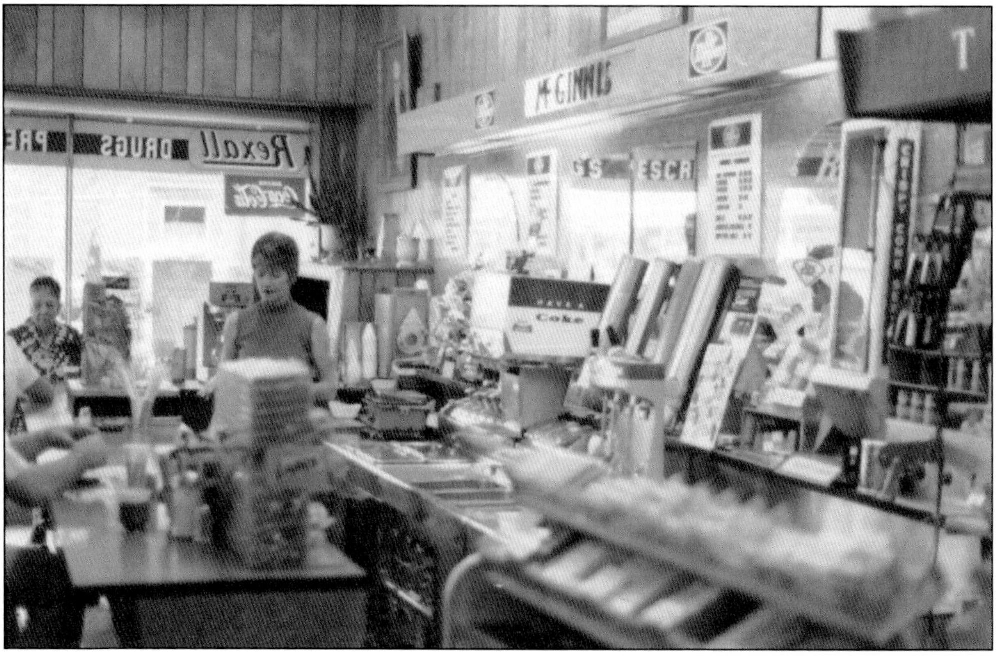

A 1974 photograph of McGinnis Drug Store shows Dorothy Wilson working behind the counter. Vivian Turner, shown on the left, was a daily customer and ran a beauty shop upstairs in the same building. (Courtesy of Gene McGinnis.)

Three

Newsworthy and Notable

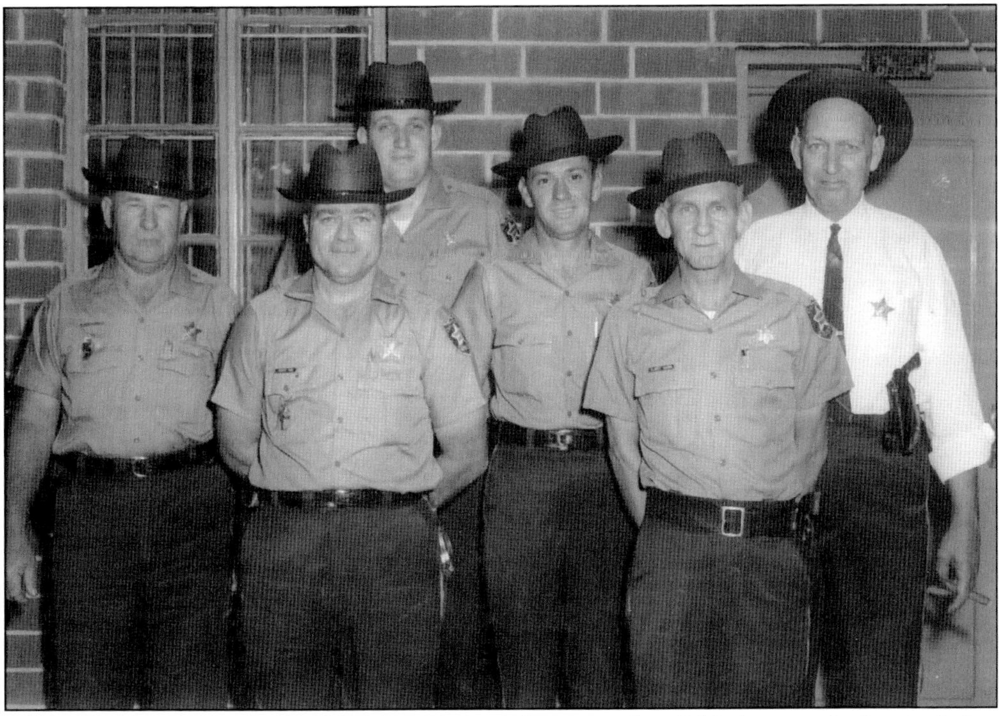

The Chattooga County Sheriff's Department is shown in this 1966 photograph that includes, from left to right, W.R. Coker, Robert King, Gary McConnell, J.D. Miller, Elbert Tucker, and Sheriff John Frank McConnell. When Sheriff McConnell died in office in 1967, his son, Gary, replaced him, and Gary later became the youngest sheriff ever elected in the United States at the time. (Courtesy of Mike King.)

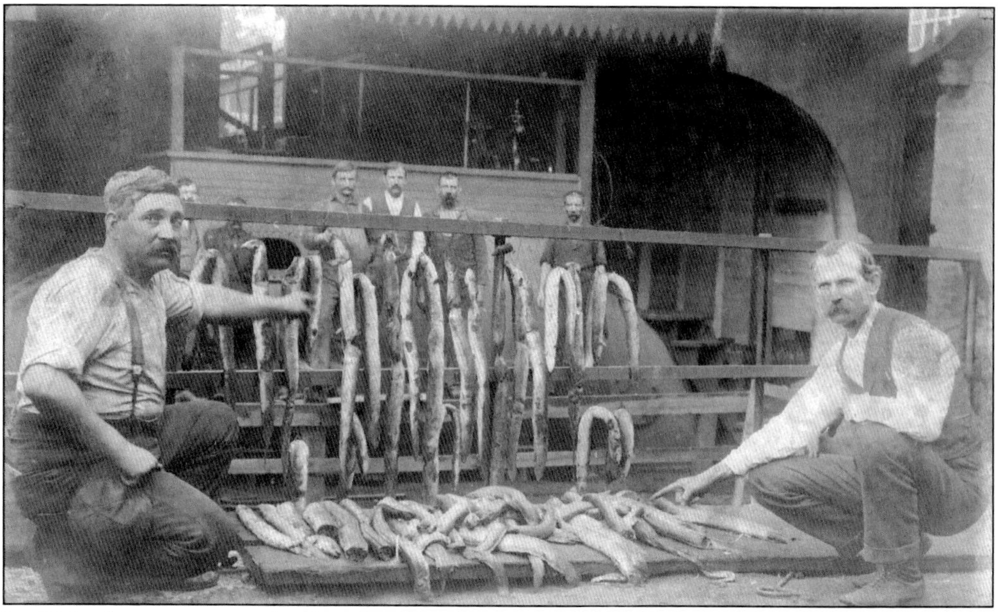

In 1896, eels migrating up the Chattooga River were stopped by the dam at the Trion Manufacturing Company. They turned downstream and were caught in a raceway that led to a waterwheel. When the waterwheel jammed, the mill's only source of power was cut off. It required three two-horse wagons to load all the eels for disposal. (Courtesy of the family collection of Alexander McMillan Myers Jr.)

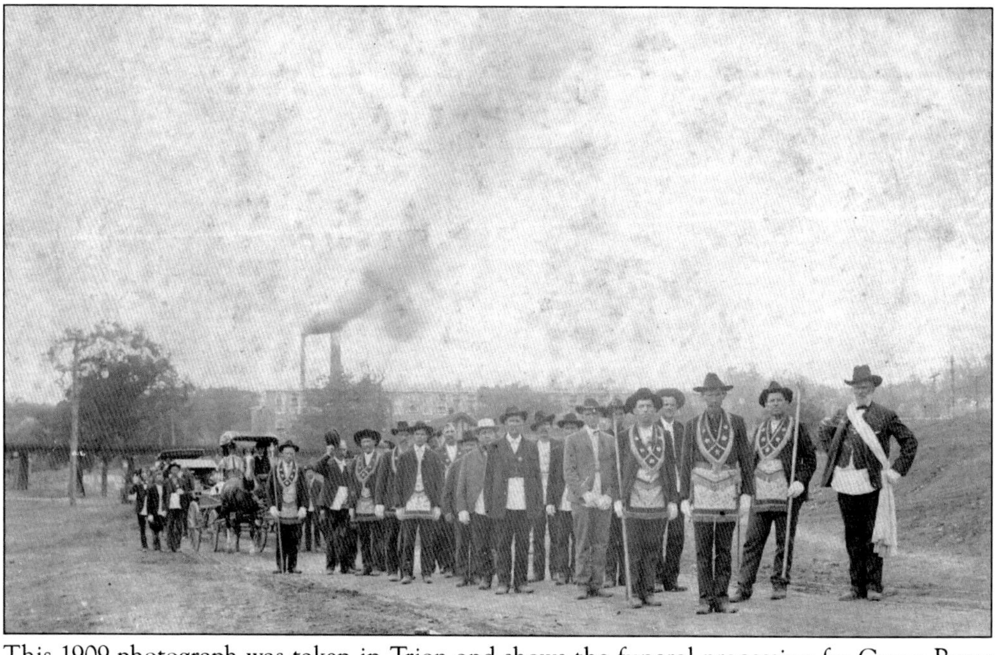

This 1909 photograph was taken in Trion and shows the funeral procession for Green Berry Myers. Myers was a Civil War veteran of the 60th Georgia Regiment and later rose to the position of secretary-treasurer of the Trion Mill. The man on the right is William Ham Penn, leading a group of Red Men and Odd Fellows from Trion Lodge F&AM. (Courtesy of the family collection of Alexander McMillan Myers Jr.)

William B. Hair was born in 1892 and graduated from Emory School of Medicine. By chance, a friend saw a note on a bulletin board stating that Summerville needed a doctor. The note was forwarded to Dr. Hair, who, after consulting with his fiancée, moved to Summerville in 1923. The newlyweds later relocated to a home on East Washington Street. (Courtesy of Will and Judy Hair.)

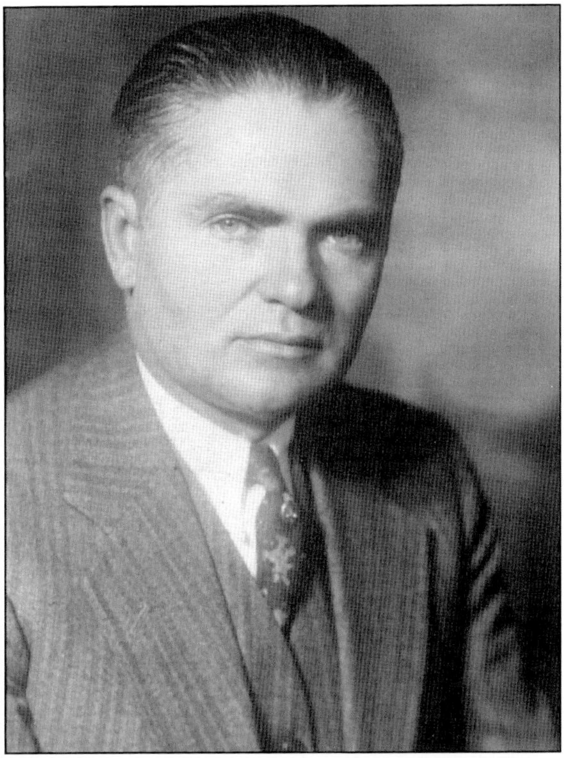

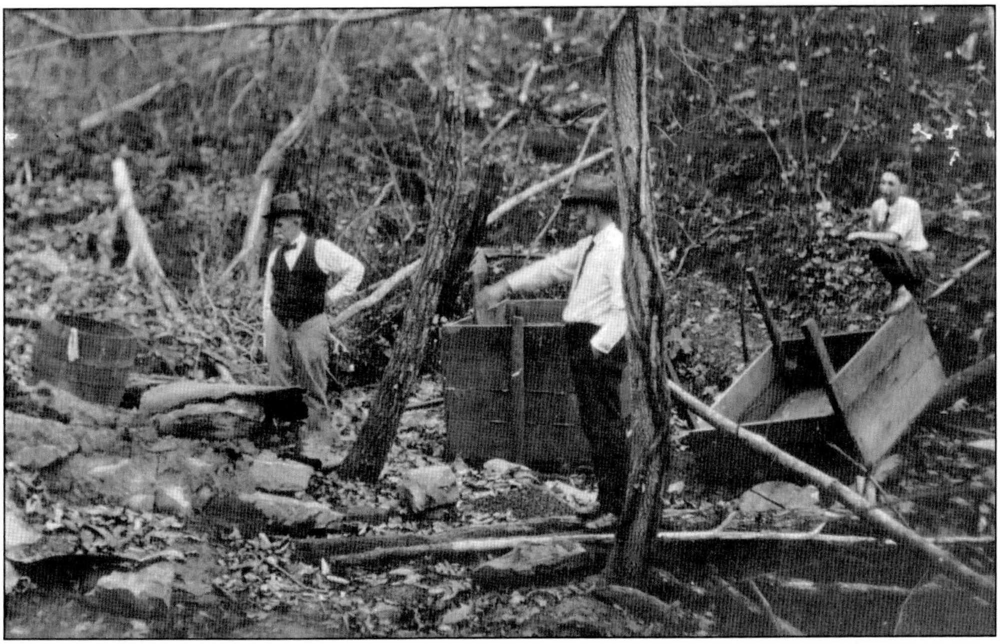

Wesley Shropshire (left) surveys the destruction of a still found on his farm near the Chattooga River. Shropshire was mayor of Summerville and served in the state senate. His grandfather of the same name was an influential Chattooga County farmer and politician who voted against secession from the Union in 1861. Shropshire's daughter, Beulah, was a well-known businesswoman. (Courtesy of Rex Evans.)

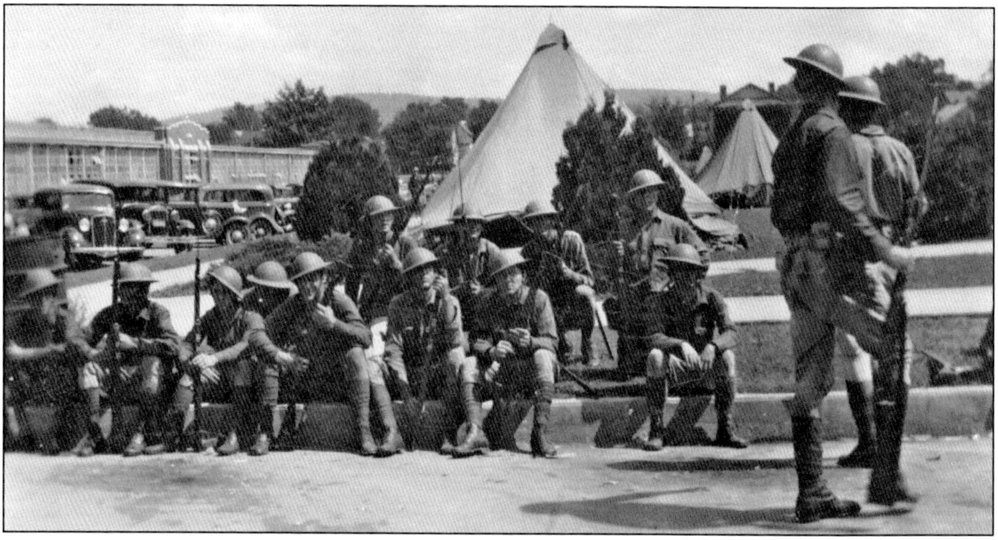

Soldiers from the National Guard are shown bivouacked on the plaza at the Trion Mill in 1934. Efforts to unionize textile workers had closed most of the mills in the South and, despite B.D. Riegel's efforts to keep his plant open, half of the workers at Trion stayed home out of sympathy for the union or fear of violence from pickets. (Courtesy of Larry Langston.)

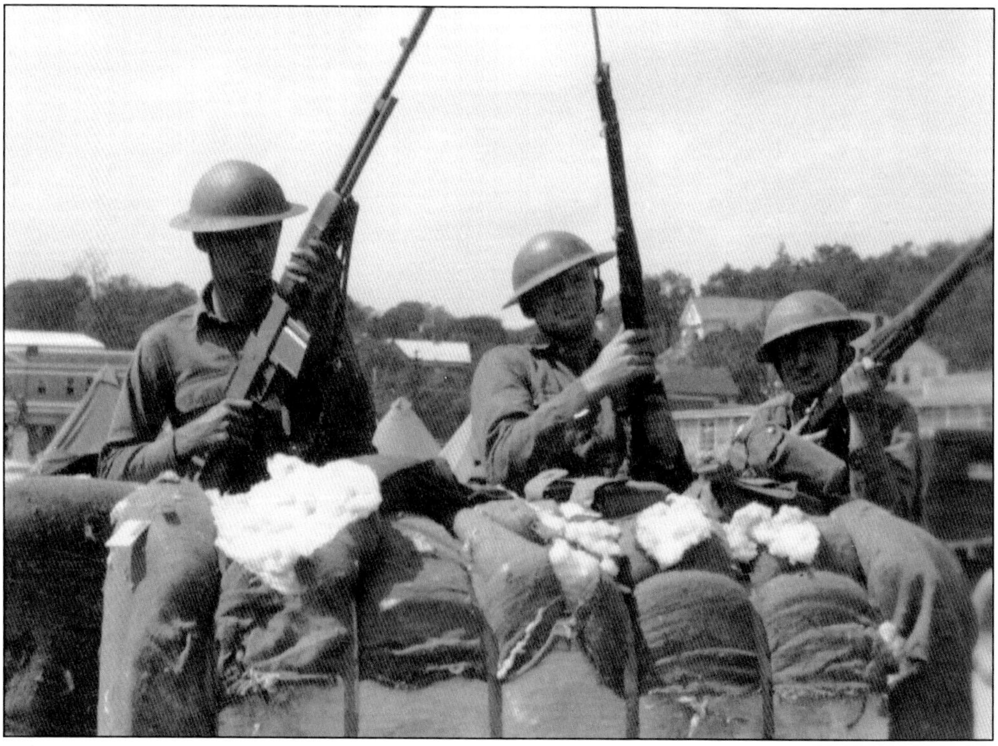

Following the shooting deaths of a union organizer and a deputy sheriff, Guardsmen arrived at the mill to protect the workers and the plant. Bales of cotton were positioned around the mill as protection from possible gunfire. Management, positioned near the soldiers, identified workers and kept others away. The attempt to unionize the mill ended soon afterward. (Courtesy of Larry Langston.)

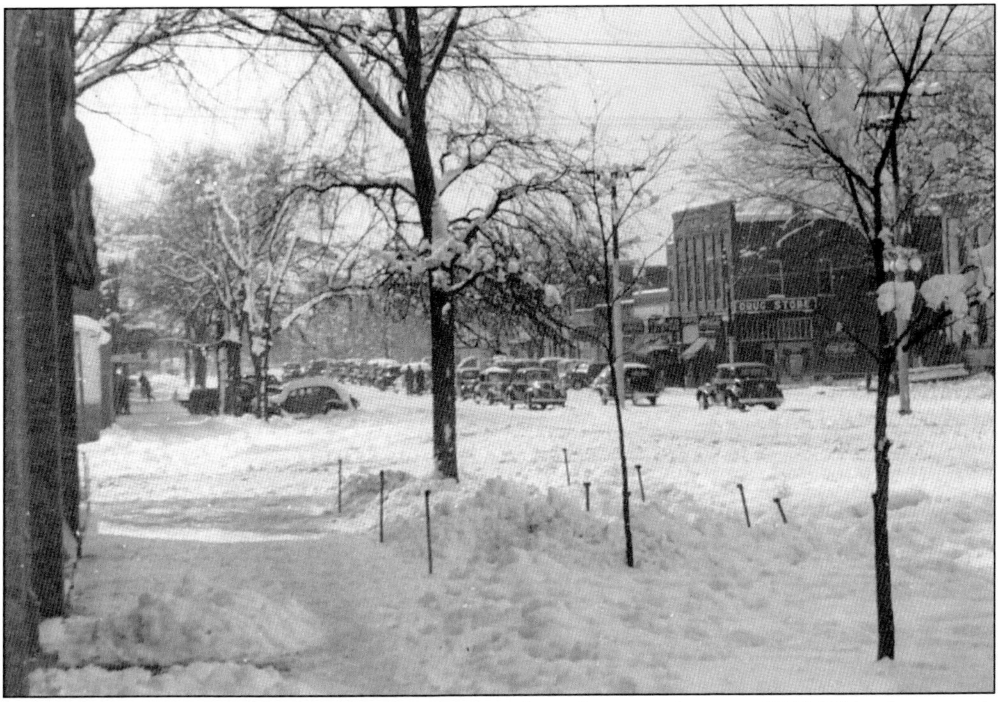

Chattooga County was blanketed with over 11 inches of snow in January 1940. This photograph shows Commerce Street in Summerville. (Courtesy of L.C. Smith.)

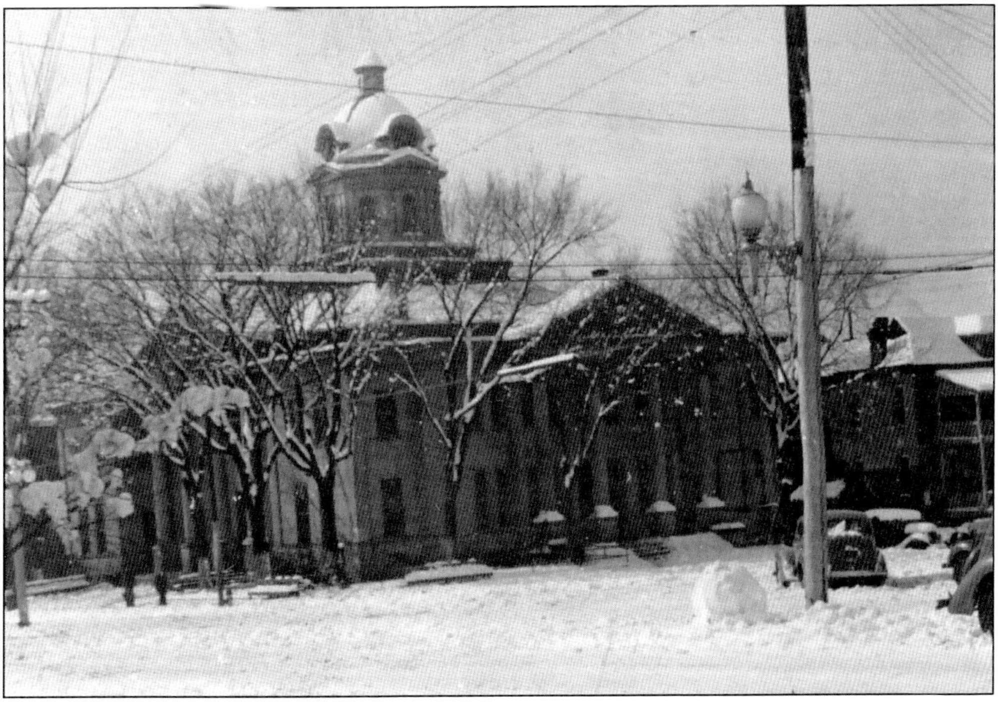

Another photograph of the snowstorm of 1940 shows the county courthouse and, behind it, the county jail. School superintendent Frank Dillard closed schools since many roads were impassable. (Courtesy of L.C. Smith.)

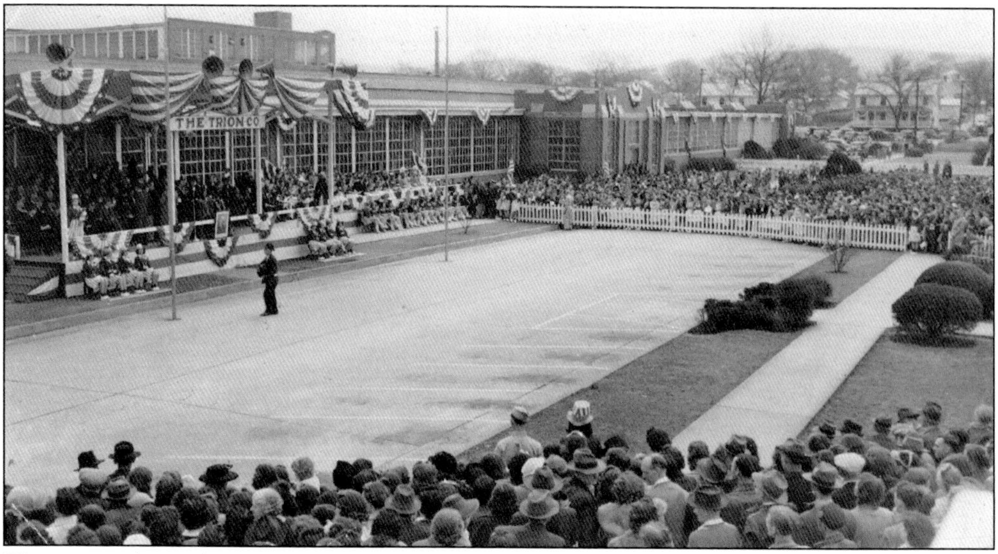

This image shows the presentation ceremony of the Army-Navy Production Award to the men and women of the Trion Company, Trion, Georgia, on March 18, 1943. The "E" Award was given for excellence to plants producing weapons, equipment, and materials needed for World War II. A silver "E" insignia pin was presented to all employees in recognition of their contributions to the production of war equipment. (Courtesy of Bill Barker.)

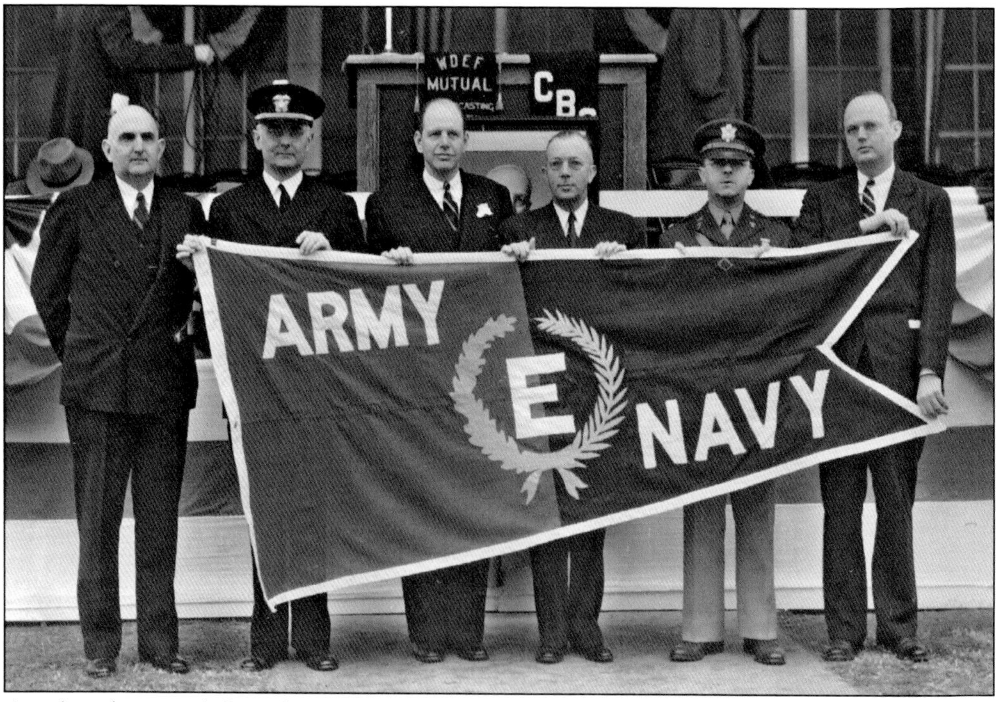

Another photograph from the presentation ceremony shows representatives from the military and officers of the Trion Company, which owned the mill. Shown from left to right are Dr. C.R. Wilcox, headmaster of the Darlington School for Boys and master of ceremonies; Lt. A.S. Lewis; John L. Riegel, chairman of the board; N. Bernard Murphy, president; Lt. Col. Harold M. Manderbach; and German H.H. Emory, treasurer. (Courtesy of Mount Vernon Mills.)

During World War II, Archibald A. Farrar fought in the battle for Leipzig, Germany, in 1945 and was subsequently awarded the Distinguished Service Cross, the French Croix de Guerre, and a Bronze Star, among others. After the war, he returned to Summerville to practice law. His firm continued after his death in 1992 under the leadership of his eldest son, Arch Farrar Jr. (Courtesy of Janet Farrar Byington.)

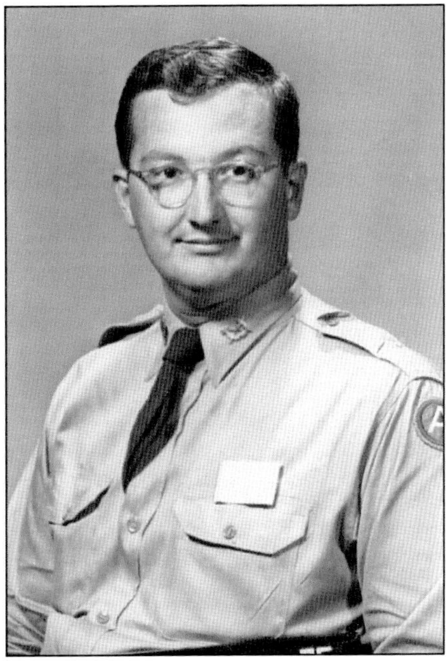

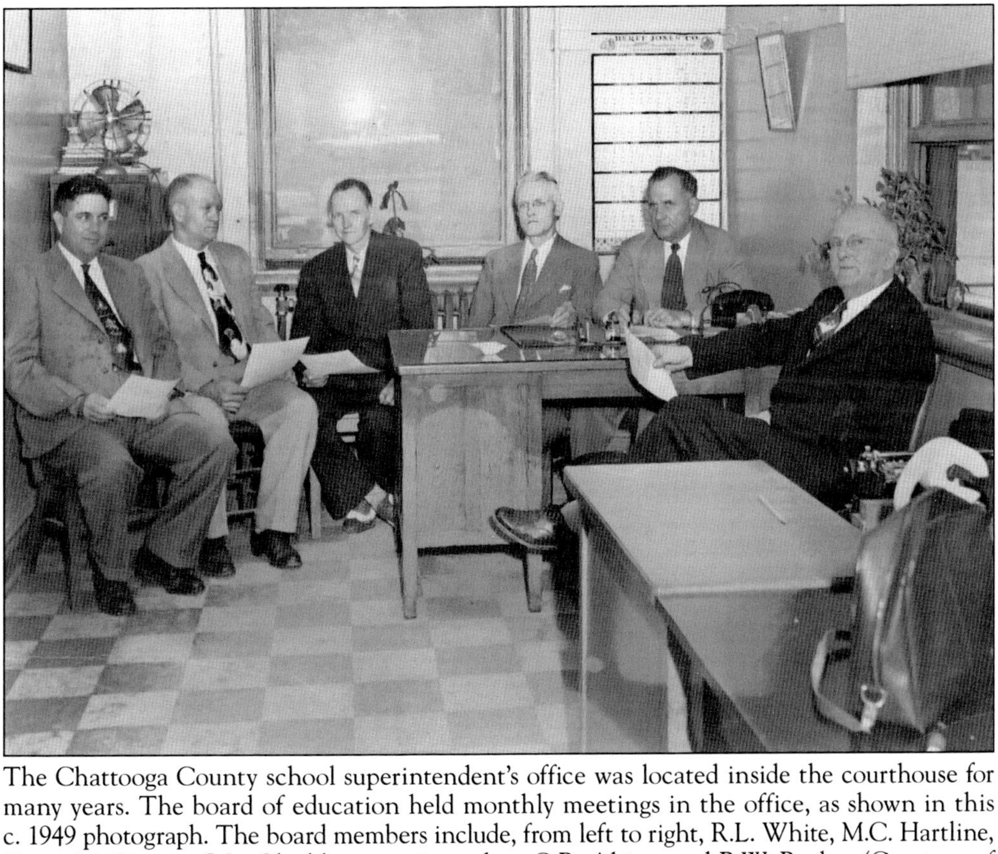

The Chattooga County school superintendent's office was located inside the courthouse for many years. The board of education held monthly meetings in the office, as shown in this c. 1949 photograph. The board members include, from left to right, R.L. White, M.C. Hartline, Harry McGinnis, O.L. Cleckler, superintendent C.B. Akins, and R.W. Bagley. (Courtesy of Gene McGinnis.)

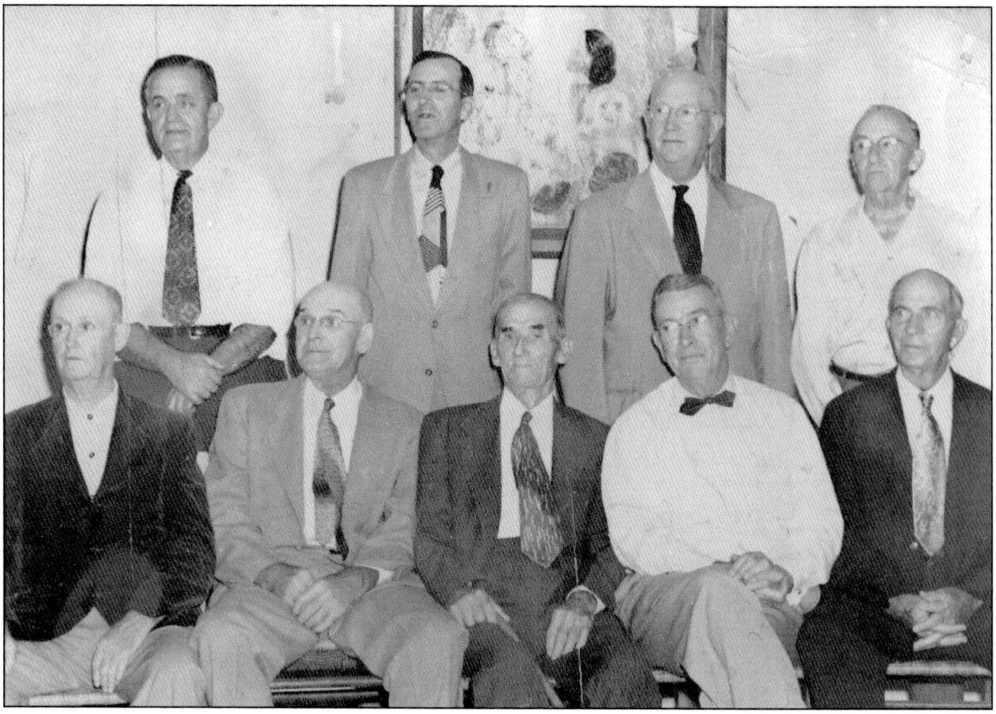

A Layman's Association meeting includes, from left to right, (first row) Rowland Henry, Henry Powell, Mid Allen Sr., Wyatt Ransom, and John Agnew; (second row) John D. Taylor Jr., Henry McWhorter, Baker Farrar, and Carl Wilson. (Courtesy of Janet Farrar Byington)

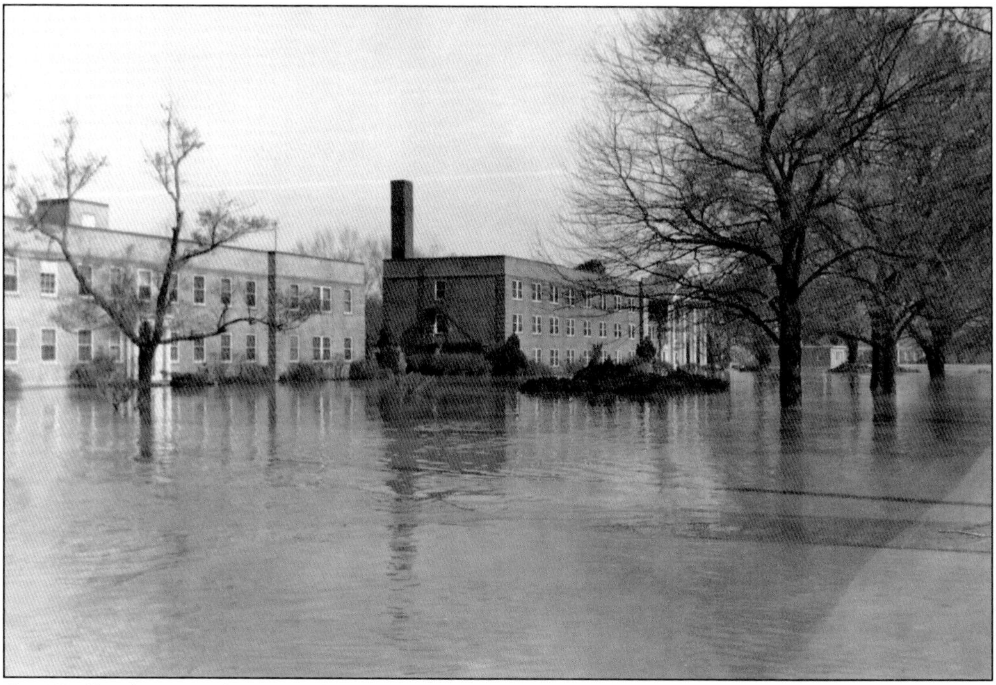

A 1951 flood covers the ground along Park Avenue in Trion. This photograph shows the Trion Hospital on the left and the Trion Inn in the center. (Courtesy of Charles Logan.)

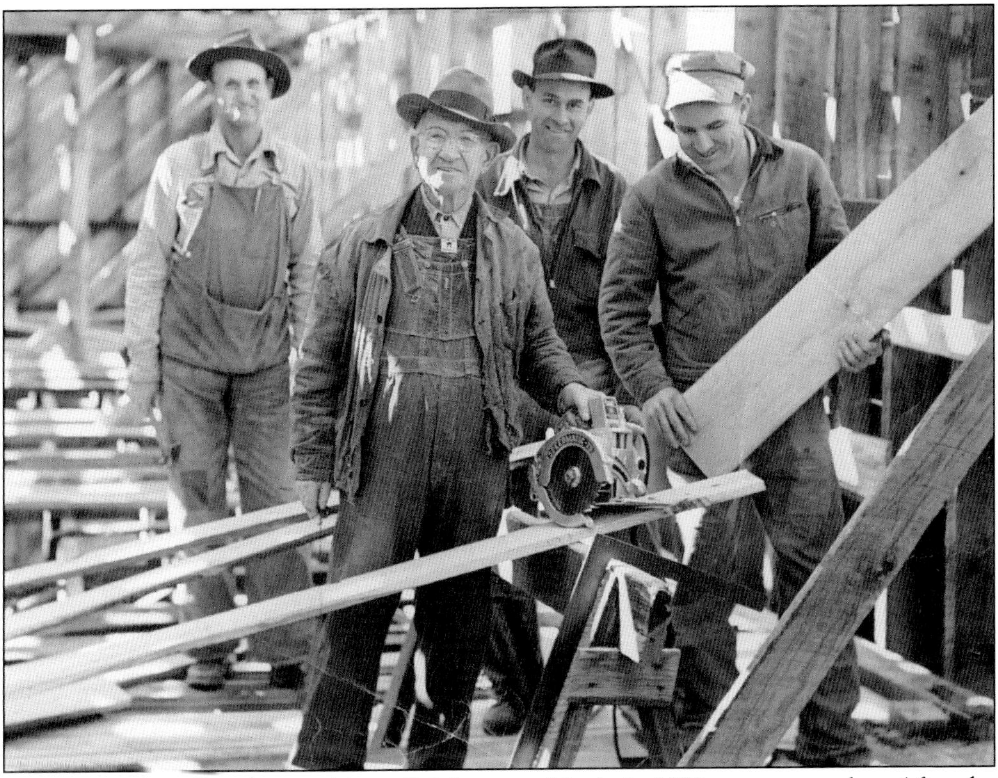

George A. Kling (front) moved from California to Menlo in 1898 to grow peaches. After the "peach bust," he operated a cotton gin for 41 years, served two terms as county commissioner, was elected mayor of Menlo, and served on the Menlo City Council for 13 years. This 1953 photograph also shows, from left to right, George Romine, Fay Grigsby, and George Kling Jr. (Courtesy of Phyllis Grigsby Howell.)

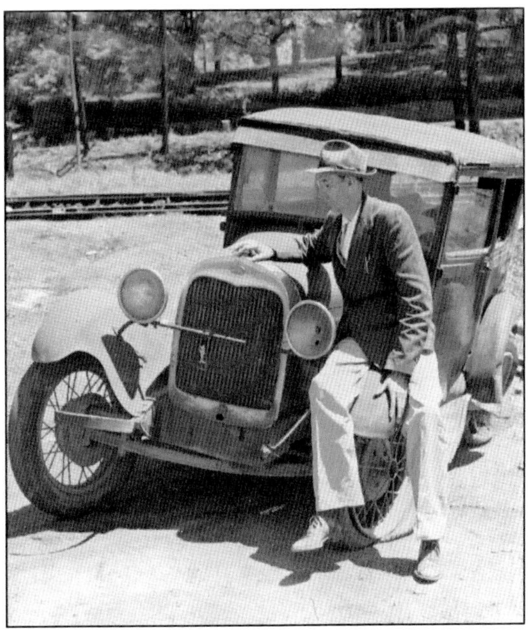

In 1929, Henry McWhorter bought his new Ford Model A. While approaching the crossing at the Summerville depot in 1954, the car's brakes failed, and the 60-year-old McWhorter and his vehicle were pushed 200 feet down the track by a passing freight train. Although he escaped with only a few scratches, McWhorter lamented having to replace his first new car. (Courtesy of Gene McGinnis.)

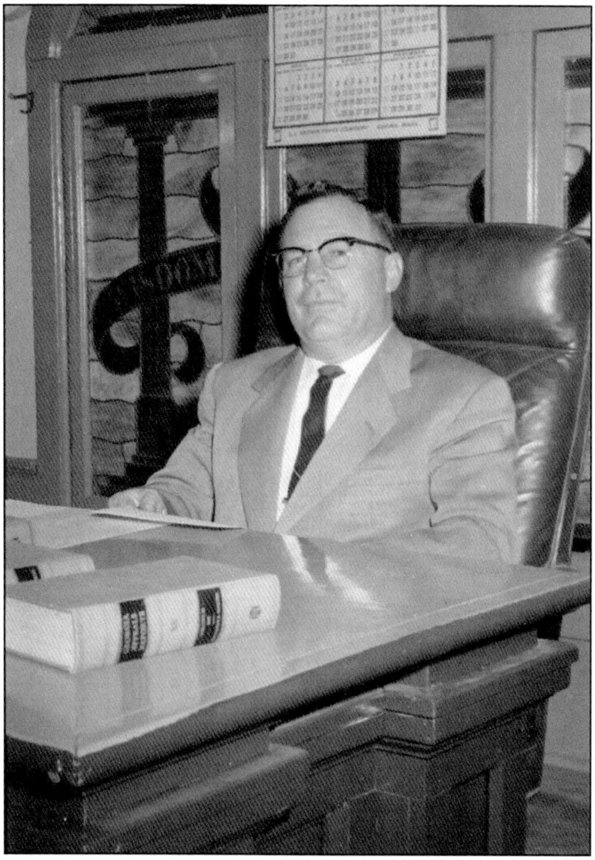

Shown in a 1959 photograph, F.H. "Pete" Boney was a teacher and football coach at Summerville High School before moving to Trion High School in 1937. After a stint in the Navy during World War II, he returned to Summerville to open a law office in 1955. His wife, Virginia, was principal of Summerville Elementary School for many years. (Photograph by T. Emmett Nunn, courtesy of Betty Morris Rice.)

A 1960 snow and ice storm closed schools and businesses, knocked out telephone service for hundreds of county households, and made local roads impassable. This photograph shows John D. Taylor Jr. and his wife, Nell, crossing Commerce Street in Summerville. (Courtesy of Gene McGinnis.)

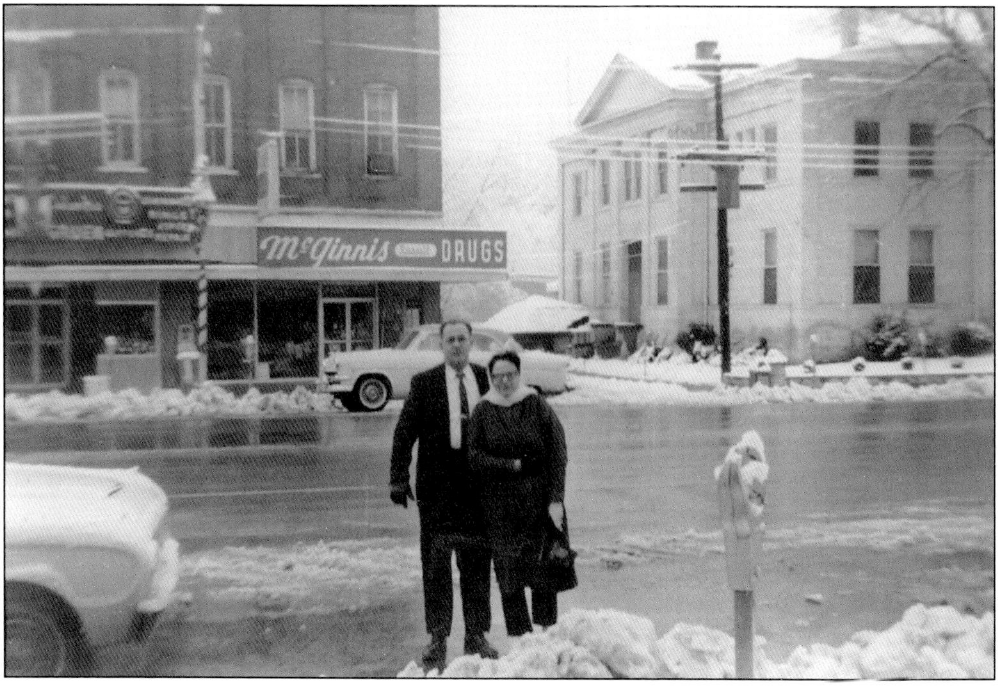

Blanche Toles graduated from Menlo High School in 1934 and began her teaching career two years later at the Pine Grove School, located between Menlo and Lyerly. She and another teacher supervised 100 students in a school with no electricity or running water. In 1946, she transferred to the Menlo School, where she remained until retiring in 1986 after a remarkable 50-year teaching career. (Courtesy of Chattooga County Library.)

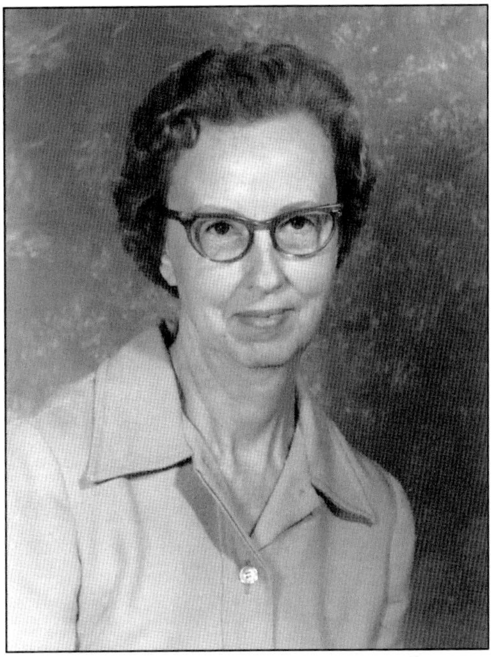

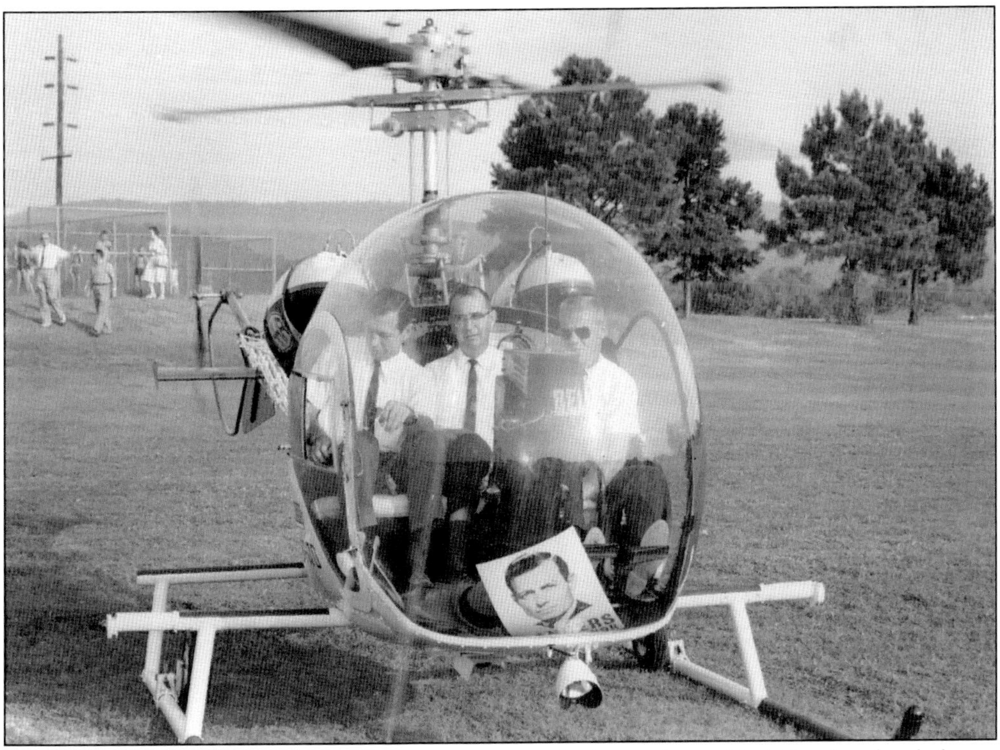

In 1962, while campaigning for governor against the incumbent, Carl Sanders landed in a helicopter next to the Summerville Recreation Center accompanied by his local campaign manager, Summerville attorney Joseph "Bo" Loggins. Shown here are Sanders (left), Loggins (center), and an unidentified pilot. Sanders won the race and, at age 37, became one of America's youngest governors. (Photograph by T. Emmett Nunn, courtesy of Betty Morris Rice.)

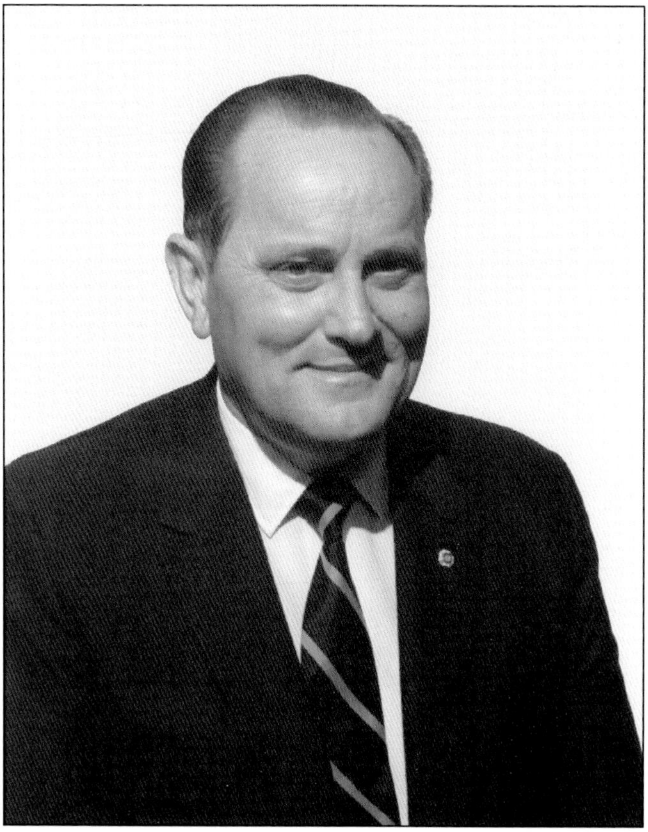

James H. "Sloppy" Floyd was born in Chattooga County in 1920. He served 22 years as a state representative and became known as one of Georgia's most powerful legislators as chairman of the state House Appropriations Committee. Following his death in 1974, new offices for the Georgia Senate and House of Representatives were named in his honor, as was a state park near Summerville. (Courtesy of Jimmy Floyd.)

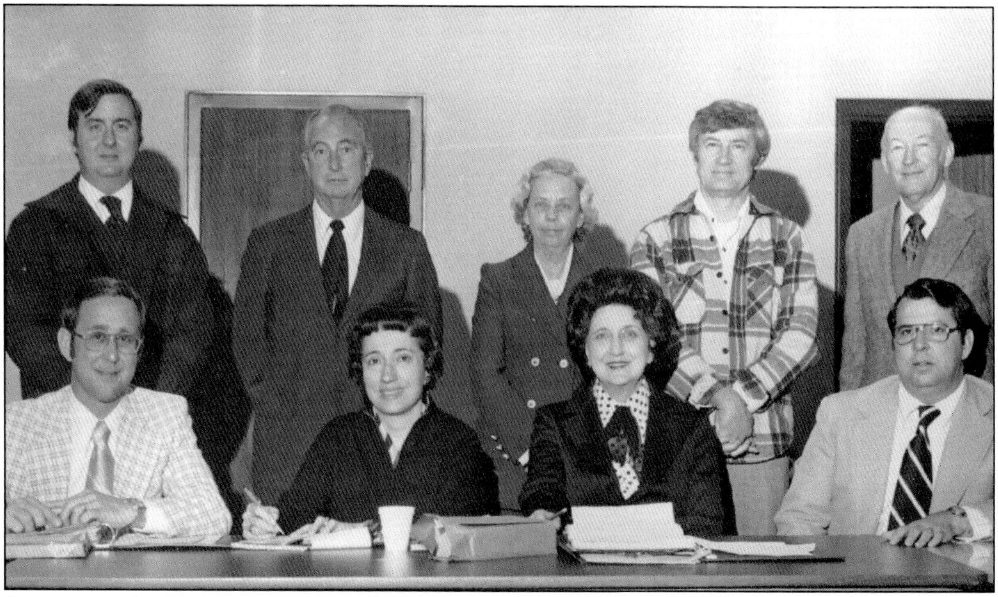

Community leaders meet in 1975 to plan the annual Christmas parade for downtown Summerville. The group includes, from left to right, (first row) unidentified, Sue Spivey, Carrie B. Freeman, and Henry Watson; (second row) J.R. "Bud" Jackson, Bill Farrar, Conner Allen, Boyce Dooley, and Bob Guffin. (Courtesy of Sue Spivey.)

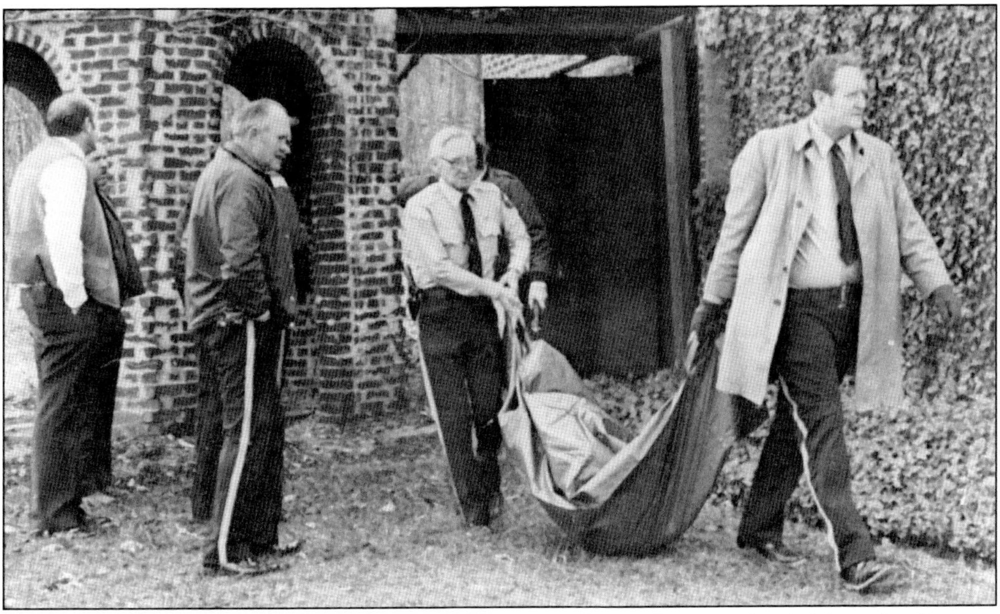

One of the most notorious crimes to occur in Chattooga County happened in 1982 in what became known as the Corpsewood murders. This photograph shows the body of one of the two victims being removed from his home, described as a castle-like fortress with no electricity or running water. Sheriff Gary McConnell is shown on the left. (Courtesy of the *Summerville News*.)

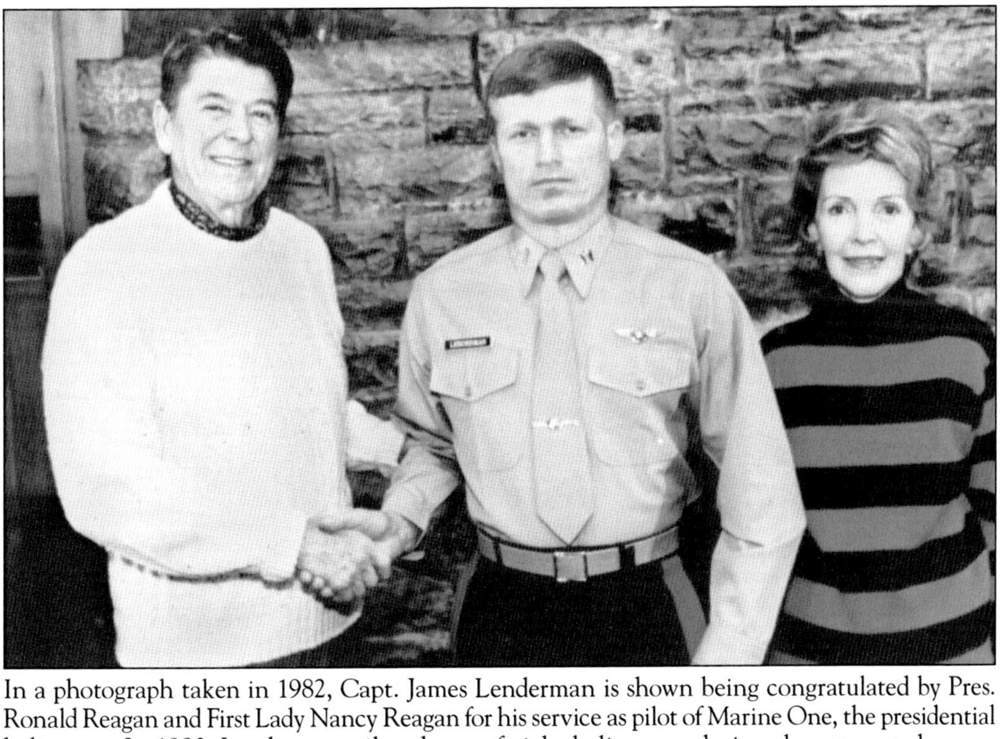

In a photograph taken in 1982, Capt. James Lenderman is shown being congratulated by Pres. Ronald Reagan and First Lady Nancy Reagan for his service as pilot of Marine One, the presidential helicopter. In 1980, Lenderman piloted one of eight helicopters during the attempted rescue of Americans held hostage in Iran. He later became principal of Chattooga High School and Chattooga County school superintendent. (Courtesy of Jim Lenderman.)

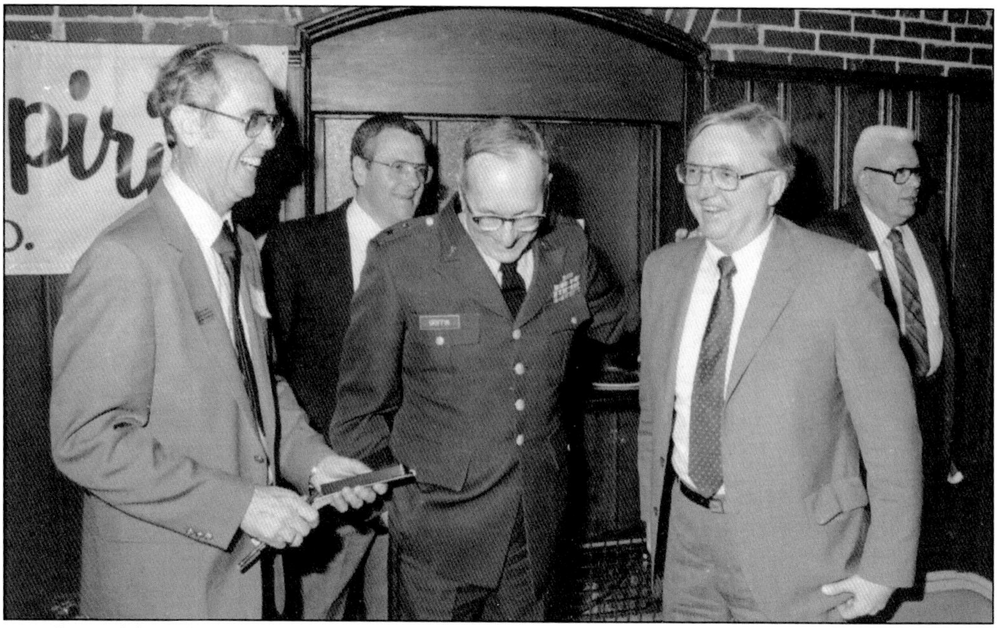

Members of the Chattooga County Chamber of Commerce met with a Gen. Joseph Griffin of the Georgia National Guard to lobby for an armory for the county. Shown in this 1980s photograph are, from left to right, Summerville mayor Sewell Cash, superintendent of Trion schools Bill Kinzey, General Griffin, Will Hair, and "Tip" McCollum. Cash served as mayor of Summerville for two decades. (Courtesy of Sue Spivey.)

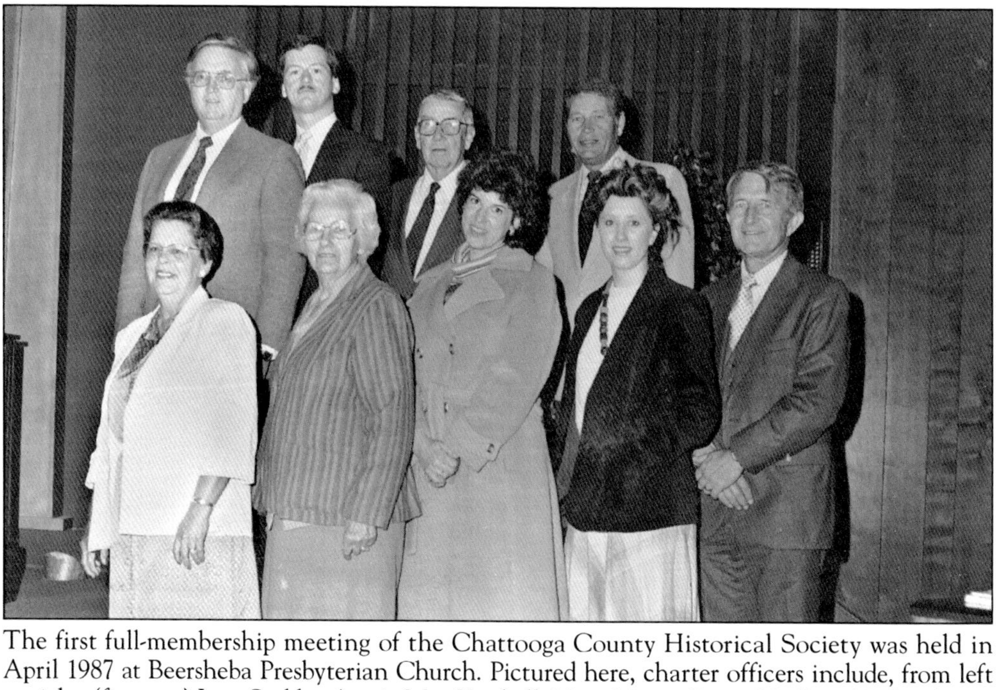

The first full-membership meeting of the Chattooga County Historical Society was held in April 1987 at Beersheba Presbyterian Church. Pictured here, charter officers include, from left to right, (first row) Jean Stubbs, Annie Mae Kimbell, Mary Myers, Susan Huff, and Bill Selman; (second row) Will Hair, Steven Strickland, A.J. Strickland, and Jerry Sprayberry. (Courtesy of Steven Strickland.)

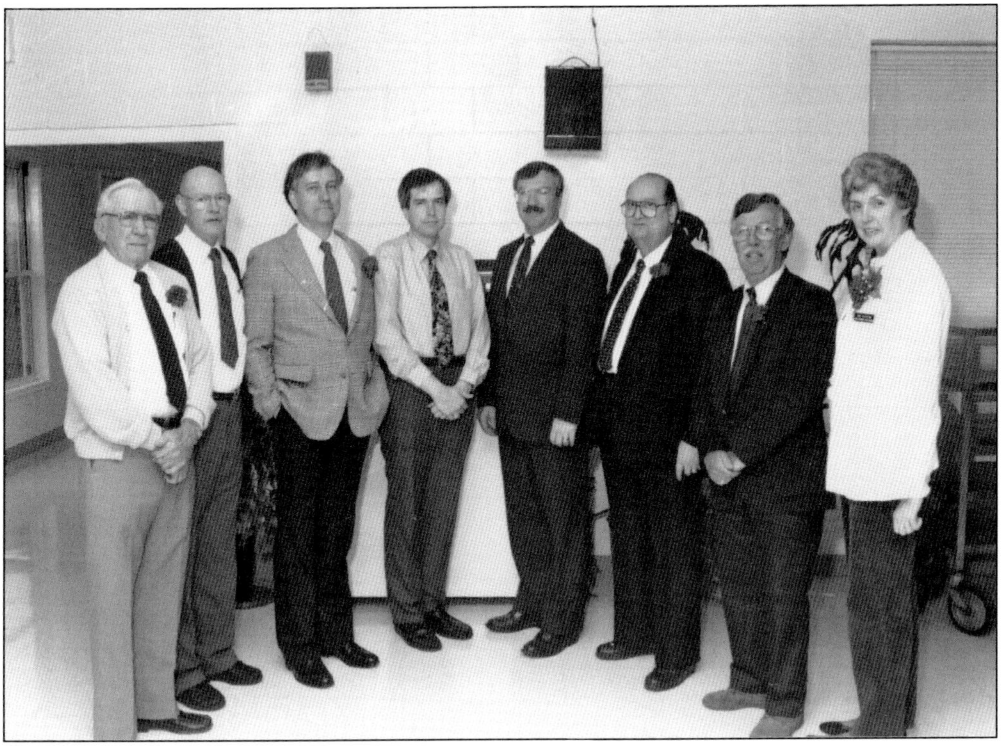

Chattooga County physicians were honored in 1991 at a luncheon hosted by the county hospital. Shown are, from left to right, Drs. Hugh Goodwin, Herman Spivey, and Stephen Wohlgemuth; Gene McGinnis, hospital authority chairman; Dan Sweitzer, hospital executive director; Drs. Jack Meacham and Gary Smith; and Gail Allen, nurse practitioner. (Courtesy of Sue Spivey.)

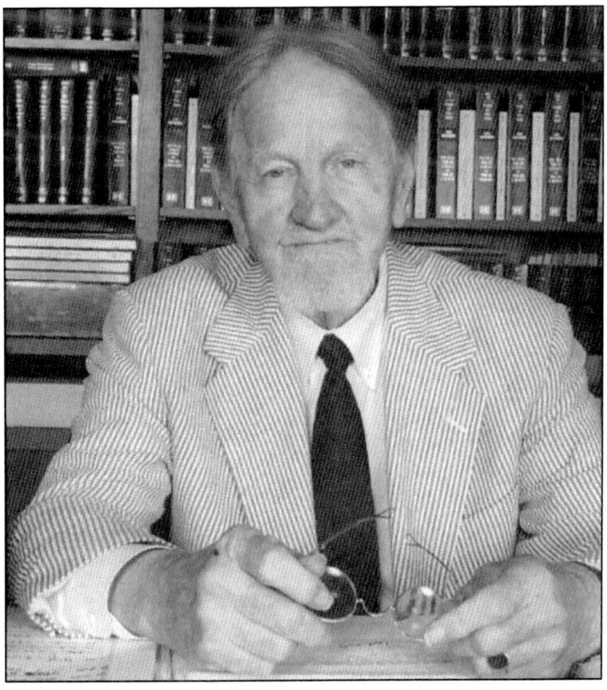

Bobby Lee Cook was born in 1927 at the family home in Chattoogaville and worked at his father's general store as a boy. After attending Vanderbilt University, Cook began practicing law in 1949 and is now a nationally known criminal defense attorney. His law firm, Cook & Connelly, continues practicing from offices in Summerville. (Courtesy of Bobby Lee Cook.)

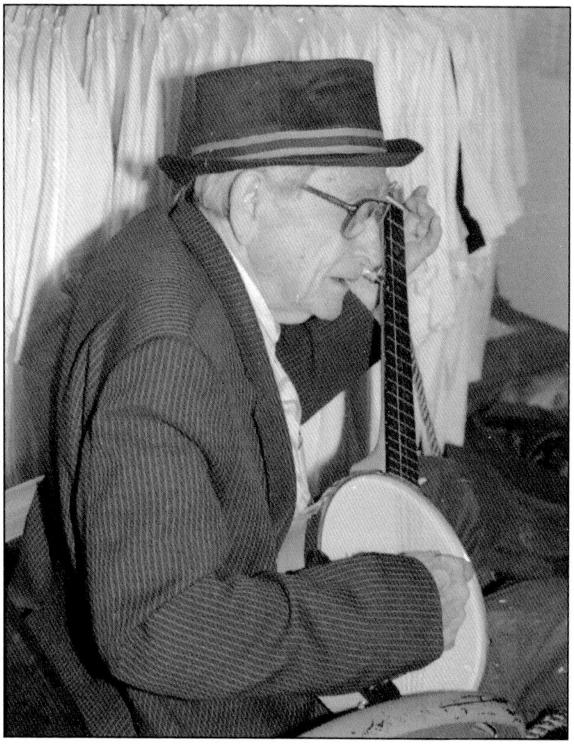

Howard Finster was known as a part-time country preacher and bicycle repairman in the Pennville community before becoming one of the most recognized folk artists in the world. According to Finster, he heard a voice compelling him to create sacred art. Afterward, the indefatigable Finster created tens of thousands of paintings and other art at his Paradise Gardens north of Summerville. (Courtesy of Nancy L. Smith.)

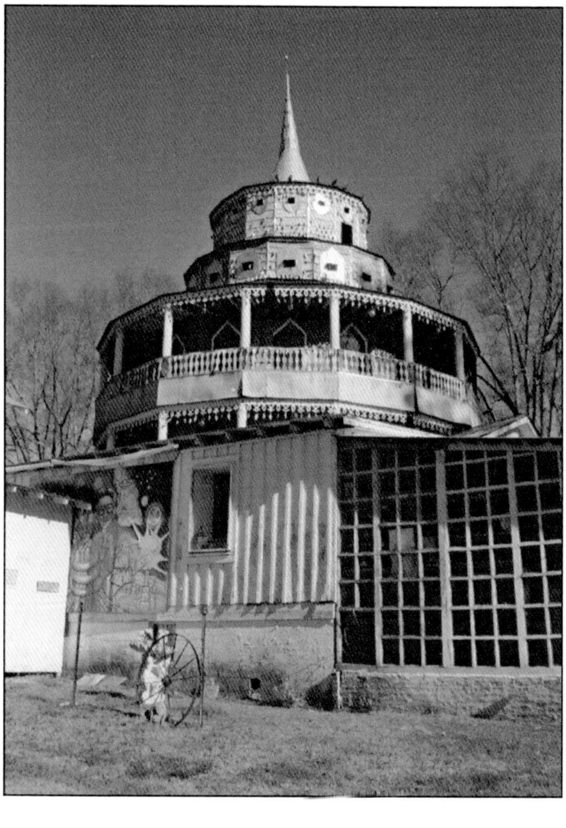

The need for restoration of Finster's most visible creation, Folk Art Chapel, has greatly increased since this photograph was made in 1999. Art critics, rock stars, celebrities, and fans once flocked to this site. Finster died in 2001 at the age of 84. (Courtesy of Nancy L. Smith.)

Four

Churches and Congregations

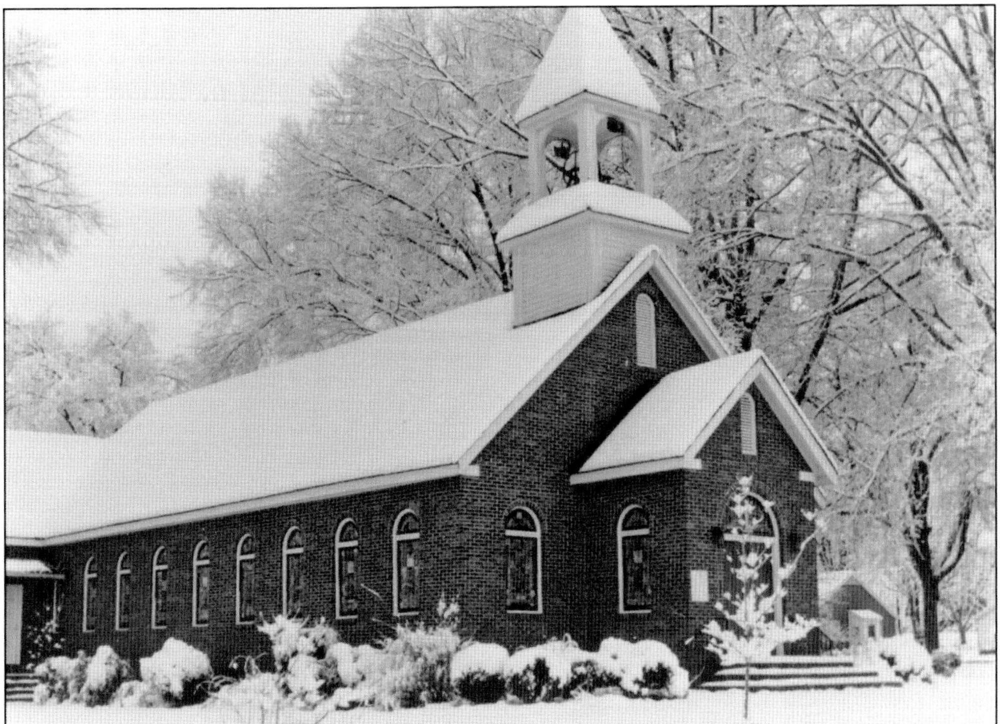

The Menlo Presbyterian Church is pictured after a rare snowfall in this c. 1986 photograph. The church was founded in 1908 by members of Alpine Presbyterian Church. The original wooden structure burned in 1938 and was replaced by the present brick sanctuary the following year. (Courtesy of Chattooga County Library.)

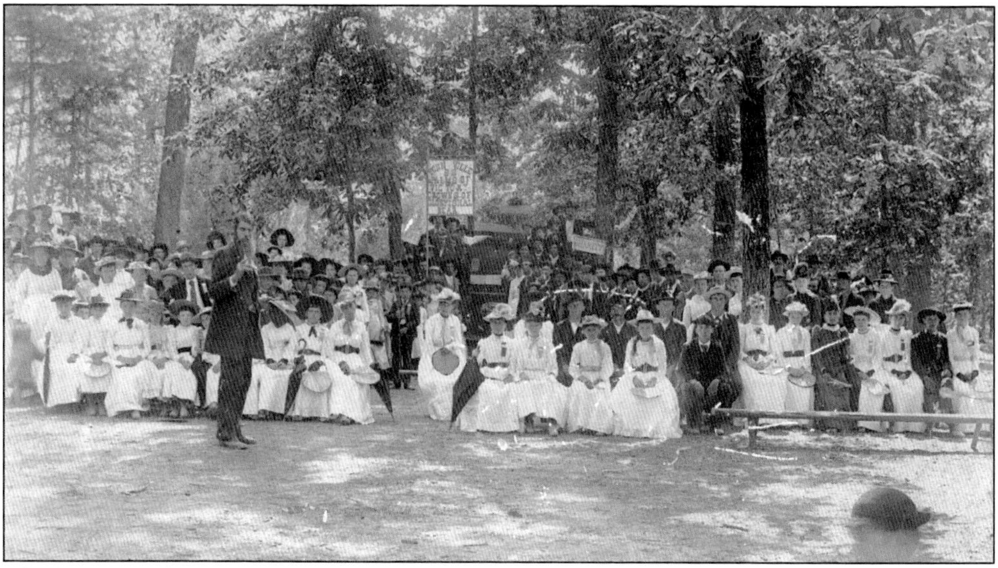

The banner reads, "Penn Ville SS. Palms of Victory. Crowns of Glory. I Shall Bear." Other banners include the single words "Hope" and "Charity." Music for the gathering was provided by an organ shown in the center of the photograph. Based on the clothing, the photograph may have been taken some time between 1895 and 1910. (Courtesy of Darlene Norton Mallonee.)

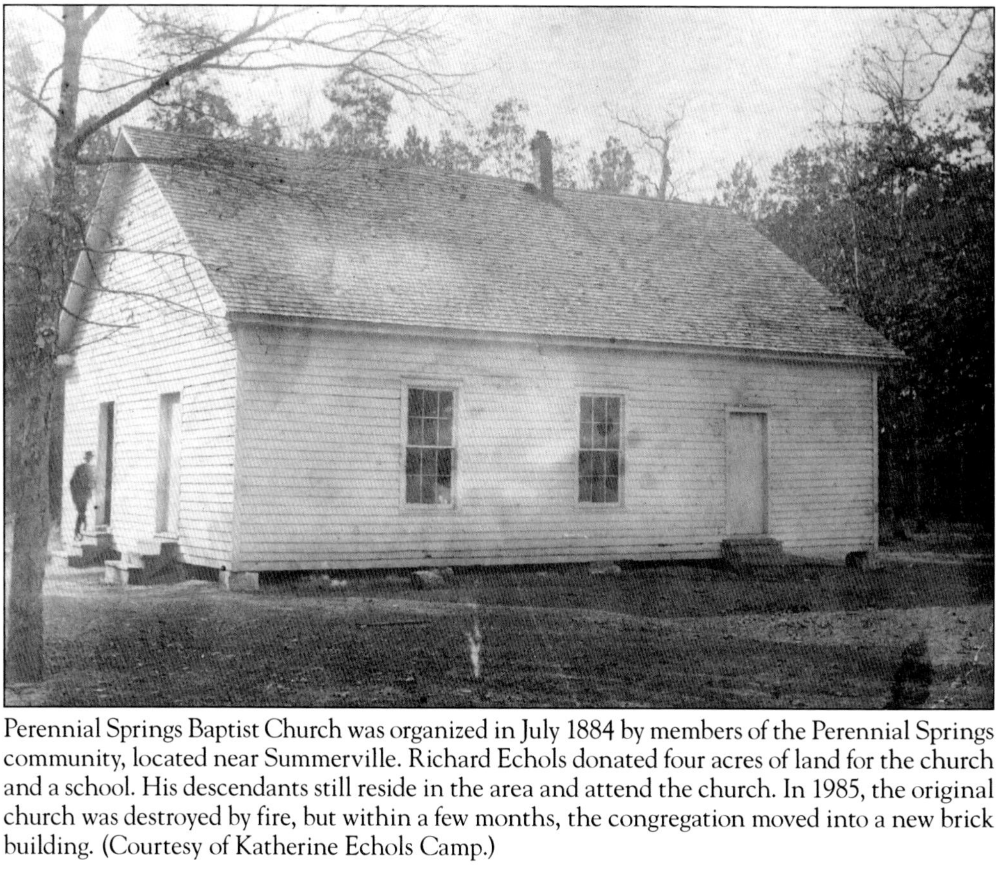

Perennial Springs Baptist Church was organized in July 1884 by members of the Perennial Springs community, located near Summerville. Richard Echols donated four acres of land for the church and a school. His descendants still reside in the area and attend the church. In 1985, the original church was destroyed by fire, but within a few months, the congregation moved into a new brick building. (Courtesy of Katherine Echols Camp.)

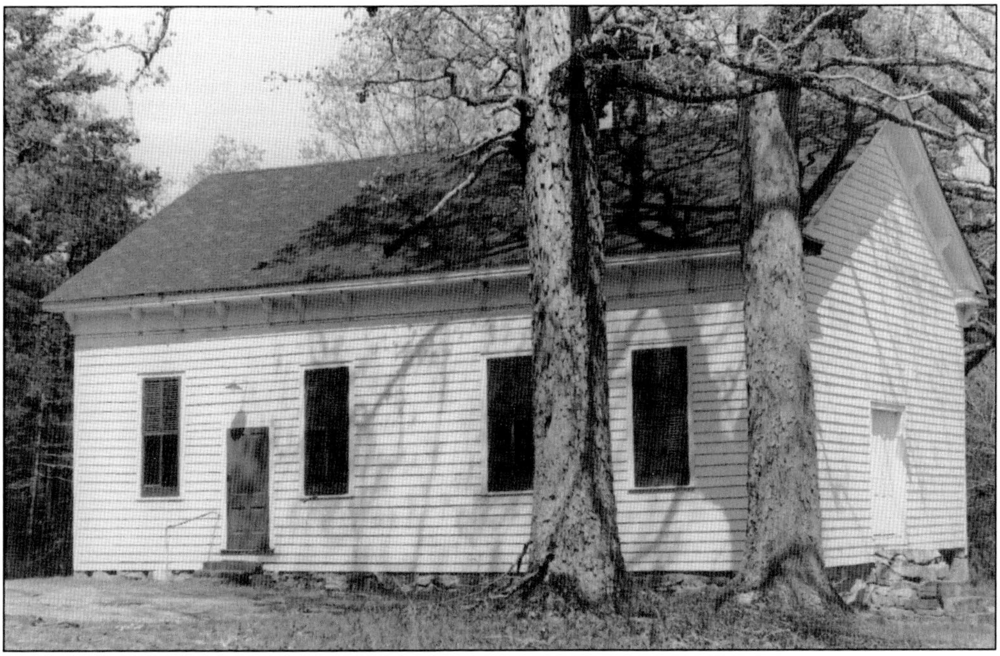

Weary of making long trips to the two Presbyterian churches in the county, the many Presbyterians residing in Dirt Town Valley organized Bethel Presbyterian Church in 1846. In 1849, the church building shown in this photograph was constructed next to an existing cemetery. The church remains standing near Gore. (Courtesy of Chattooga County Library.)

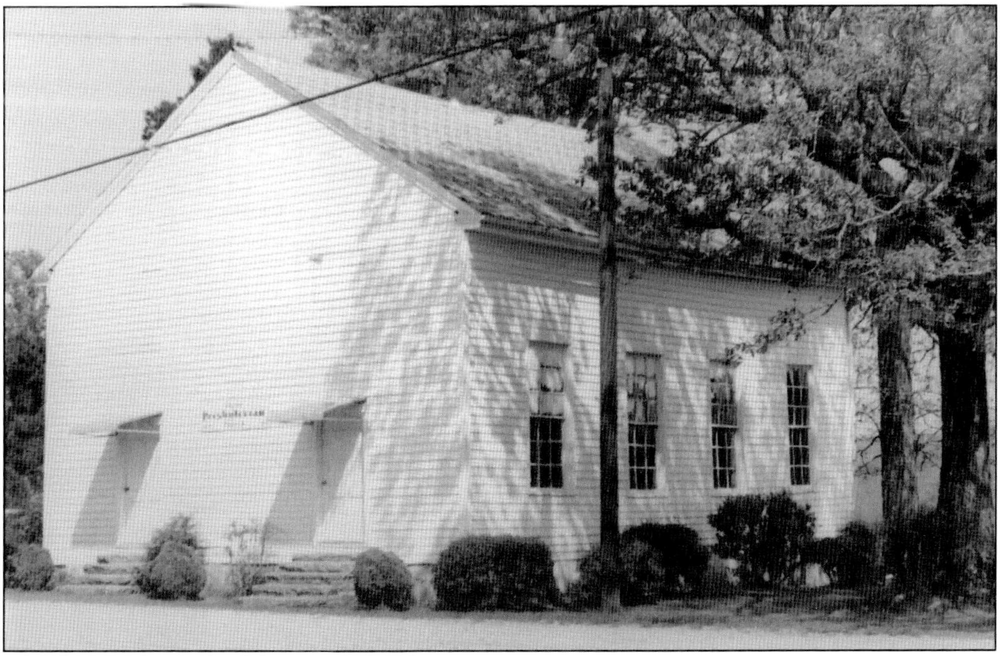

Alpine Presbyterian Church was founded in 1853 and was later used as a field hospital by Union soldiers during the Civil War. Samuel Knox, whose historic house had been built earlier on adjacent property, was a charter member. Both the church and house still stand south of Menlo. (Courtesy of Chattooga County Library.)

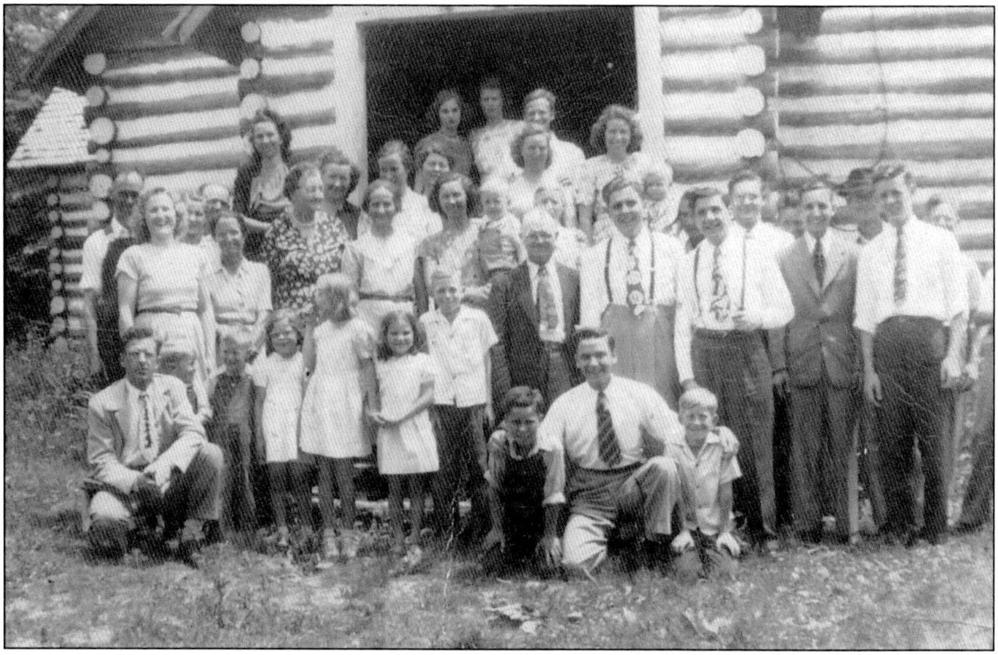

Members of the Wayside Community Chapel are shown in this photograph taken in the mid-1940s. The church later became Wayside Baptist Church. (Courtesy of Phyllis Grigsby Howell.)

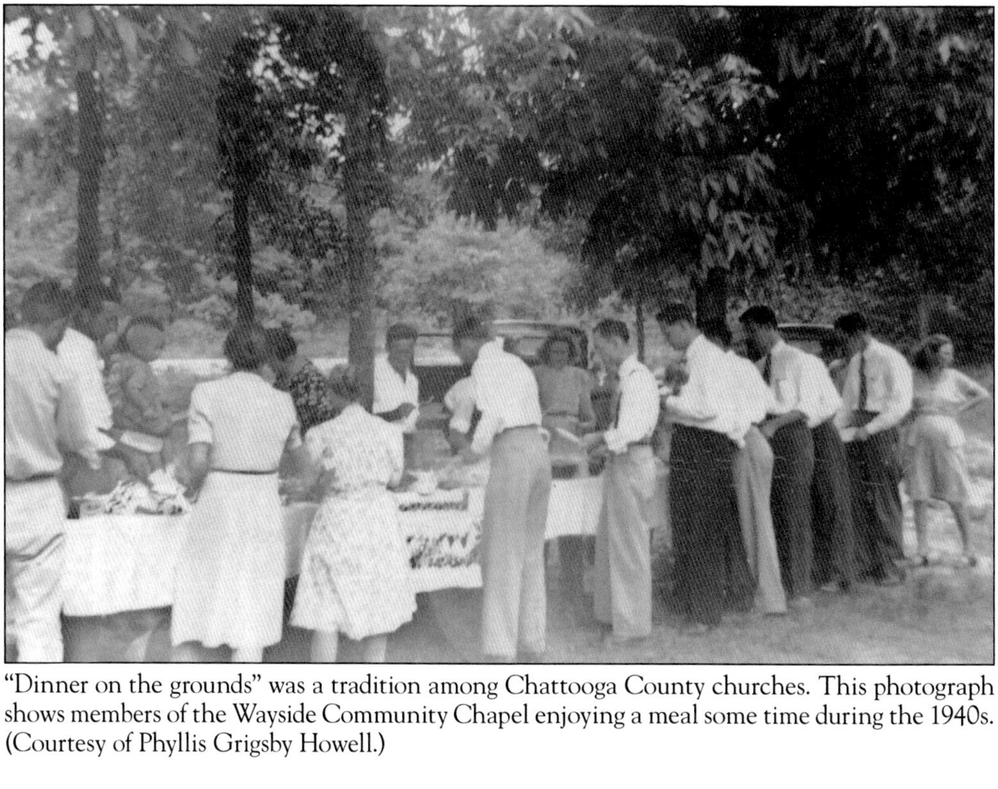

"Dinner on the grounds" was a tradition among Chattooga County churches. This photograph shows members of the Wayside Community Chapel enjoying a meal some time during the 1940s. (Courtesy of Phyllis Grigsby Howell.)

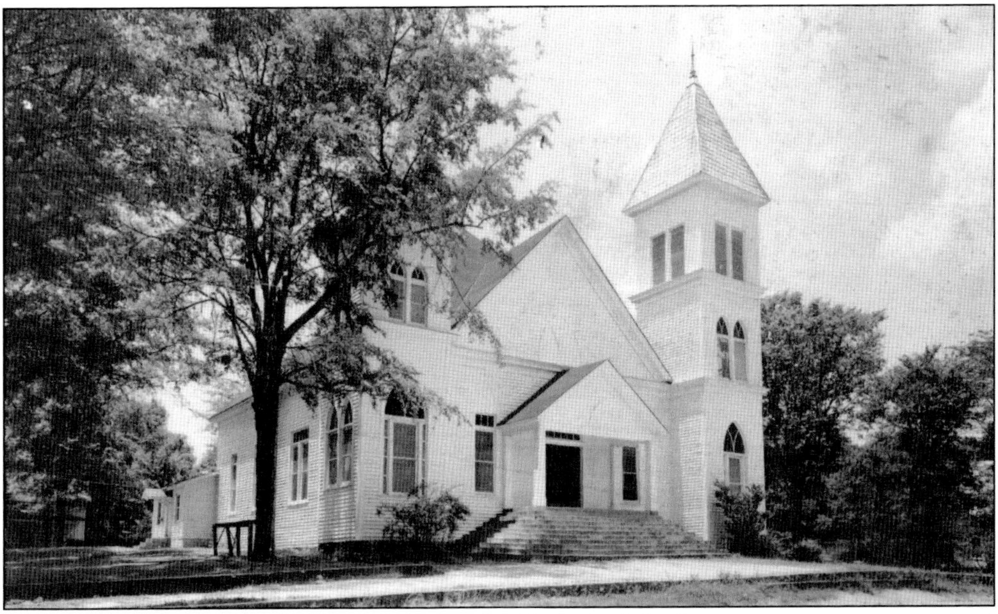

Menlo First Baptist Church was organized in the 1890s, and the first sanctuary was constructed in 1896. The building shown above was dedicated in 1908. In 1962, it was damaged by a tornado and required major renovation. (Courtesy of Menlo City Hall.)

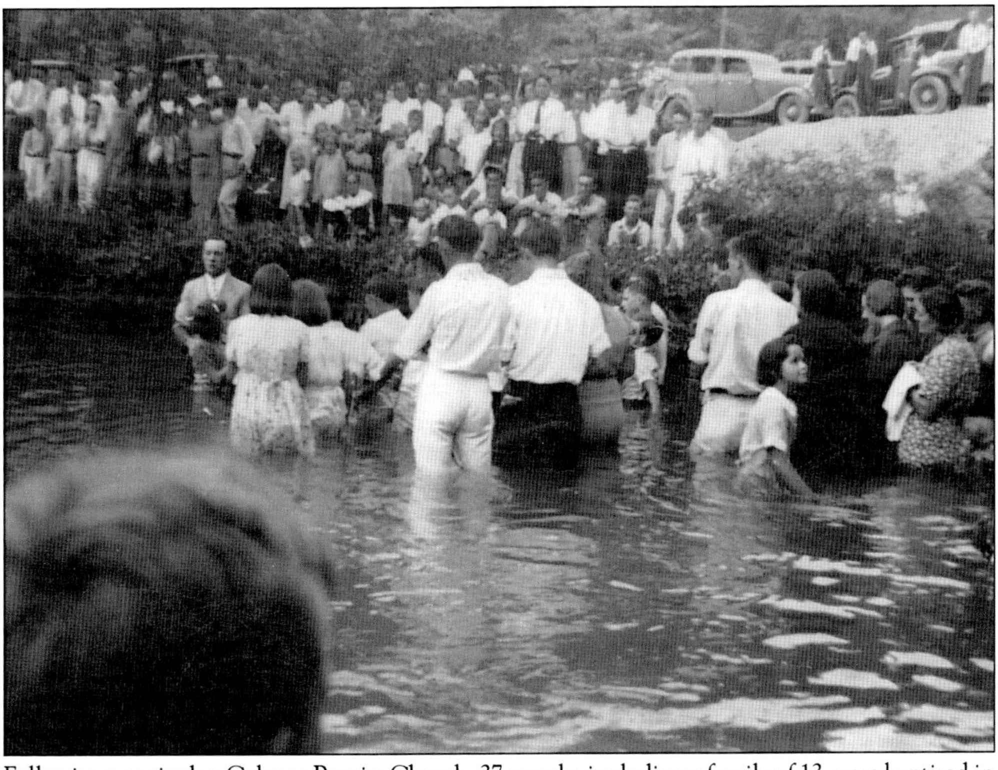

Following a revival at Calvary Baptist Church, 37 people, including a family of 13, were baptized in the Chattooga River. The Summerville church was established in 1948 with the assistance of South Summerville Baptist Church. Sidney Dooley was the first pastor. (Courtesy of Sidney Dooley.)

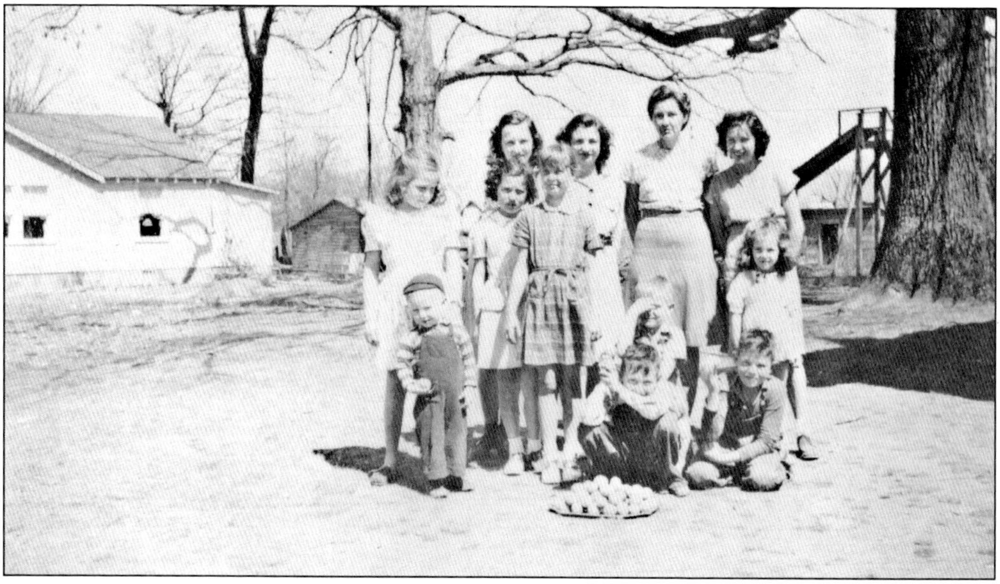

One of the highlights for children at the Lyerly Church of Christ was the annual Easter egg hunt. This 1946 photograph shows, from left to right, (on ground) Morris Hogg, Lafaughn Bishop, and Joe Frank Kimbell; (first row) unidentified, Gwen Williams, Shirley Murphy, Patsy Williams, and Brenda Hogg; (second row) Alice Murphy, Liffey Johnson, Annie Mae Kimbell, and Martha Murphy. (Courtesy of Brenda Hogg Lanier.)

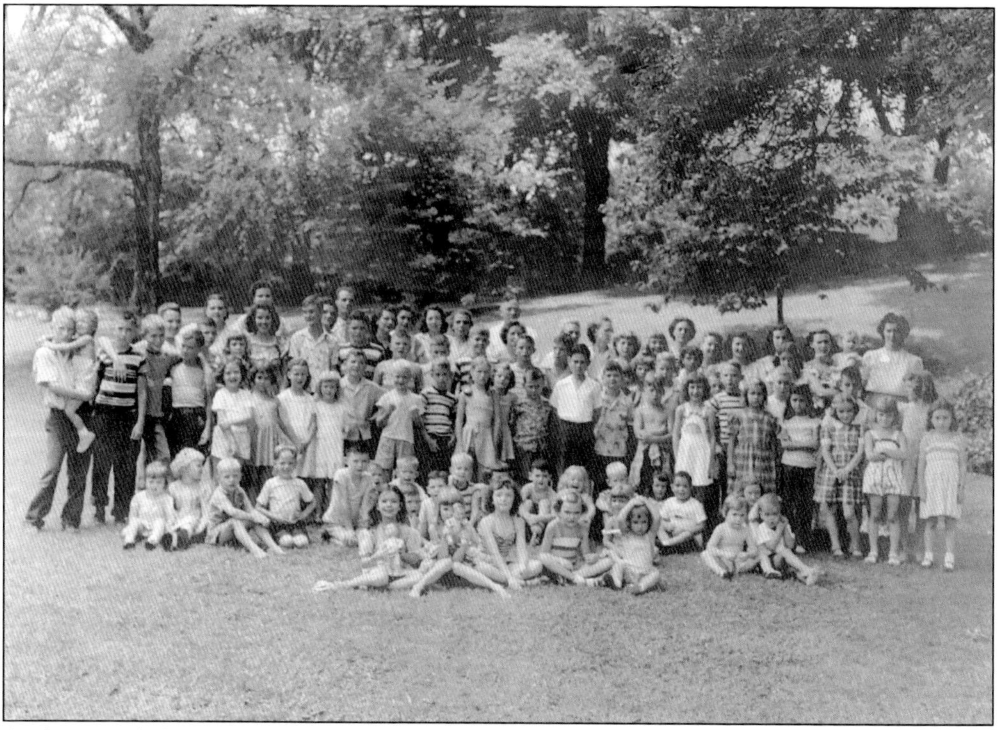

A photograph from 1949 shows members of Summerville Methodist Church and Summerville Presbyterian Church gathered for a Sunday school picnic. The Reverend Henry Grady Walker was pastor of the Methodist church at the time. (Courtesy of Alice Crouch.)

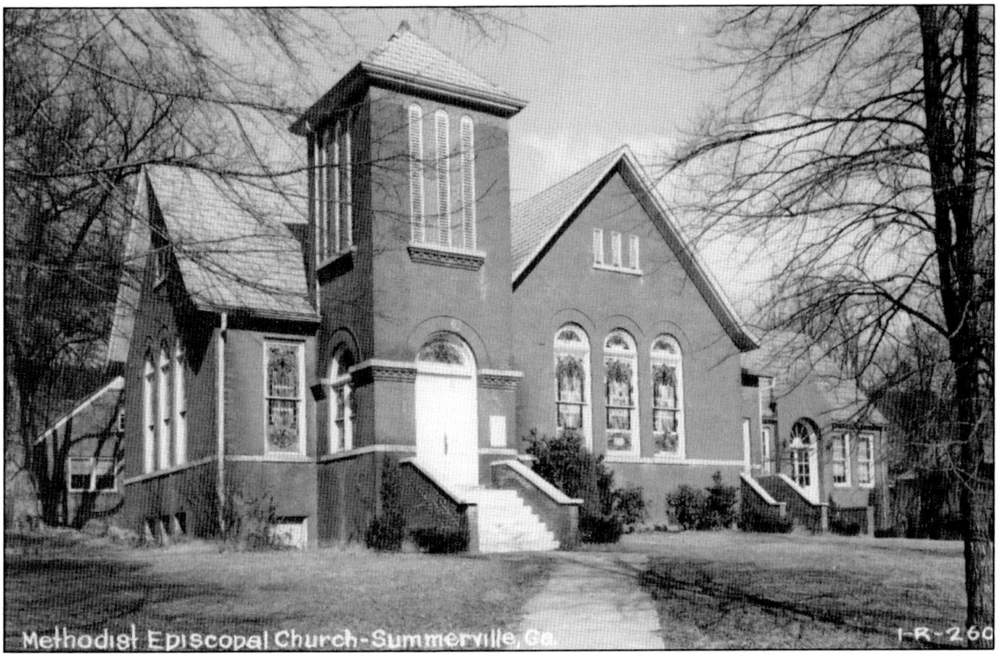

The Summerville Methodist Church originated in the 1840s and was located across West Washington Street from the present site in a building used by three congregations. In 1849, the first church was constructed at the current location, followed by the second building (shown here), begun in 1907. The church is now known as the Summerville First United Methodist Church. (Courtesy of Chattooga County Library.)

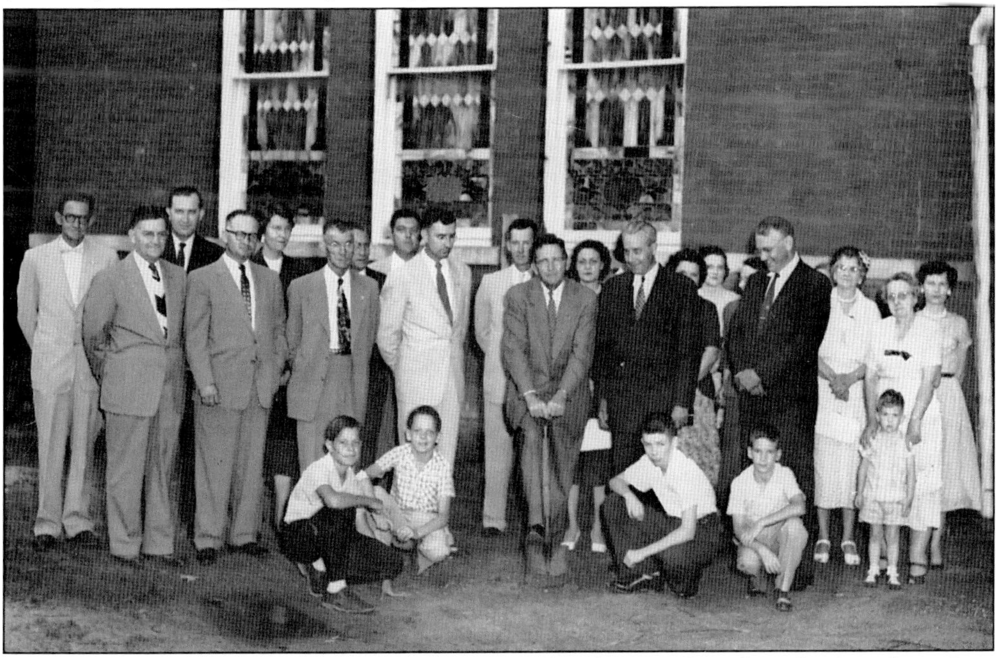

In 1954, members of the Summerville Methodist Church are gathered on the front lawn for a ground-breaking ceremony for a new fellowship hall. The new addition was completed the following year under the leadership of the Reverend Frank Barfield. (Courtesy of Alice Crouch.)

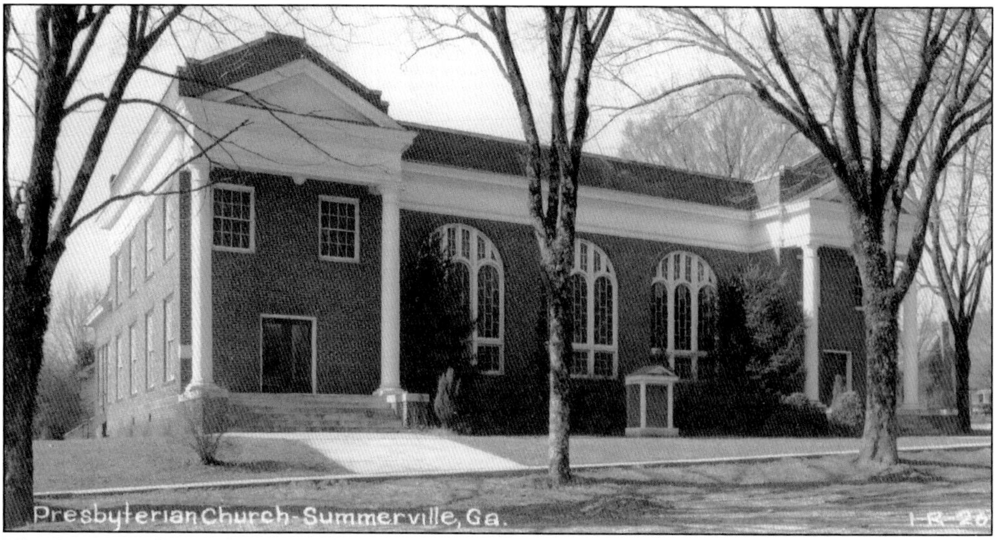

The Summerville Presbyterian Church was established in 1841 by Presbyterians attending Pleasant Green Church four miles west of town at Gamble Springs. The church building pictured in this 1950s photograph was constructed in 1924. In 1961, a new addition included space for Sunday school, a kitchen, and a fellowship hall. (Courtesy of the *Summerville News*.)

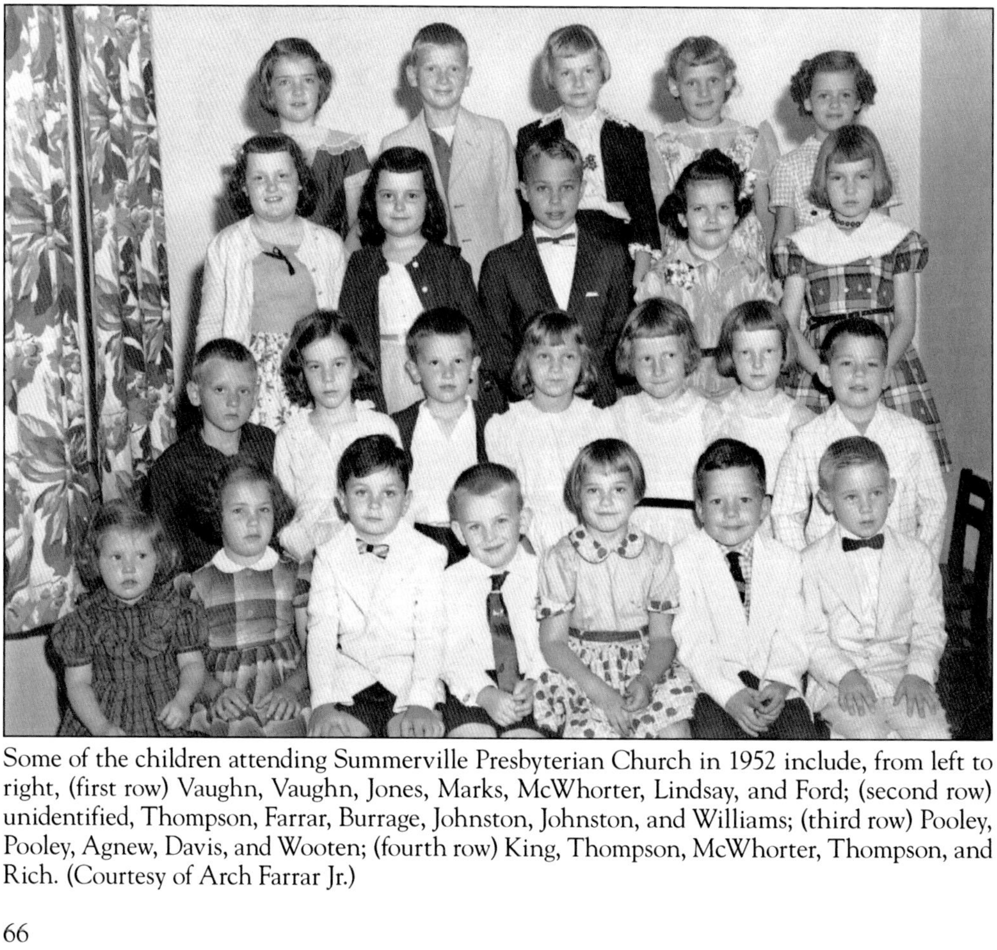
Some of the children attending Summerville Presbyterian Church in 1952 include, from left to right, (first row) Vaughn, Vaughn, Jones, Marks, McWhorter, Lindsay, and Ford; (second row) unidentified, Thompson, Farrar, Burrage, Johnston, Johnston, and Williams; (third row) Pooley, Pooley, Agnew, Davis, and Wooten; (fourth row) King, Thompson, McWhorter, Thompson, and Rich. (Courtesy of Arch Farrar Jr.)

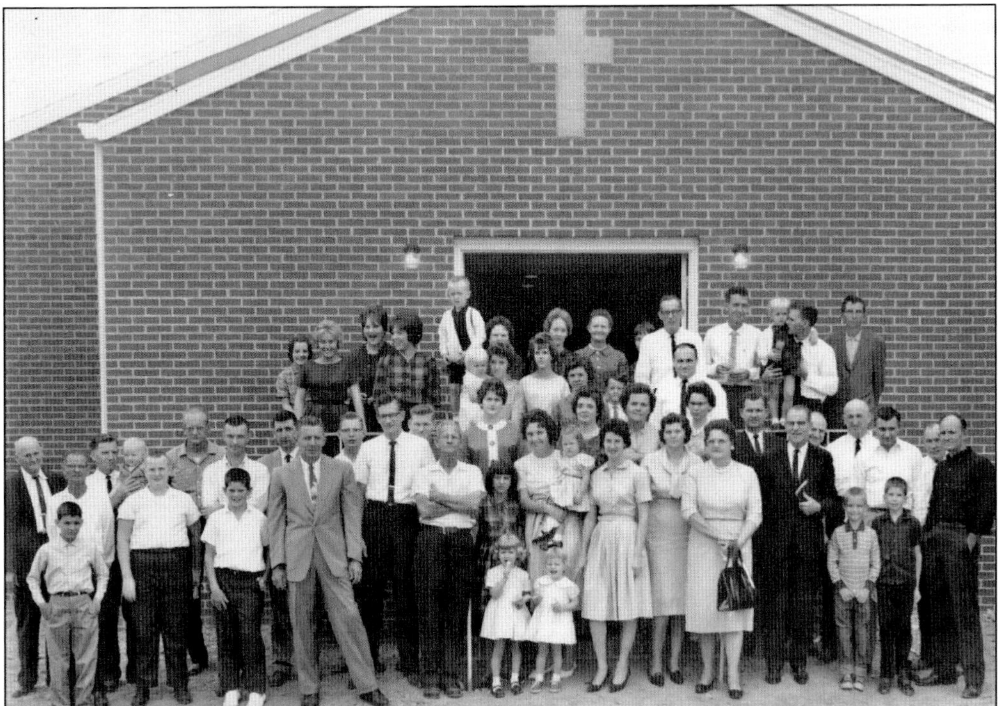

The congregation of the Dry Valley Baptist Church in Trion is shown in this c. 1962 photograph. This was the first Sunday gathering in the newly built sanctuary after an earlier one was destroyed by fire. (Courtesy of Mackie Carson.)

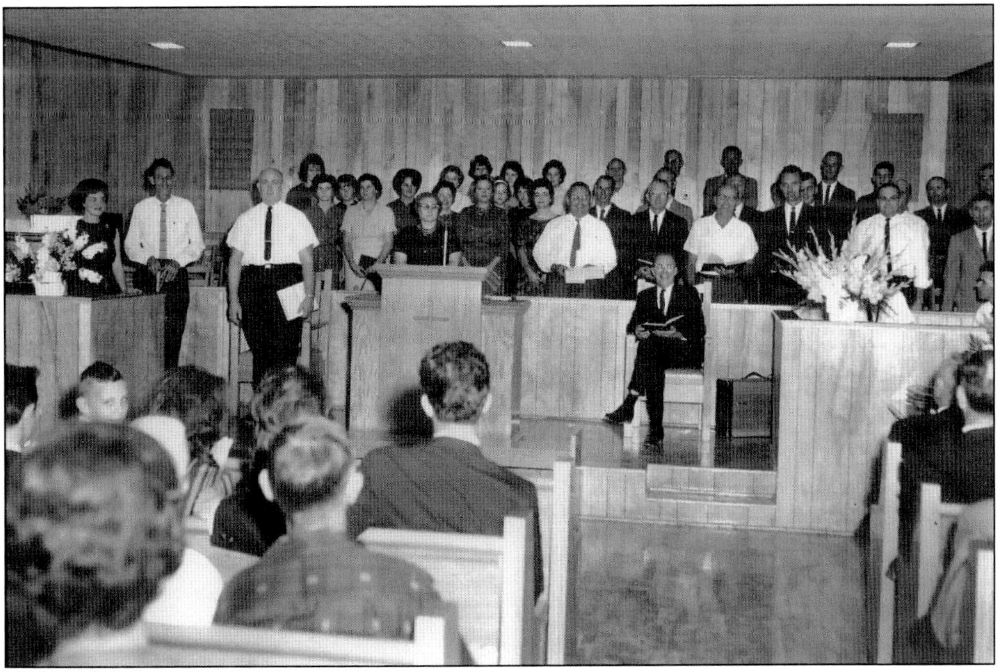

The interior of the Dry Valley Baptist Church is shown in this photograph taken around 1962. E.H. Carson was the church pastor. (Courtesy of Mackie Carson.)

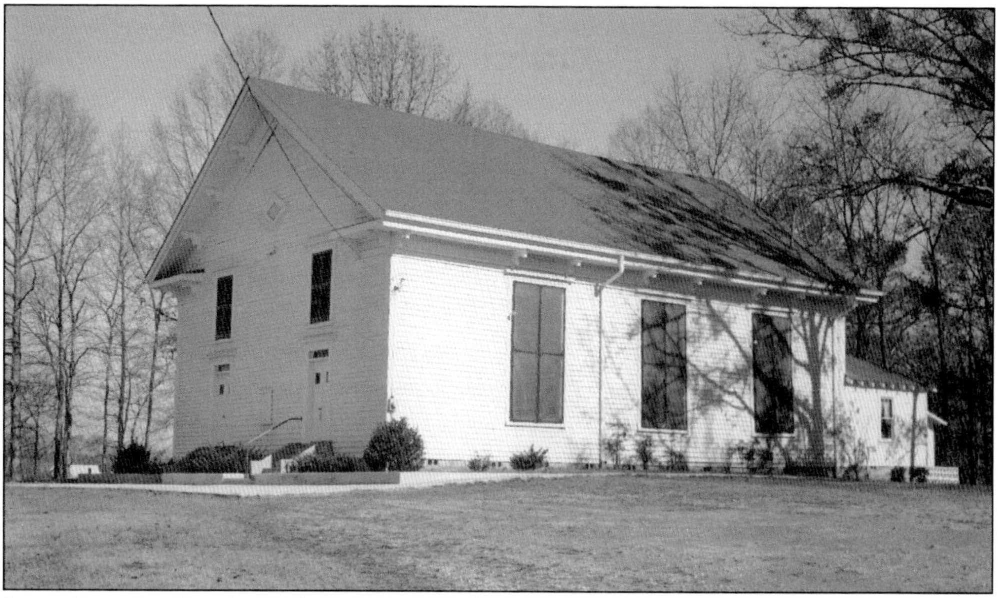

Located south of Lyerly, Sardis Baptist Church was organized around 1835 on land donated by Sarah Young Price. The sanctuary, shown in this 1970s photograph, was built some time during the 1850s. Prior to the Civil War, a gallery at the rear of the sanctuary was used by slaves who attended as members along with their owners. A partition built down the middle of the sanctuary separated the male and female worshipers and remains to this day. (Courtesy of Chattooga County Library.)

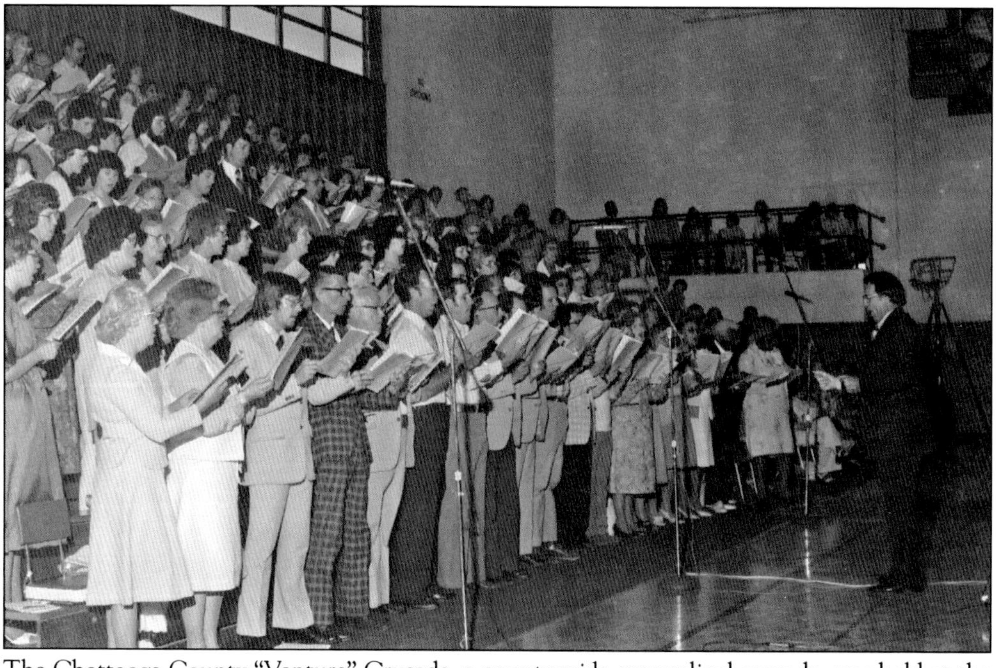

The Chattooga County "Venture" Crusade, a county-wide evangelical crusade, was held at the Chattooga High School gymnasium in 1979. Over 1,000 people attended the first in a weeklong series of services sponsored by 37 local churches. (Photograph by Earl McConnell, courtesy of Rebecca and Susan McConnell.)

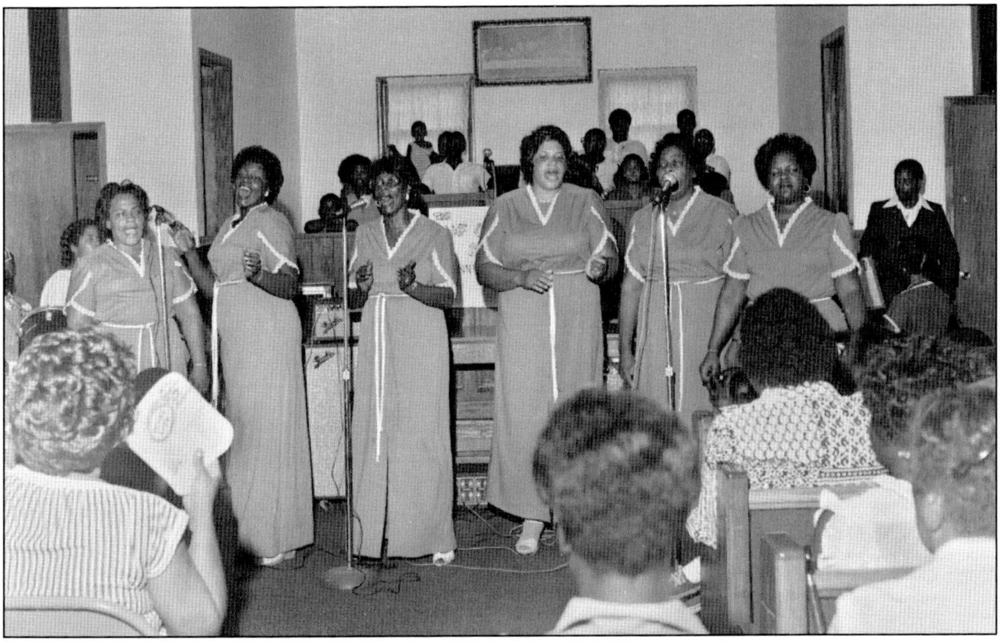

The A.M.F. Quintet was formed in 1960 by members of the Adams, Favors, and Mosley families, all of whom attended Oak Hill Missionary Baptist Church near Gore. This photograph shows a 23rd-anniversary performance by group members, from left to right, Louise Adams Favors, Jeneal Farmer Johnson, Deloise Farmer Booker, Aileen Adams Mosley, Jessie Perry Mosley, and Linda Farmer Hawkins. (Photograph by Earl McConnell, courtesy of Rebecca and Susan McConnell.)

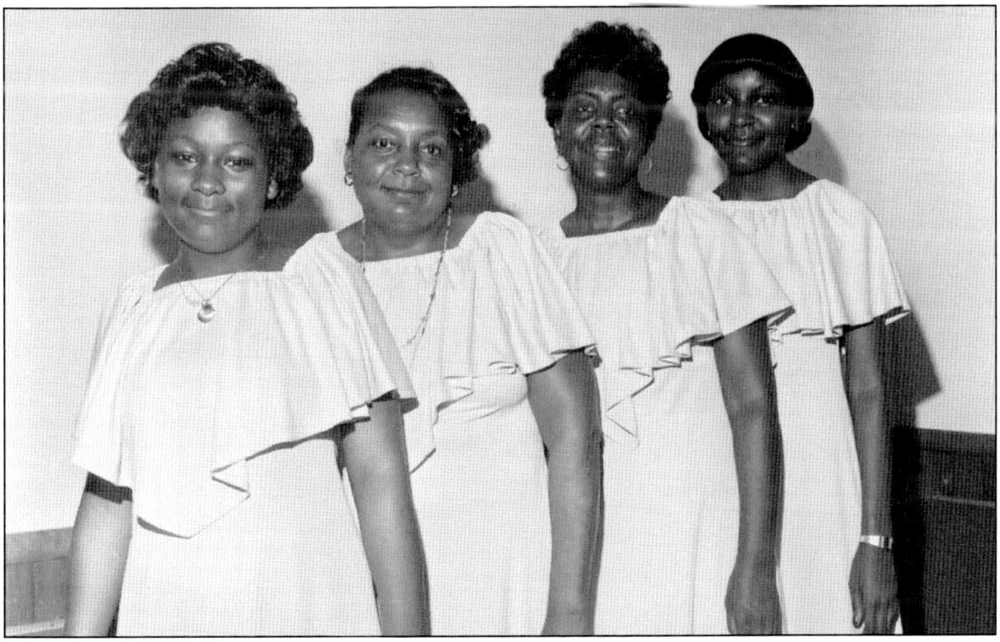

A mother and three daughters formed Mary Ware and the Caravans, another gospel group from Oak Hill Missionary Baptist Church. Shown in this c. 1983 photograph are, from left to right, Gail Ware, Henrietta Smith, Mary Ware, and Sue Adams London. (Photograph by Earl McConnell, courtesy of Rebecca and Susan McConnell.)

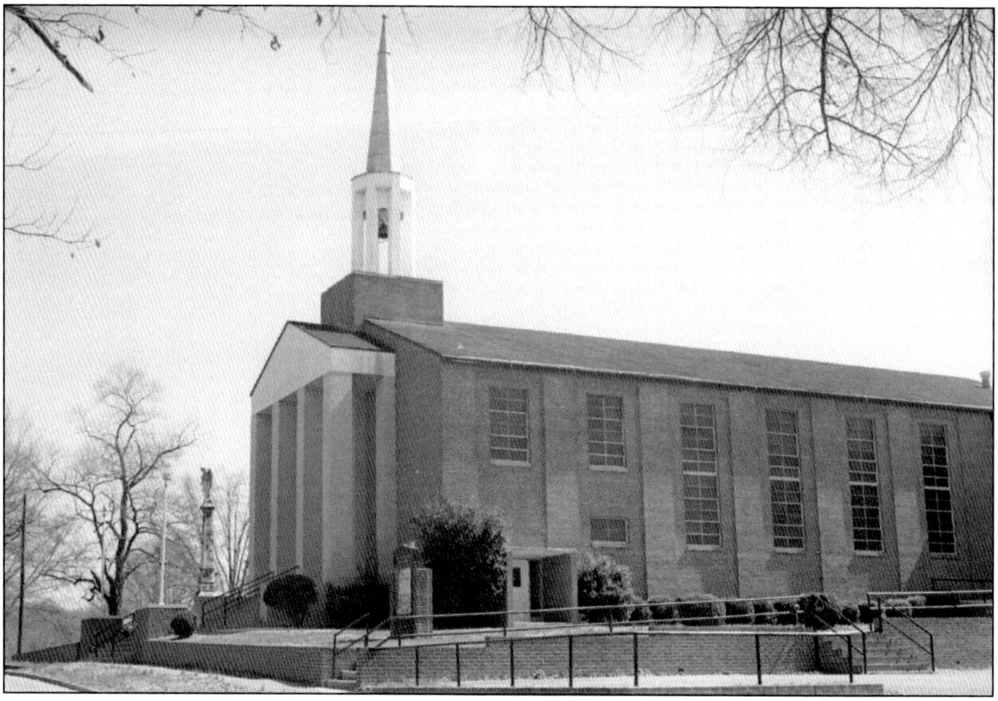

Trion First Baptist Church began as Penn's Chapel in the 1840s and held worship services for both Baptists and Methodists. After the Civil War, the church was called the Trion Factory Baptist Church and, later, the DeForest Allgood Memorial Baptist Church. (Photograph by Earl McConnell, courtesy of Rebecca and Susan McConnell.)

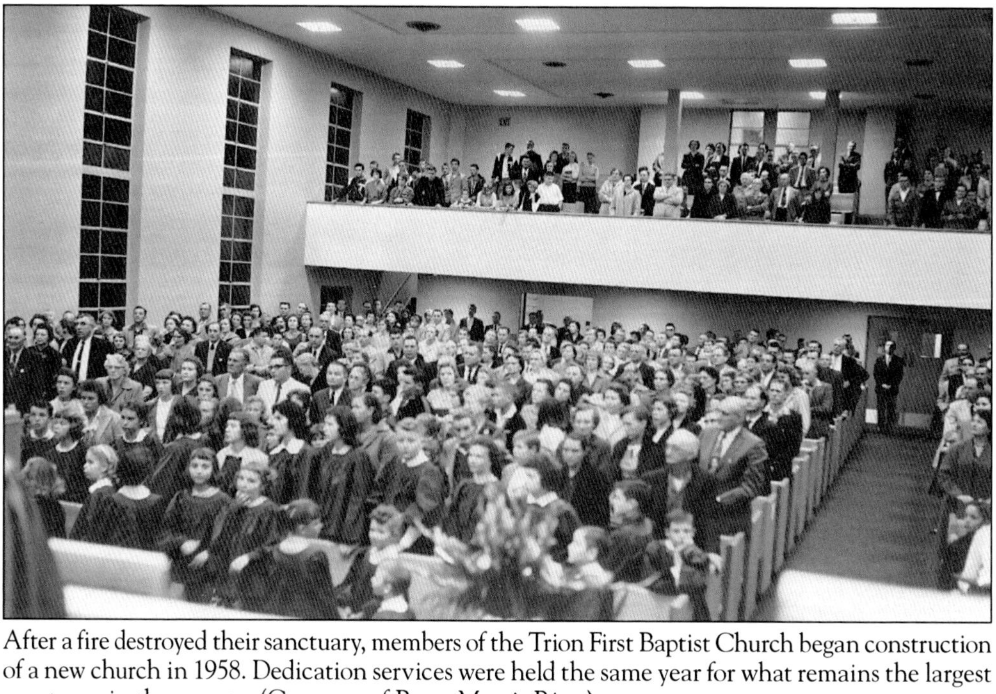

After a fire destroyed their sanctuary, members of the Trion First Baptist Church began construction of a new church in 1958. Dedication services were held the same year for what remains the largest sanctuary in the county. (Courtesy of Betty Morris Rice.)

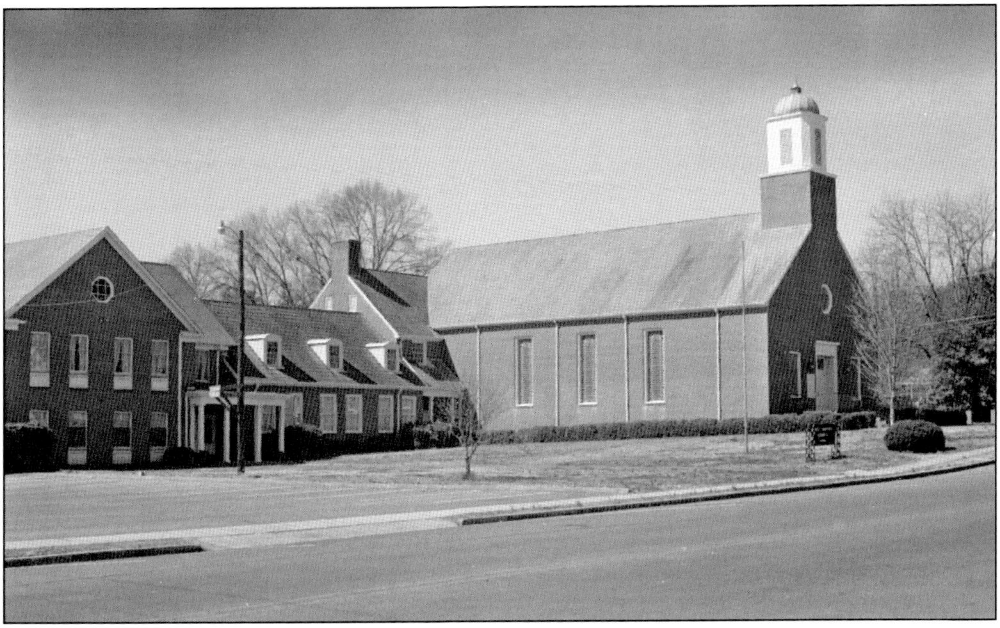

The Summerville First Baptist Church was organized at least as early as 1848 and possibly years earlier. The original sanctuary was located on Congress Street. In 1903, the Summerville First Baptist Church moved to its present site on Georgia Avenue. A 1937 fire destroyed the wooden structure, but the members rebuilt and moved into the present sanctuary the following year. (Photograph by Earl McConnell, courtesy of Rebecca and Susan McConnell.)

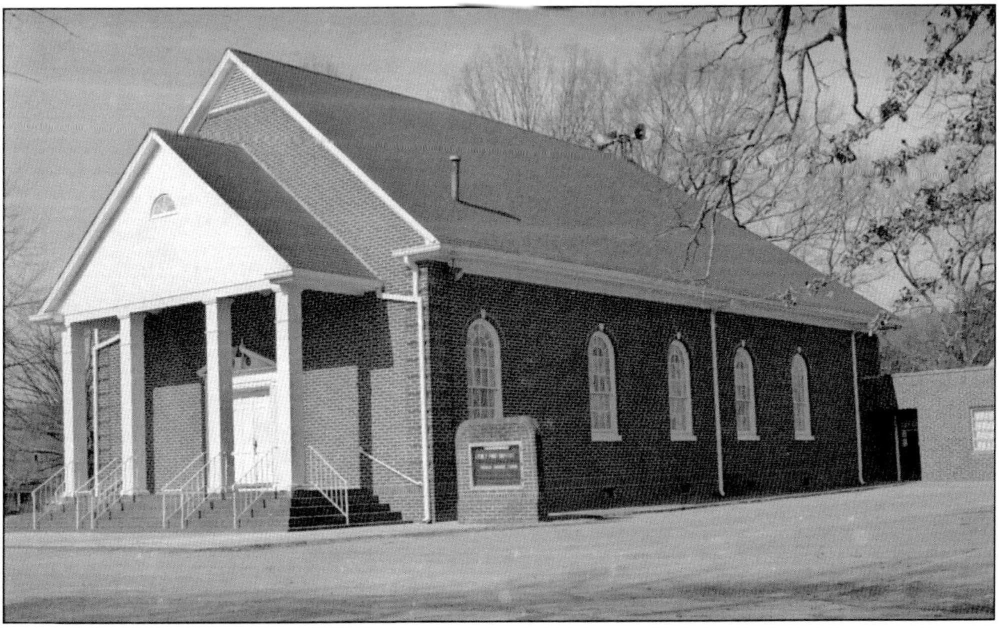

The Lyerly First Baptist Church was originally located near the Lyerly Cemetery and was known as the Melville Baptist Church when it was organized in 1886. In 1897, a new sanctuary was built on Tennessee Avenue. It was destroyed by a windstorm in 1909 but was replaced the next year by the current sanctuary. (Photograph by Earl McConnell, courtesy of Rebecca and Susan McConnell.)

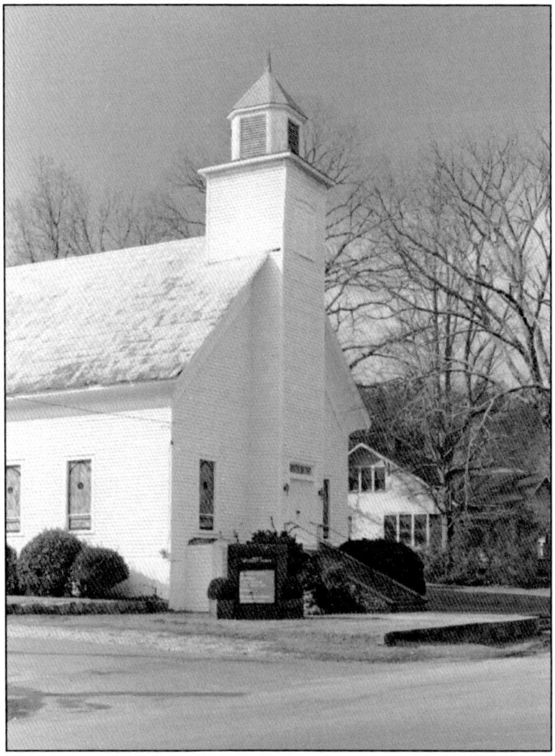

The Menlo Methodist Church was founded in 1834 as Ami Methodist Church, located two miles south of present-day Menlo. In 1897, the church relocated to Menlo on land donated by J.M. Lawrence. A fellowship hall, educational building, kitchen, and stained-glass windows were added during the 1950s. The church is now known as the Menlo United Methodist Church. (Courtesy of Barbara Pickle McCollum.)

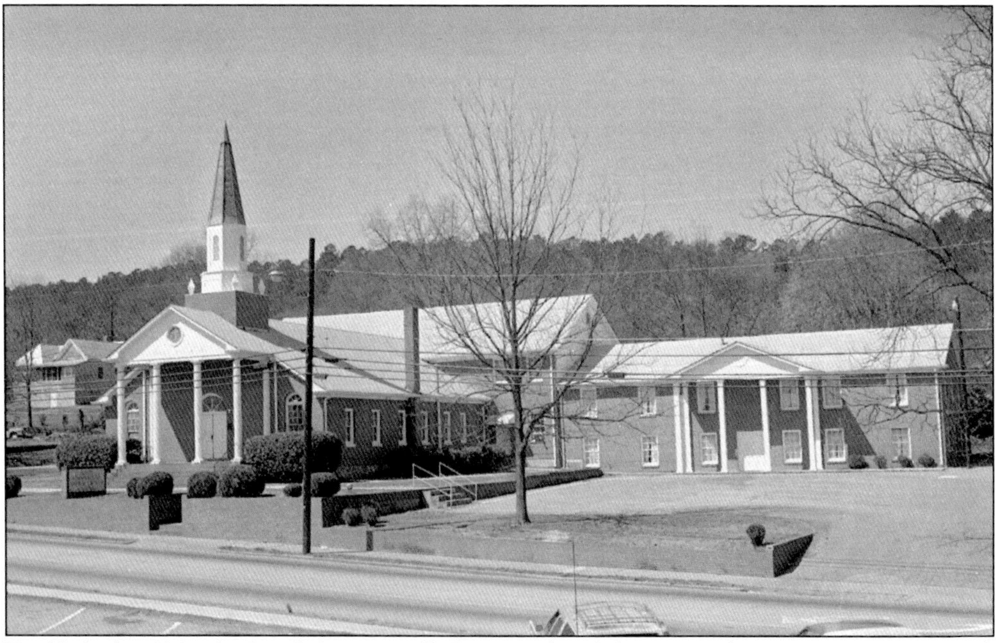

Established in 1914, the South Summerville Baptist Church began worship services in a store and, later, moved to a livery stable. The first church, a simple frame building, was erected on Union Street in 1916. Construction of the present sanctuary on South Commerce Street was started in 1932 and completed three years later. Major additions have since been added. (Photograph by Earl McConnell, courtesy of Rebecca and Susan McConnell.)

Five

Homes, Buildings, and Structures

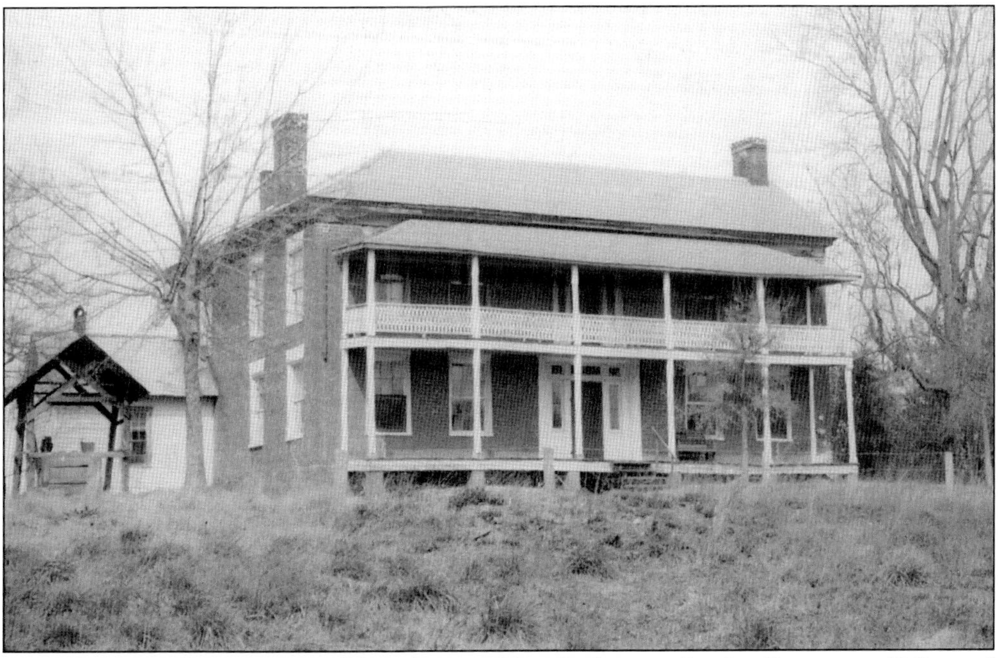

Around 1832, William McConnell bought several hundred acres of land in Broomtown Valley and built this house with bricks made by his slaves. Several barns and outbuildings, slave quarters, a dairy, and a store were also part of his plantation. After McConnell's death in 1854, the plantation was ransacked during the Civil War by neighboring Union sympathizers. (Courtesy of Chattooga County Library.)

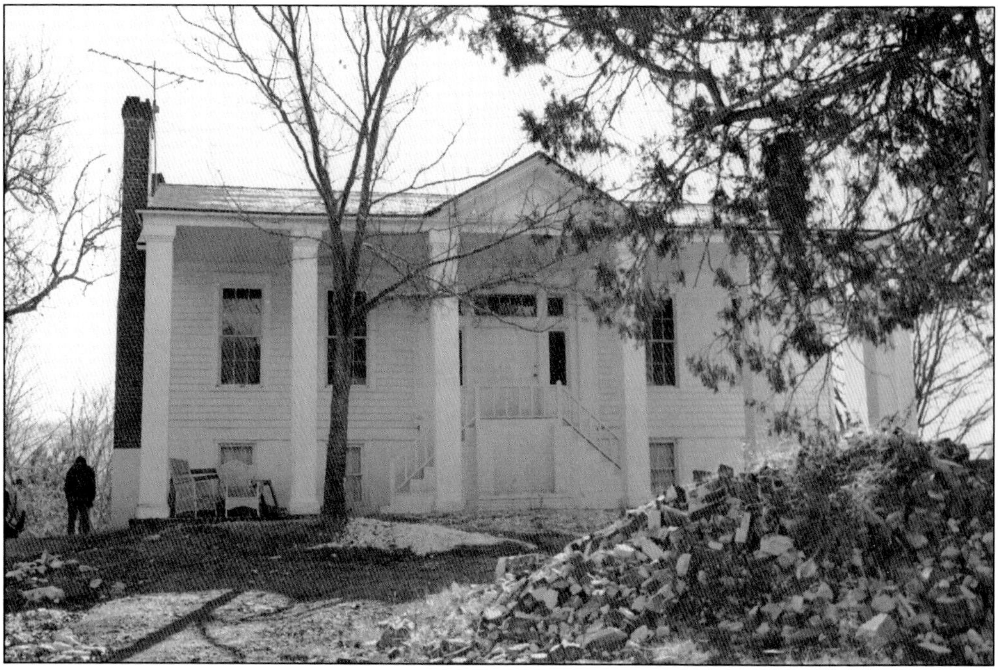

Samuel Finley arrived in the Chattoogaville area from Hall County in 1833 and completed construction of his house two years later. A prosperous farmer, Finley owned 1,200 acres and 40 slaves, many of whom assisted in the construction of the home by making bricks for the basement. After surviving the Civil War, Finley continued living in the house until his death in 1876. (Courtesy of Chattooga County Library.)

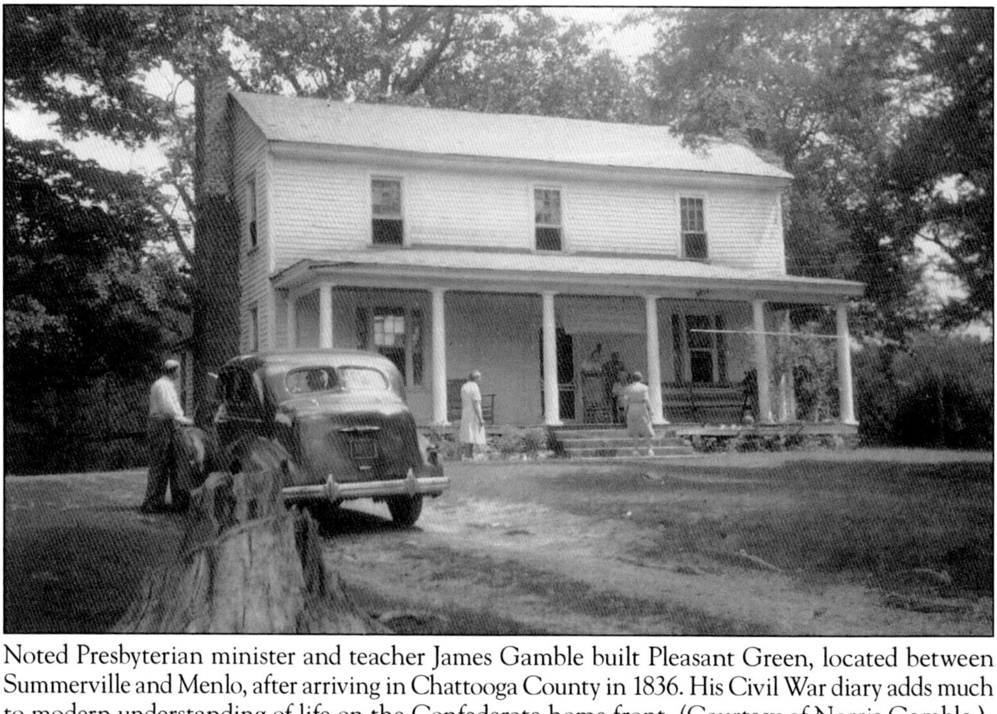

Noted Presbyterian minister and teacher James Gamble built Pleasant Green, located between Summerville and Menlo, after arriving in Chattooga County in 1836. His Civil War diary adds much to modern understanding of life on the Confederate home front. (Courtesy of Norris Gamble.)

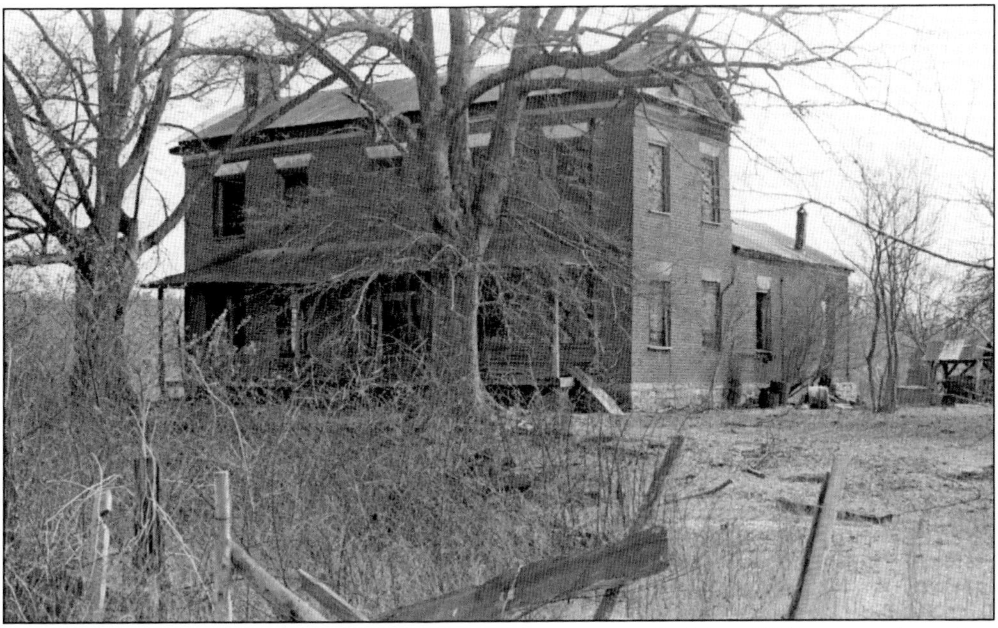

The Charles Price house was built in 1837 for his young bride, Mary Wilder, near Dirtseller Mountain west of Lyerly. It once boasted six fireplaces, walnut wainscoting, and wide-plank pine floors. At the time this photograph was made in 1979, the house was already in ruins. (Courtesy of Barbara Pickle McCollum.)

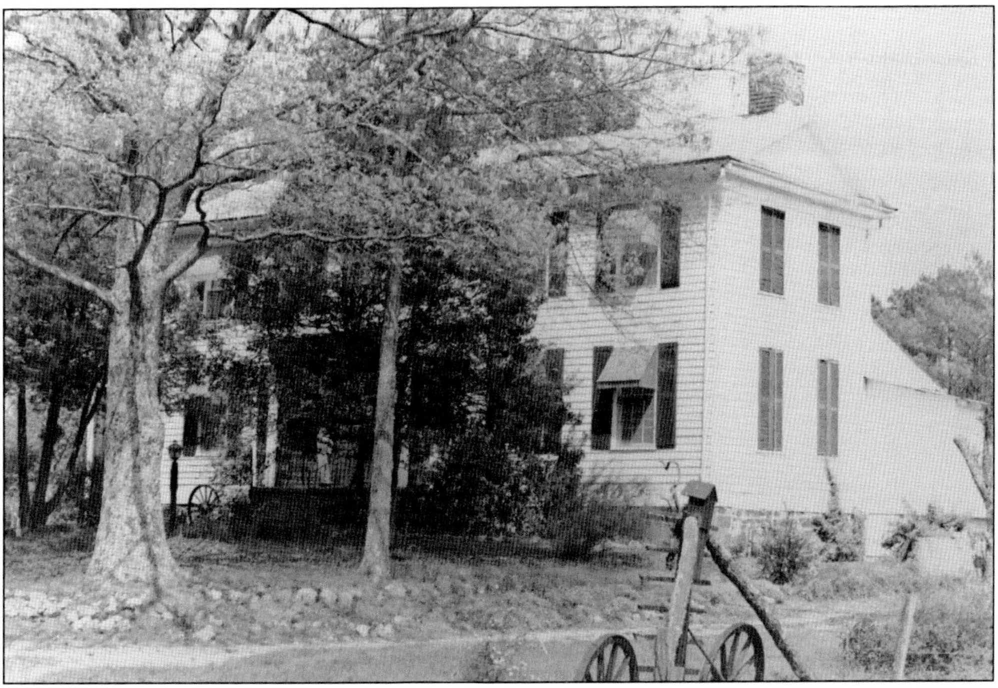

Built by Samuel Knox in 1843 to house his wife and 14 children, this home still stands at Alpine near Menlo. Much of the second floor was used as a private schoolroom for the large family. The residence was sold in 1895 and again in 1919, this time to the Dodd family. Mittie Dodd named the house Alpine Glow. (Courtesy of Chattooga County Library.)

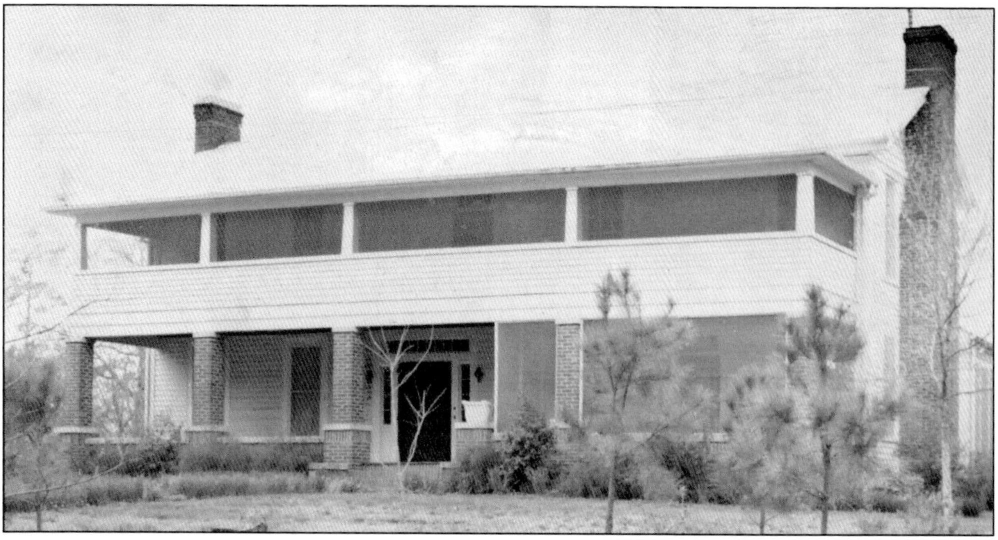

In 1846, Samuel McWhorter married Margaret Ann Knox of Alpine and built this house in Teloga. McWhorter was a farmer and operated a cotton gin, gristmill, and store. During the Civil War, Union troops took the family's food and livestock but left the house intact. It was later occupied by his great-grandson, John Stubbs Jr., and remains in the family to this day. (Courtesy of the *Summerville News.*)

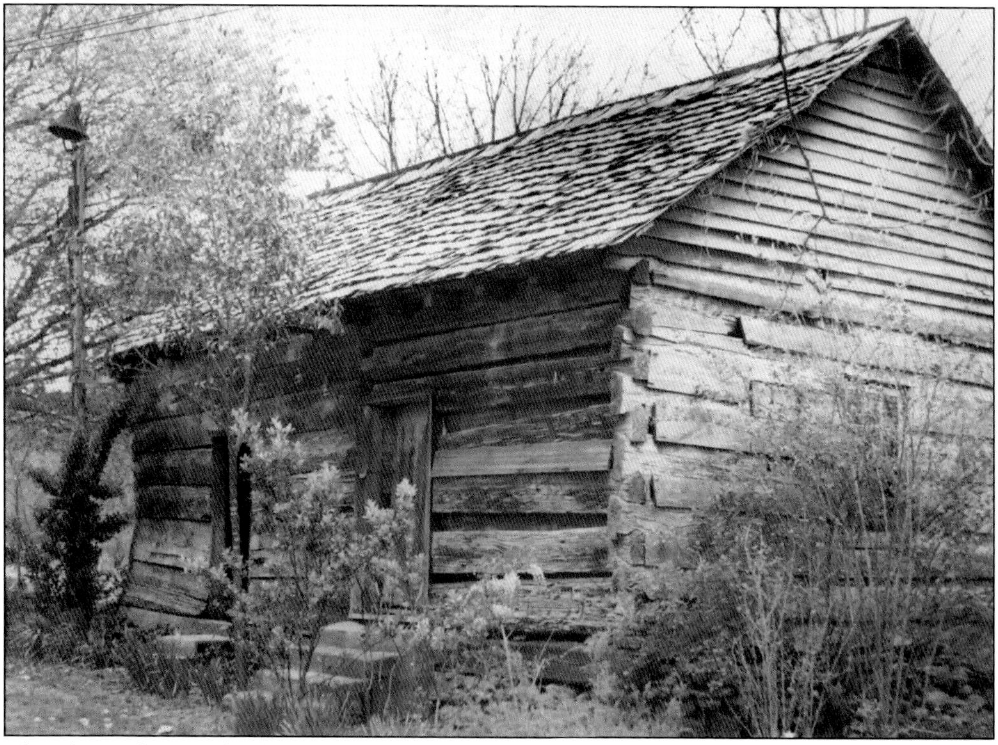

This slave cabin was built behind the Samuel McWhorter house in Teloga. The bell at the top of the pole on the left was used to call the field hands in for lunch. Samuel and Margaret Ann McWhorter had three children. She died in 1879, followed by his death in 1886. Both were buried in the Alpine Cemetery. (Courtesy of the *Summerville News.*)

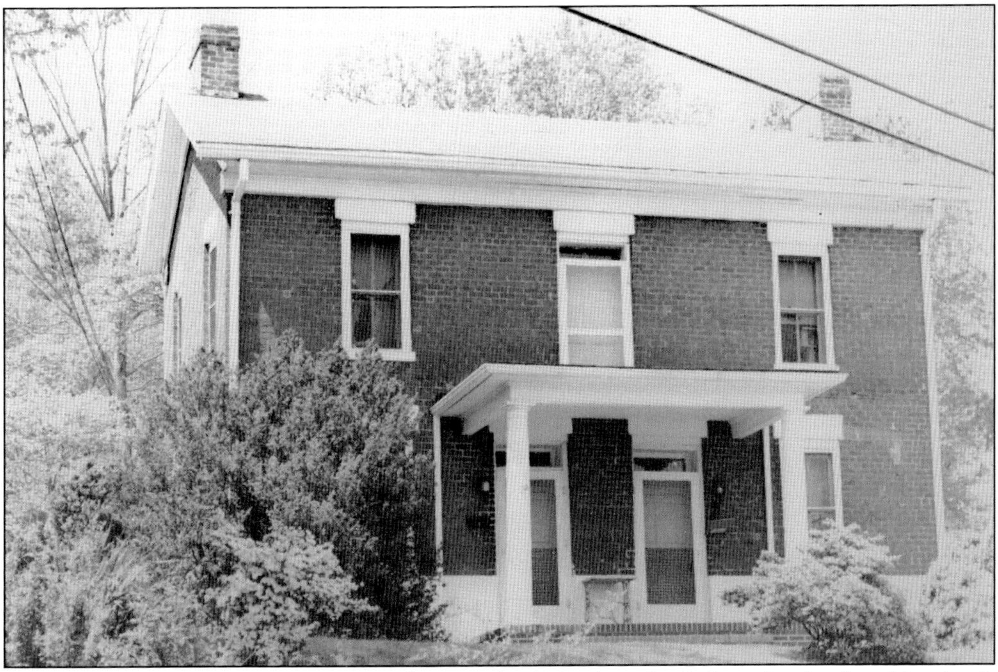

This house was built during the 1840s by Dr. John E. Park and is believed to be the oldest brick house remaining in Summerville. The home and three acres of land were deeded in 1866 by a succeeding owner to the Summerville Methodist Church to be used as a parsonage and remained as such until 1947. (Courtesy of Chattooga County Library.)

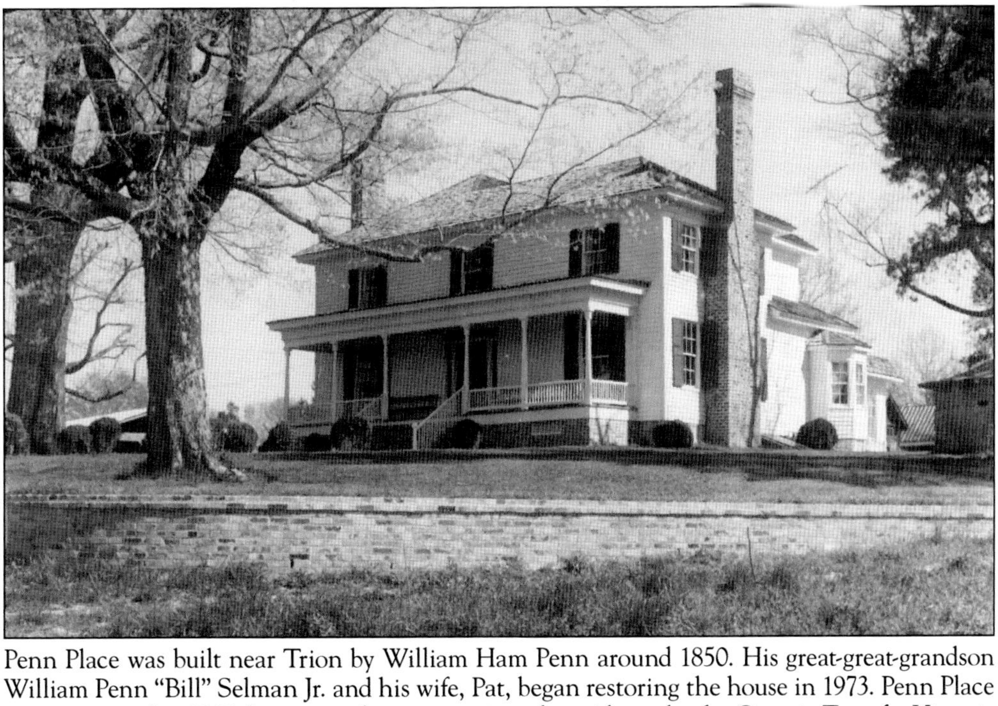

Penn Place was built near Trion by William Ham Penn around 1850. His great-great-grandson William Penn "Bill" Selman Jr. and his wife, Pat, began restoring the house in 1973. Penn Place was recognized in 1980 for outstanding restoration of a residence by the Georgia Trust for Historic Preservation. (Photograph by Earl McConnell, courtesy of Rebecca and Susan McConnell.)

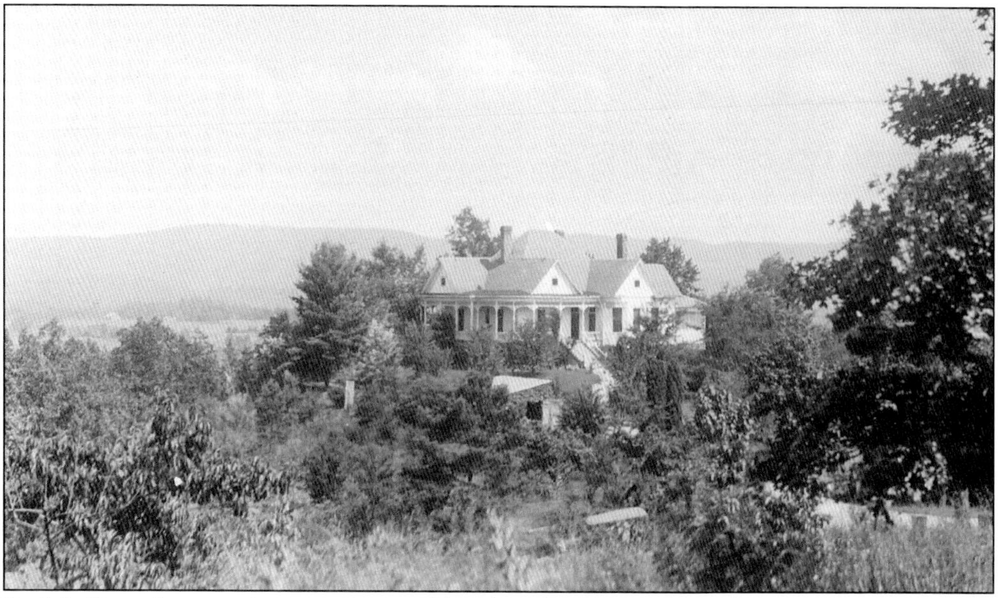

Beulah Shropshire was born in 1886 and lived in this house on a hill overlooking downtown Summerville. "Miss Beulah," as she was known, started an insurance agency in 1924 and was one of the first women in Chattooga County to register to vote. She was never married and died in 1981. The house has since been restored. (Courtesy of Rex Evans.)

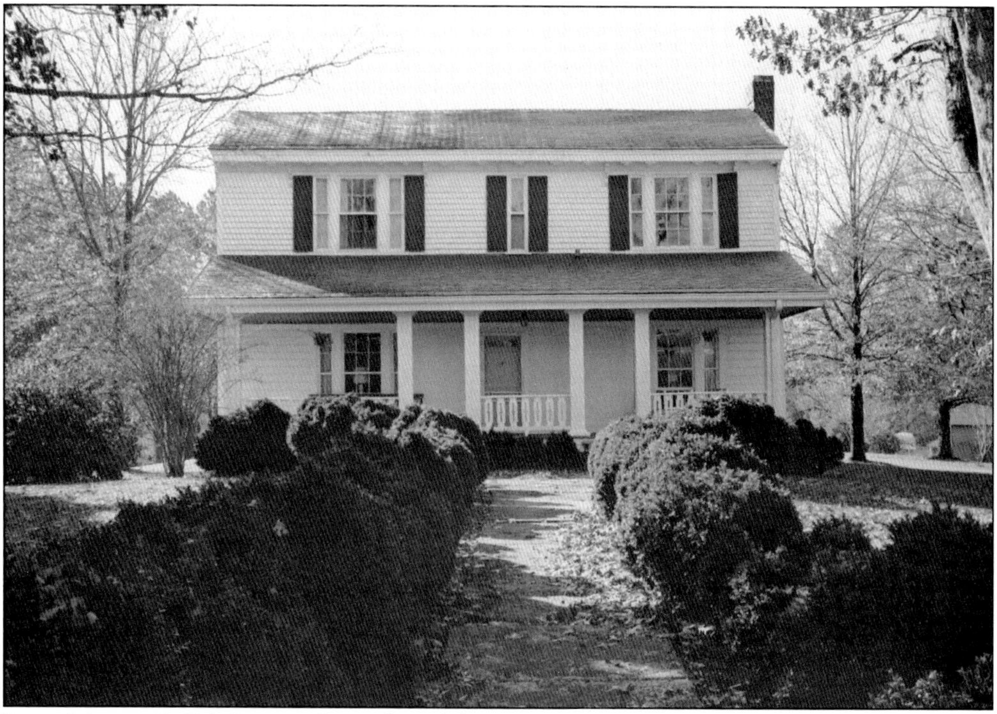

James Morgan Bellah Jr. served as judge of the county court for 34 years. He was also mayor of Summerville and represented his district in the state senate. Judge Bellah married Mary Katherine Hinton in 1886, and the couple lived in this house on the corner of Bellah Avenue and Rome Boulevard for many years. (Courtesy of Chattooga County Library.)

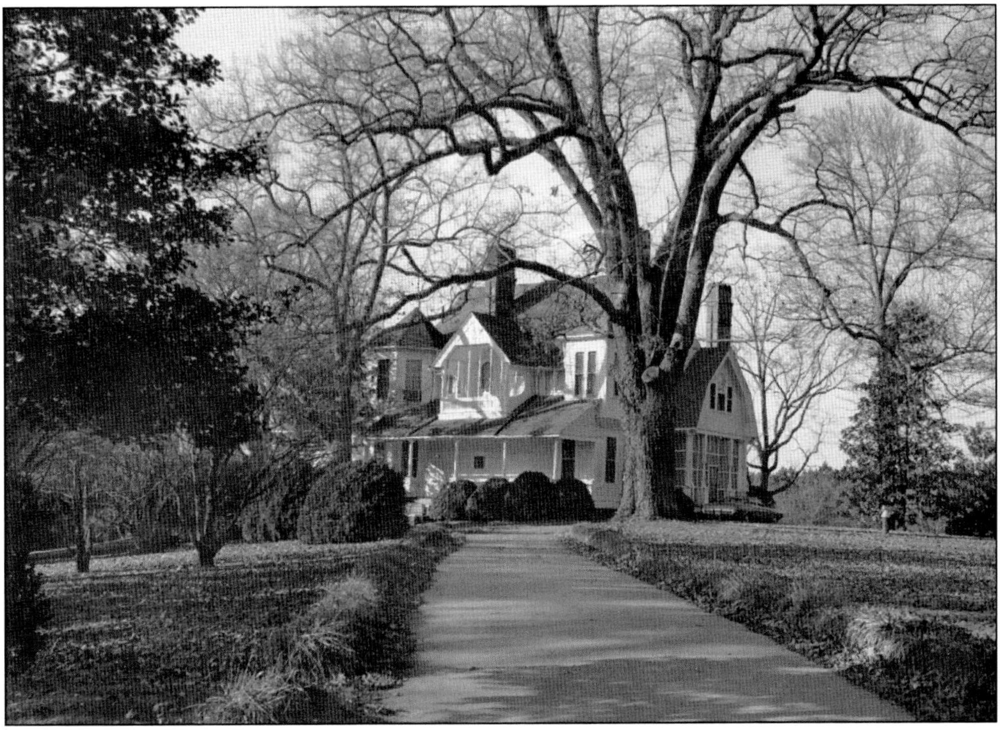

This house once stood on DeForest Avenue in Trion and was owned by A.P. Allgood, one of the founders of the Trion Mill. Built after the first Allgood house was destroyed in a 1903 fire, the home contained 20 rooms, 13 fireplaces, and 5 bathrooms. The house was used for many years as the residence of the mill's general manager. It was demolished in 1978. (Courtesy of Chattooga County Library.)

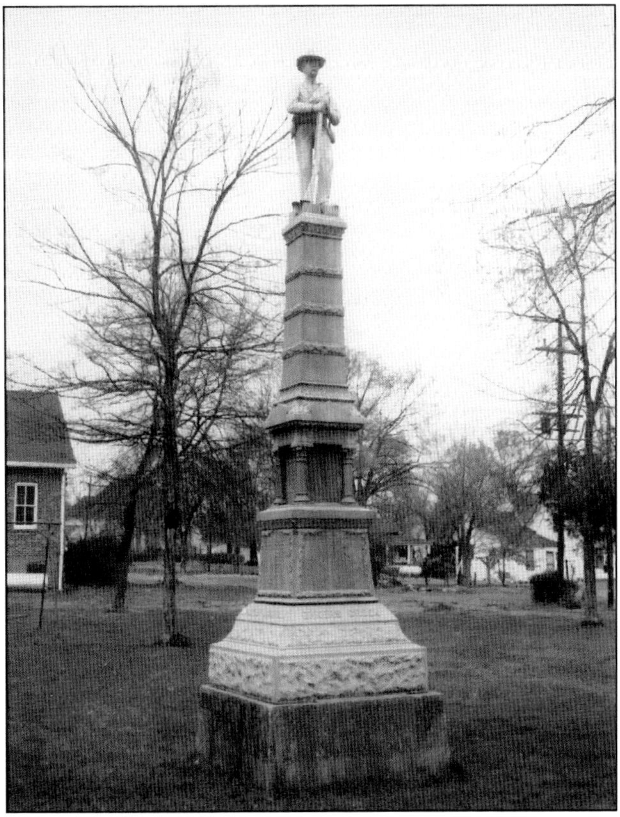

The only Confederate monument in Chattooga County was erected in 1915 in Menlo Park by Capt. Andrew Jackson Lawrence, known as the founder of Menlo. The monument pays tribute to his fellow soldiers in Company D, 34th Georgia Regiment of the Confederate States of America. (Courtesy of the *Summerville News*.)

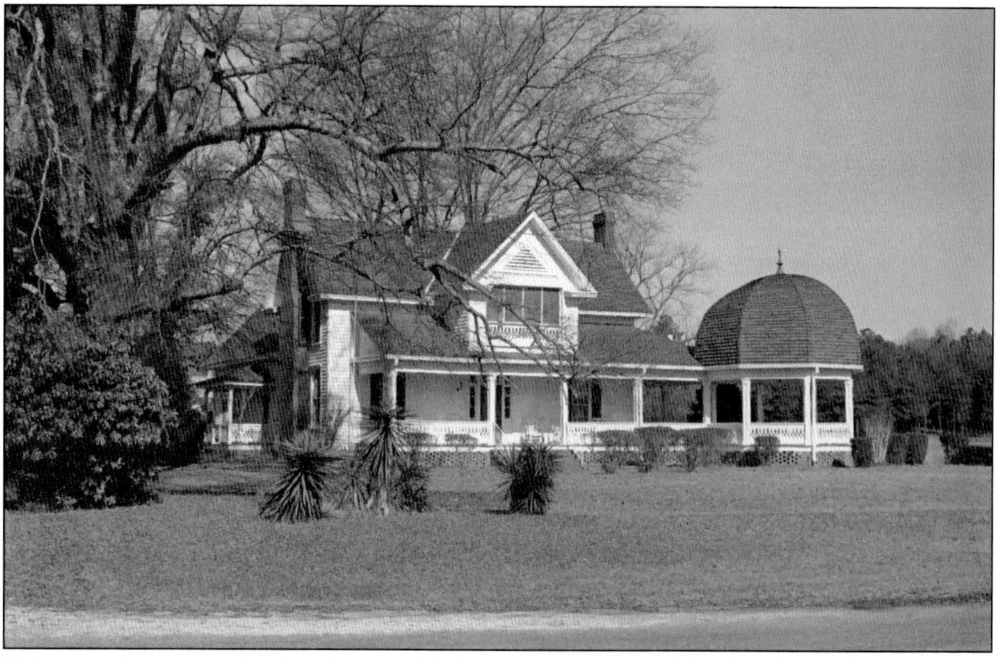

This house, located south of Lyerly in the Holland community, was built by John Pinckney Holland around 1886. The home contained a fireplace in every room, and when it was renovated in 1917, a gazebo-like pavilion was added to the front porch. A granddaughter, Mary Holland, occupied the house until her death in 1983. This Holland landmark was later destroyed by fire. (Courtesy of Chattooga County Library.)

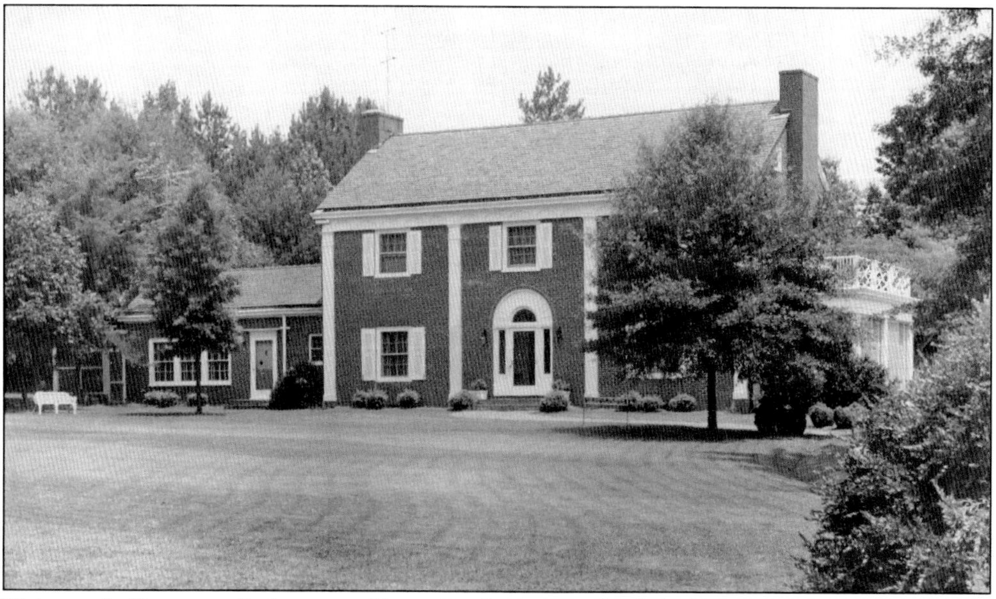

This stately Summerville home on Rome Boulevard was built by Dr. Hermon Brown in 1934. Brown arrived in Chattooga County in 1911 and began his medical practice in Lyerly. There, he met Kate Bolling, whom he married in 1913. In addition to his medical practice, Brown helped organize the Farmers & Merchants Bank and served as a director for 25 years. (Courtesy of Gene McGinnis.)

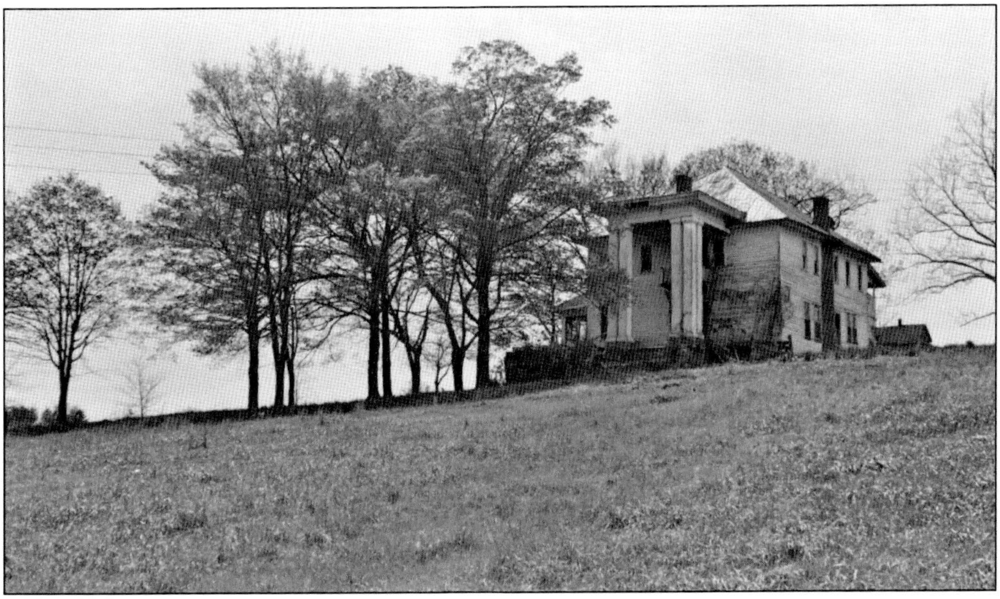

This house once stood near Chelsea, north of Menlo, and belonged to the Agnew family. When it was demolished in 1974, some of the salvaged materials were used in the restoration of the Samuel Finley house in Chattoogaville. A large, Colonial-style house now occupies this site. (Photograph by the author.)

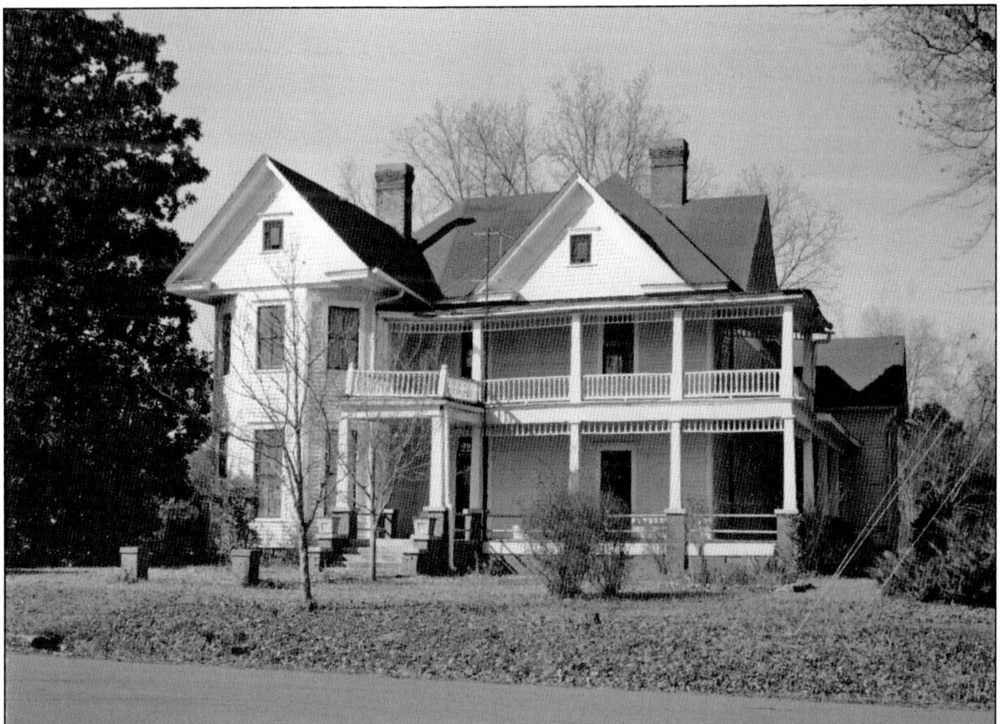

Lyerly residents Nell and Ruby Lee taught school in Chattooga County for many years. The sisters lived in this house until Ruby's death in 1976. Joe and Jan Pullen have since restored the house. (Courtesy of Chattooga County Library.)

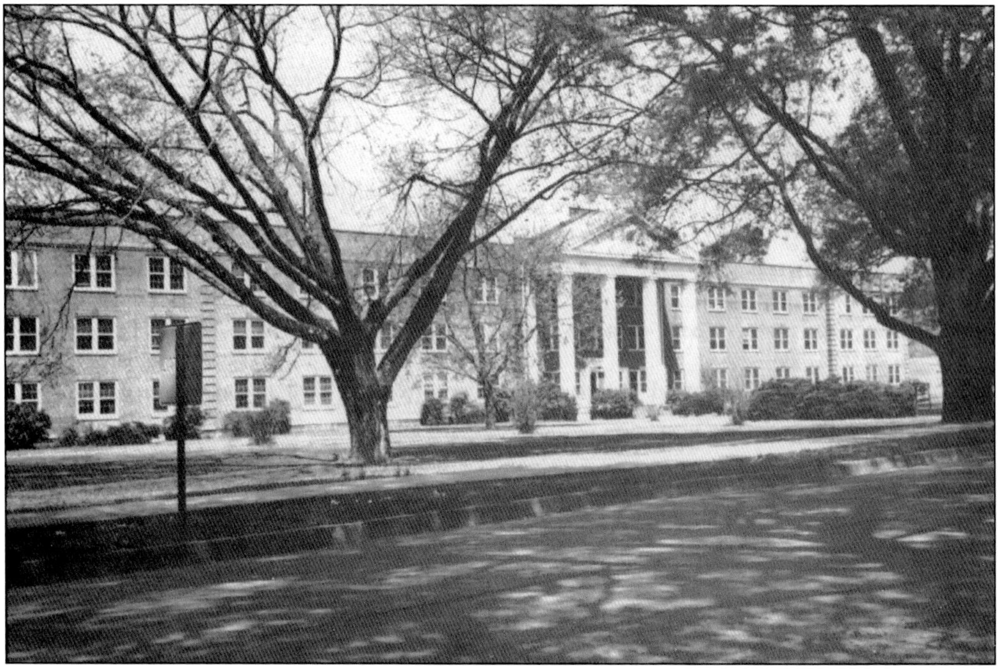

The Leila Riegel Hall was built in 1934 primarily to house women employed at the Trion Company's glove mill. After the closing of the original Trion Inn, this building became known by the same name. Guests paid $25 a month for room, board, and maid service. In 1966, Riegel closed the building and donated it to the Town of Trion. (Courtesy of Chattooga County Chamber of Commerce.)

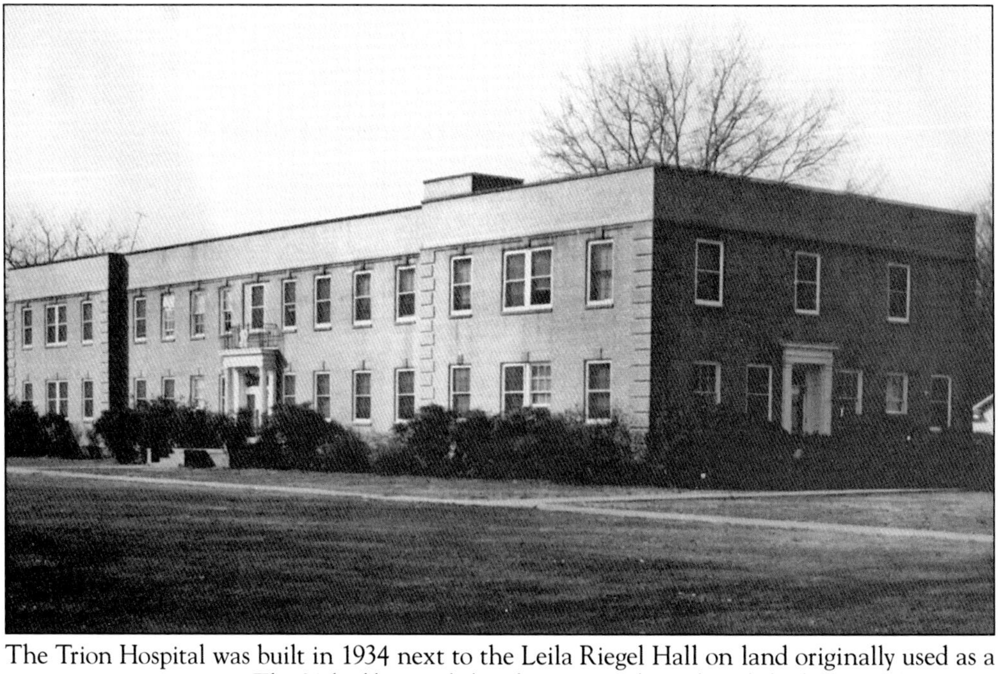

The Trion Hospital was built in 1934 next to the Leila Riegel Hall on land originally used as a community cow pasture. The 30-bed hospital closed in 1975 and was demolished in 2011. (Courtesy of Chattooga County Chamber of Commerce.)

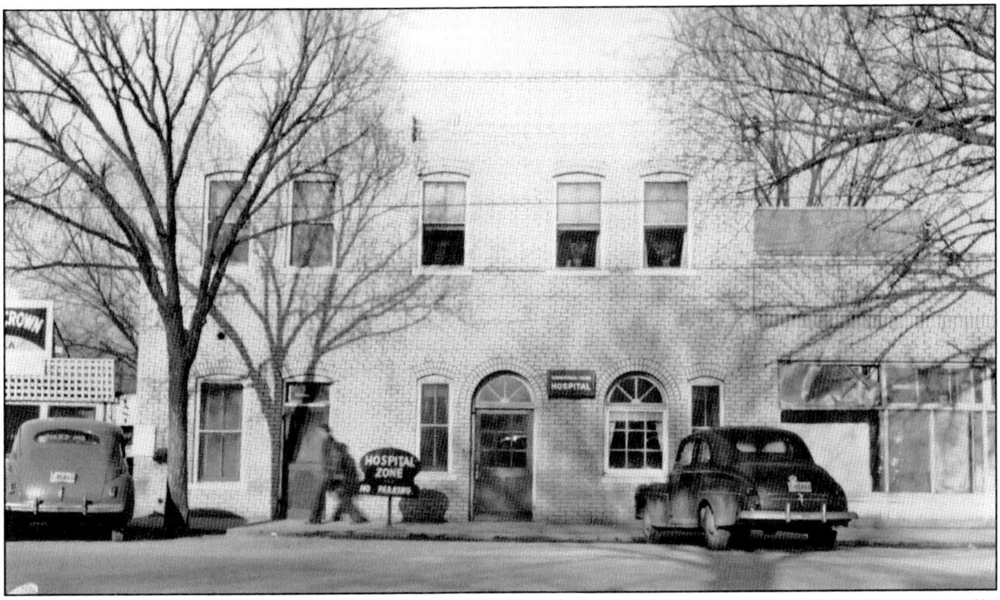

Dr. William B. Hair of Summerville and Dr. N.A. Funderburk of Trion purchased the Summerville Inn on Commerce Street, south of the courthouse. After renovating the rooms and furnishings, they opened the Summerville-Trion Hospital in 1927. The 18-bed facility featured the county's first X-ray machine. Following a heart attack in 1945, Dr. Hair closed the hospital and converted the building back to a hotel. (Courtesy of Will and Judy Hair.)

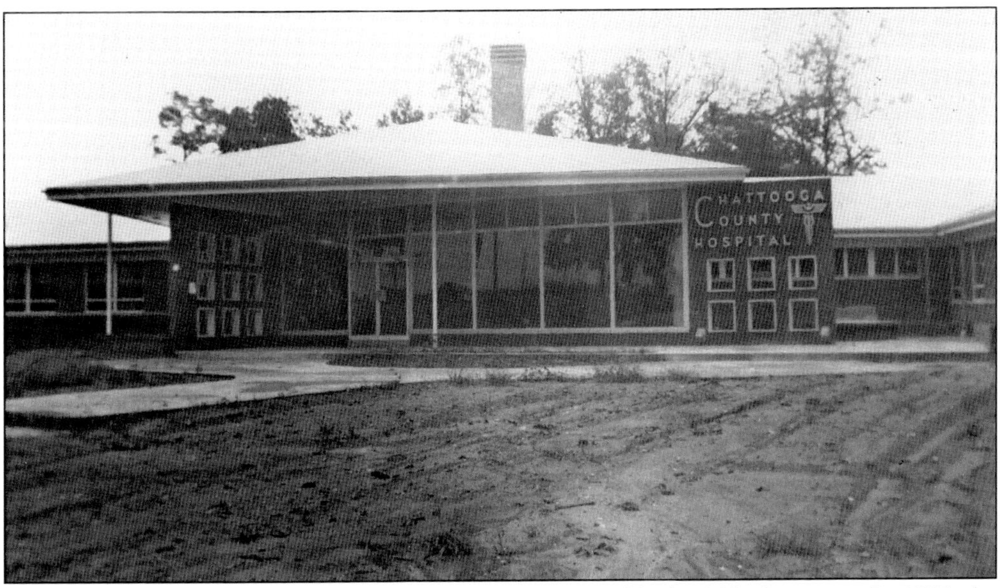

The Chattooga County Hospital was dedicated in 1952 and had a 36-bed capacity. In 1956, the county had eight doctors to serve its citizens: four in Summerville, three in Trion, and one in Menlo. There were also four dentists, two chiropractors, one optometrist, and one veterinarian. (Courtesy of Menlo City Hall.)

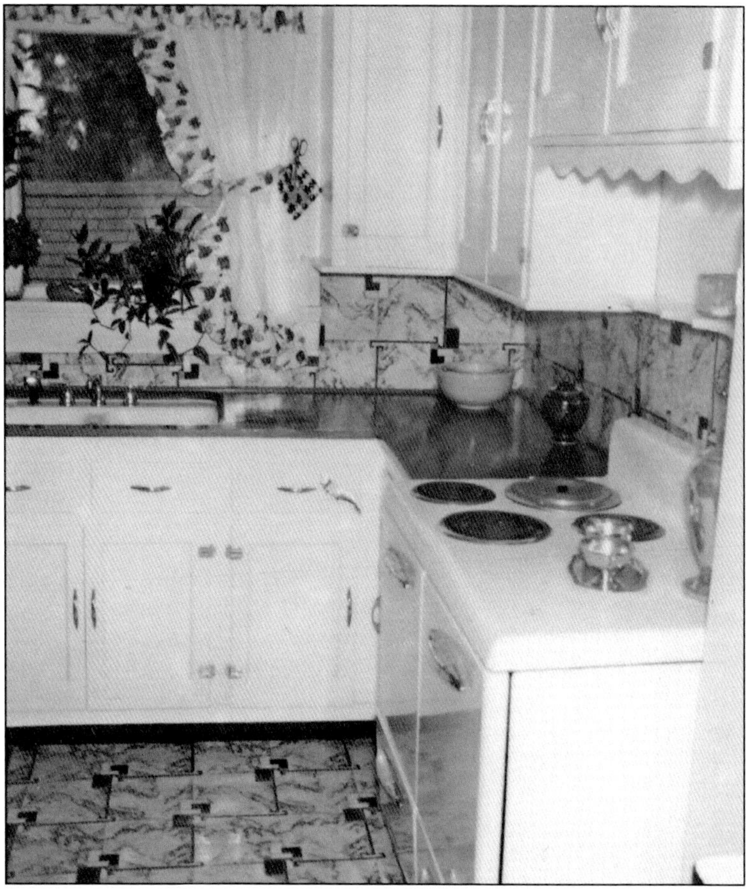

This early 1950s kitchen inside a Menlo home contained an electric stove, linoleum countertops and flooring, and, best of all, running hot and cold water. (Courtesy of Menlo City Hall.)

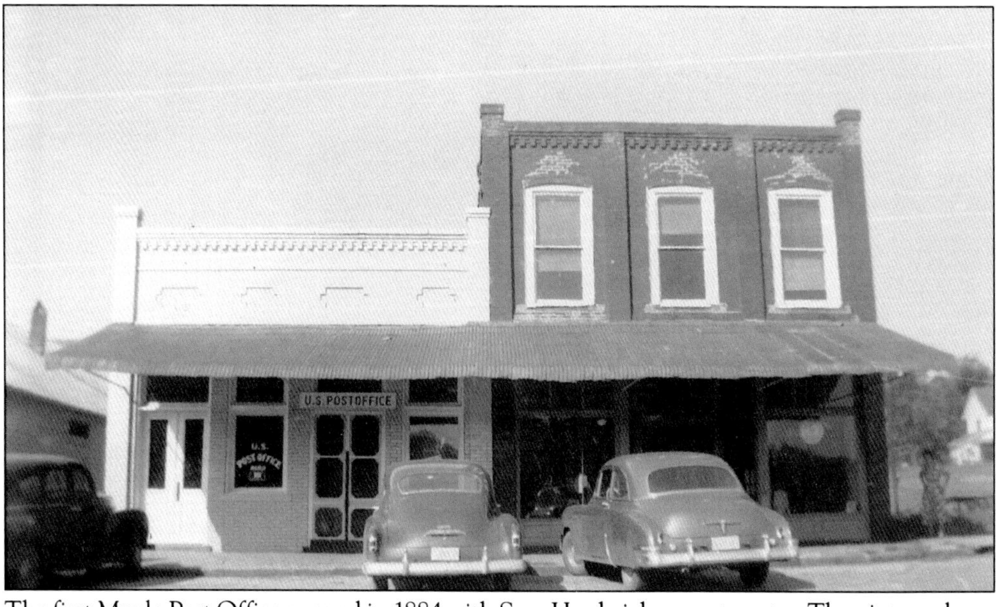

The first Menlo Post Office opened in 1884 with Sam Hardwick as postmaster. The picture above shows the Menlo Post Office as it looked in 1951. (Courtesy of Menlo City Hall.)

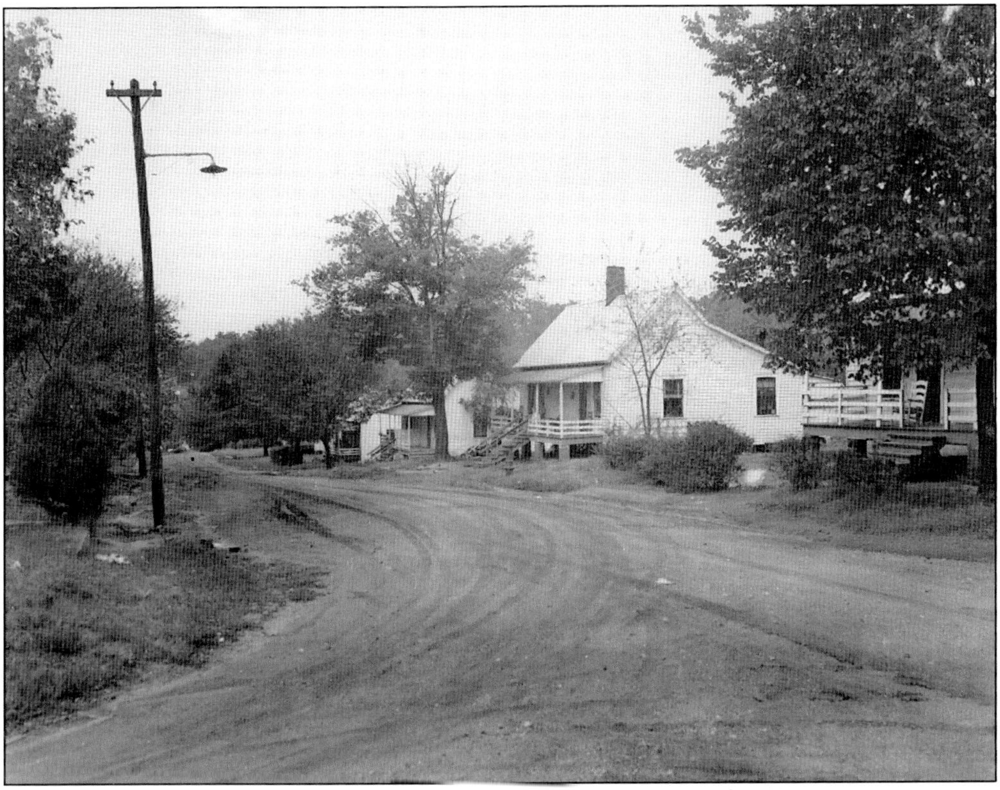

This 1950s photograph of a residential street in Trion shows a typical mill village home. Many Trion houses were owned by the mill until 1952, when the decision was made to sell them to individual buyers. (Courtesy of Charles Logan.)

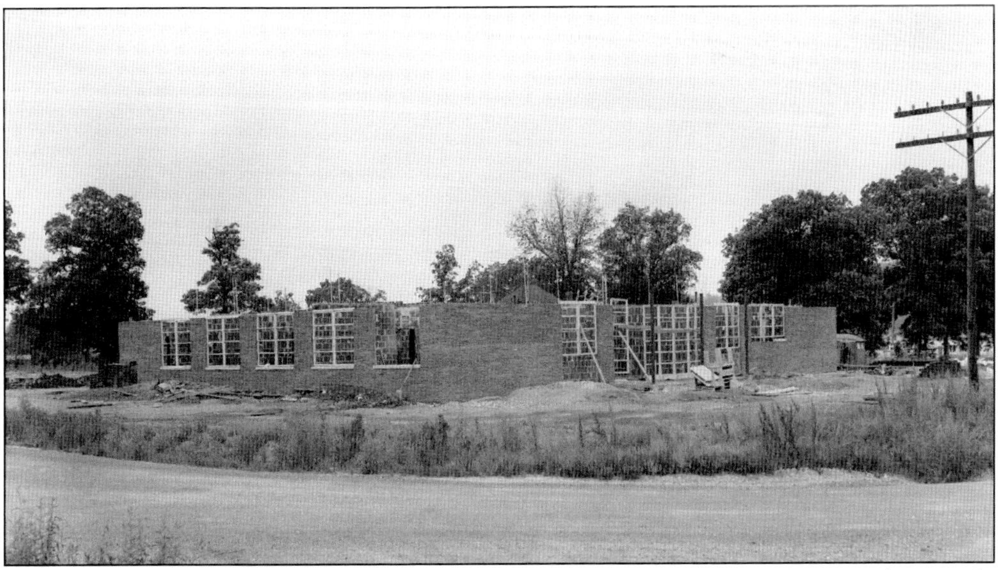

The Chattooga County Health Department is shown under construction in this 1958 photograph. The building cost $78,000 to complete and, having been greatly renovated, it still stands on Farrar Drive in Summerville. (Courtesy of the *Summerville News*.)

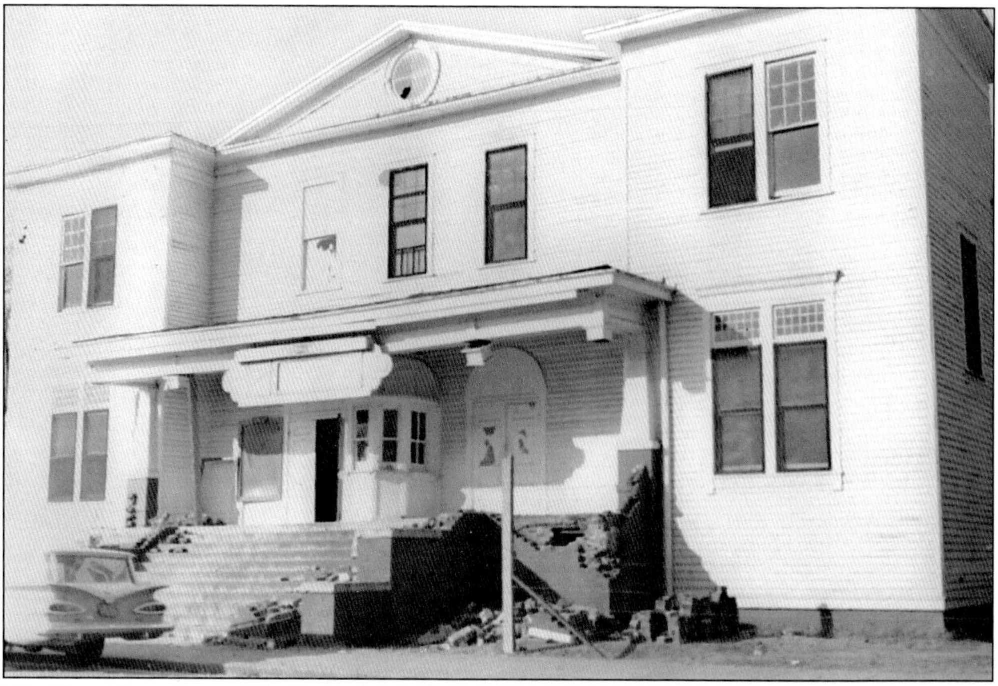

The Trion Community Theater is shown being demolished in 1960. Originally built as the Trion Opera House around 1905, the movie theater doubled as a school auditorium. The wooden structure was considered a safety hazard for school assemblies by the time this photograph was made. (Courtesy of Charles Logan.)

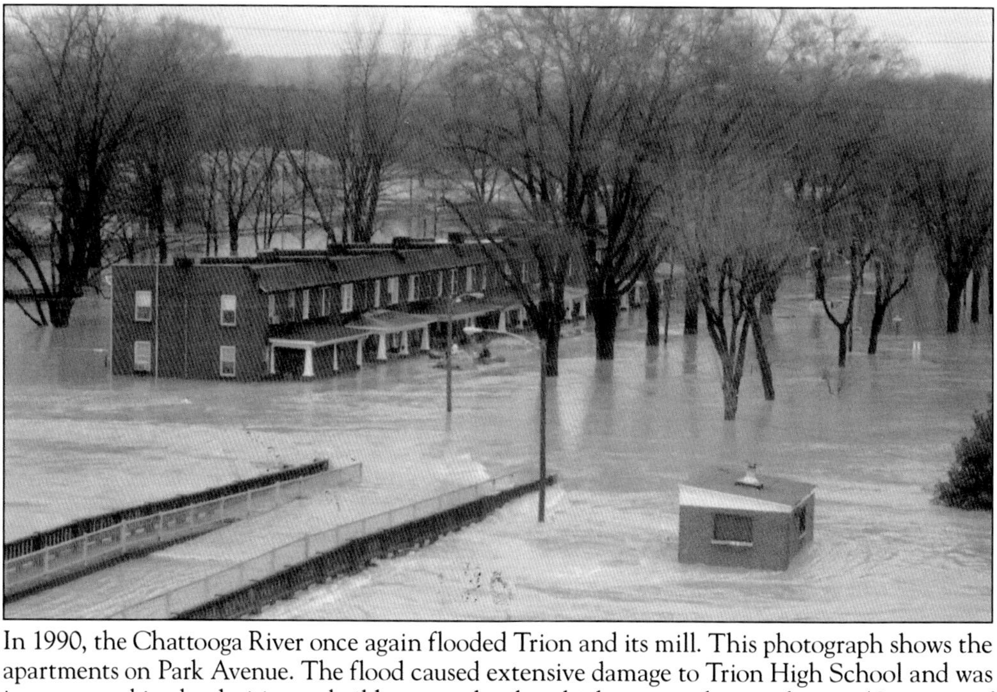

In 1990, the Chattooga River once again flooded Trion and its mill. This photograph shows the apartments on Park Avenue. The flood caused extensive damage to Trion High School and was instrumental in the decision to build a new school on higher ground west of town. (Courtesy of Mount Vernon Mills.)

Six

School Days

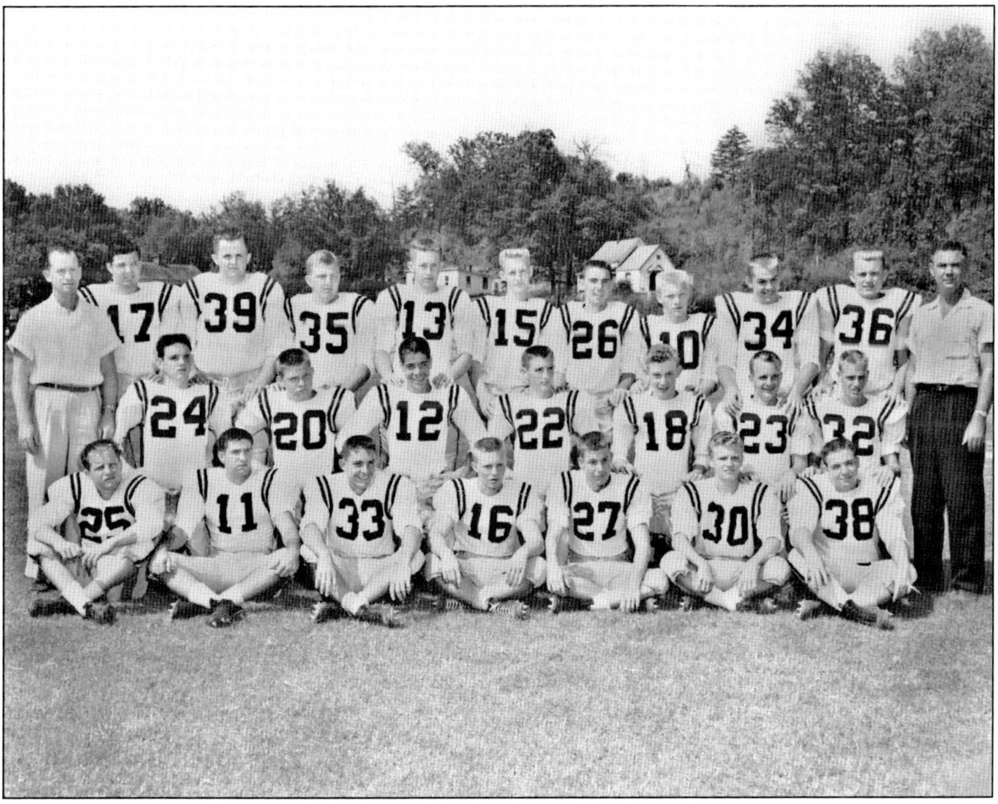

The Trion High School Bulldogs won the 1957 Class B State Football Championship. Pictured are, from left to right, (first row) Rider, B. Watson, Broome, Graoitt, Rackley, McKenzie, and R. Watson; (second row) L. Day, Whitfield, Royals, Powell, Miller, Williams, and McClellan; (third row) assistant coach Gordon Jones, Hensley, Hood, K. Day, Vines, Ingle, Finster, Daniels, Styles, Arden, and coach Sam McCain. (Courtesy of Johnny and Linda Ingle.)

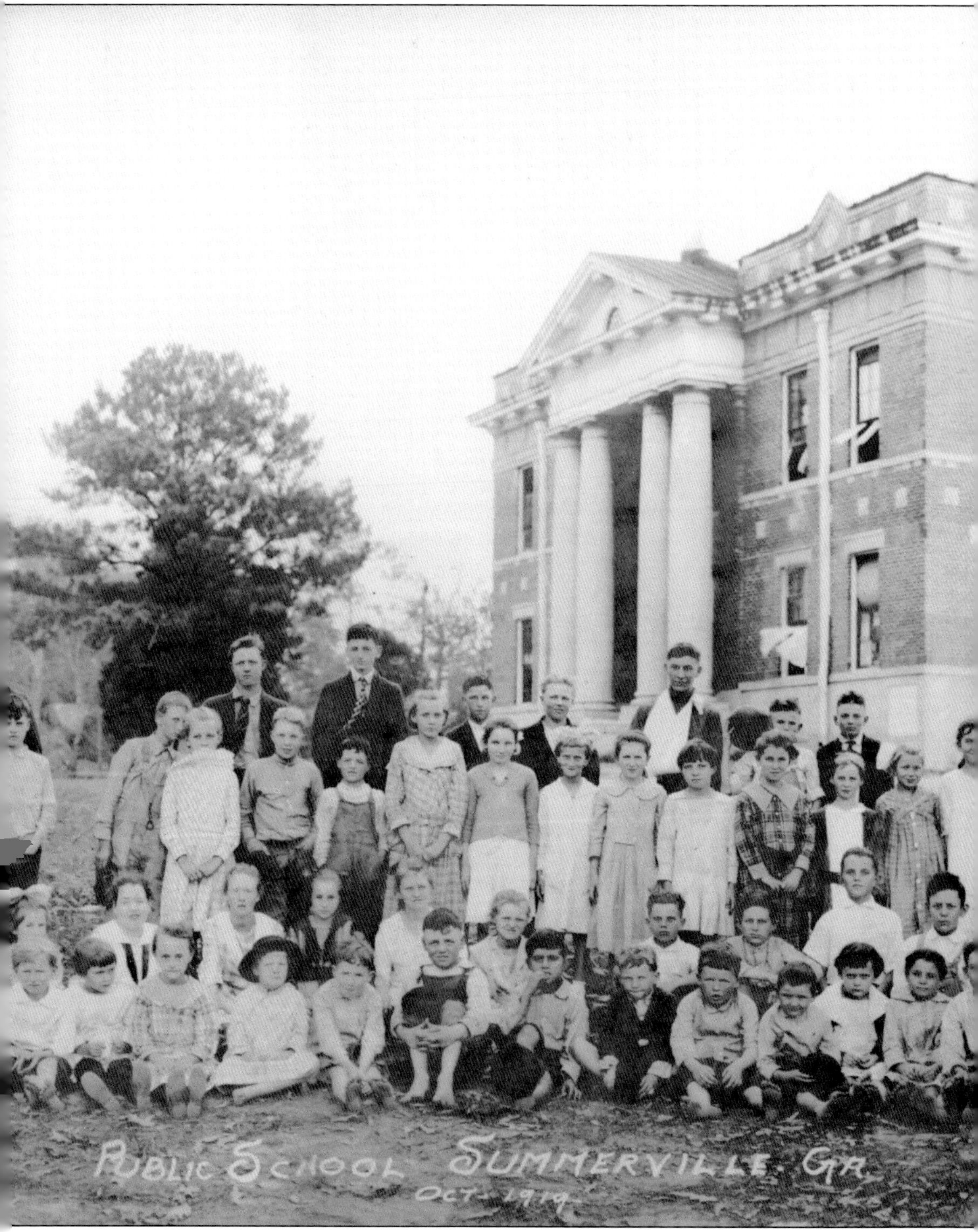

A seven-acre tract of the Middleton Allen farm was purchased by the Summerville School District in 1914, and a brick, two-story school was constructed on the site. The school contained six classrooms on the first floor and another four classrooms, plus an auditorium, on the second

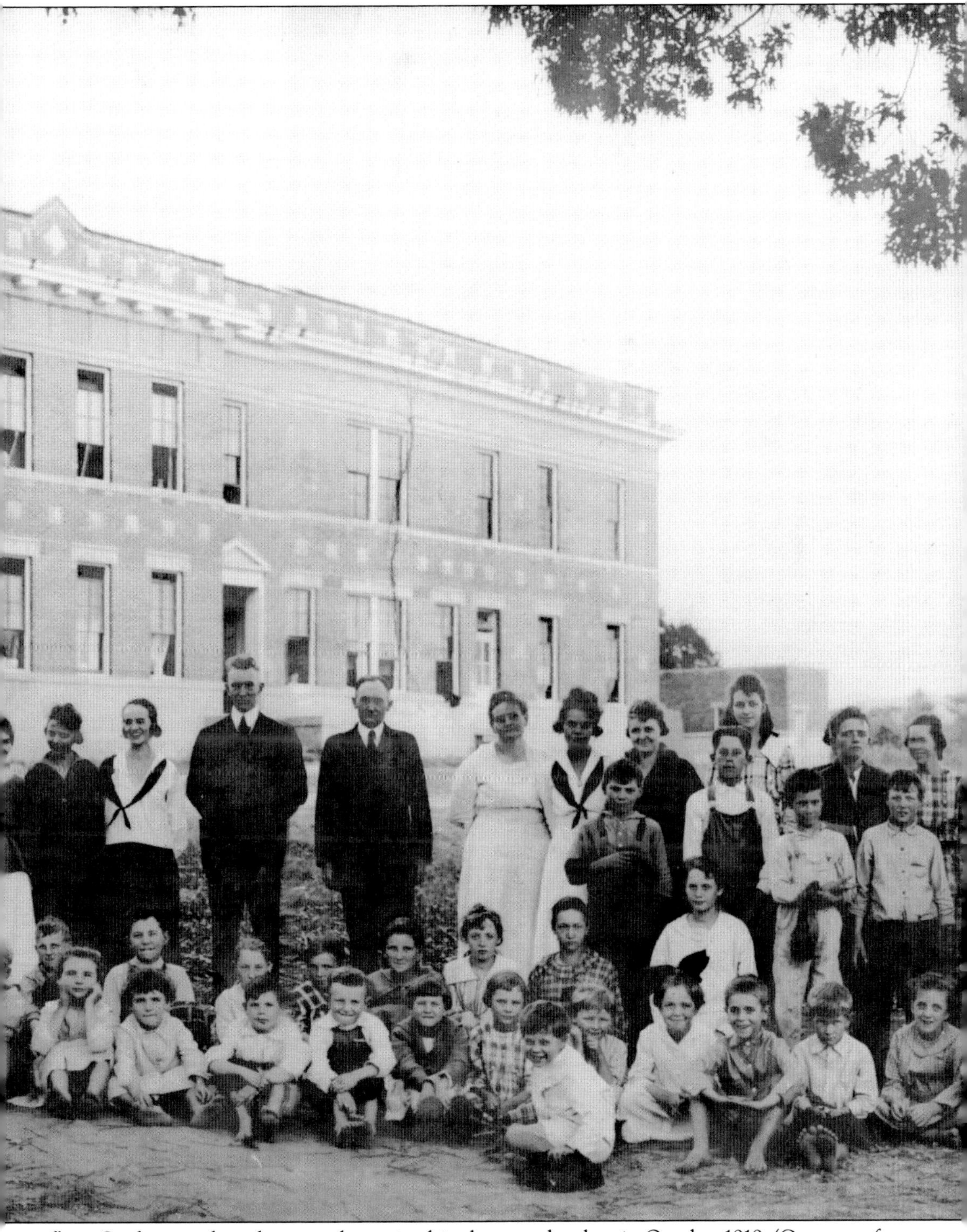

floor. Students and teachers are shown in this photograph taken in October 1919. (Courtesy of Dora Ann Lanier.)

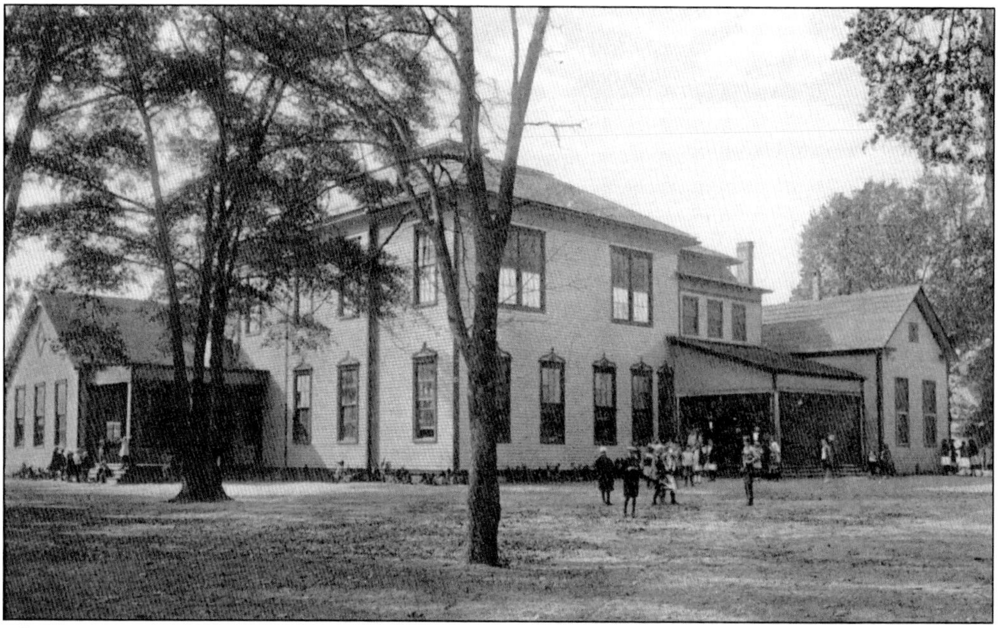

The Trion School was built in 1895 and, following minor damage from a fire, enlarged in 1902; the capacity of the school was increased to 400 students. After a new high school was built in 1929 and a new elementary school opened in 1949, this building was demolished. (Courtesy of Chattooga County Library.)

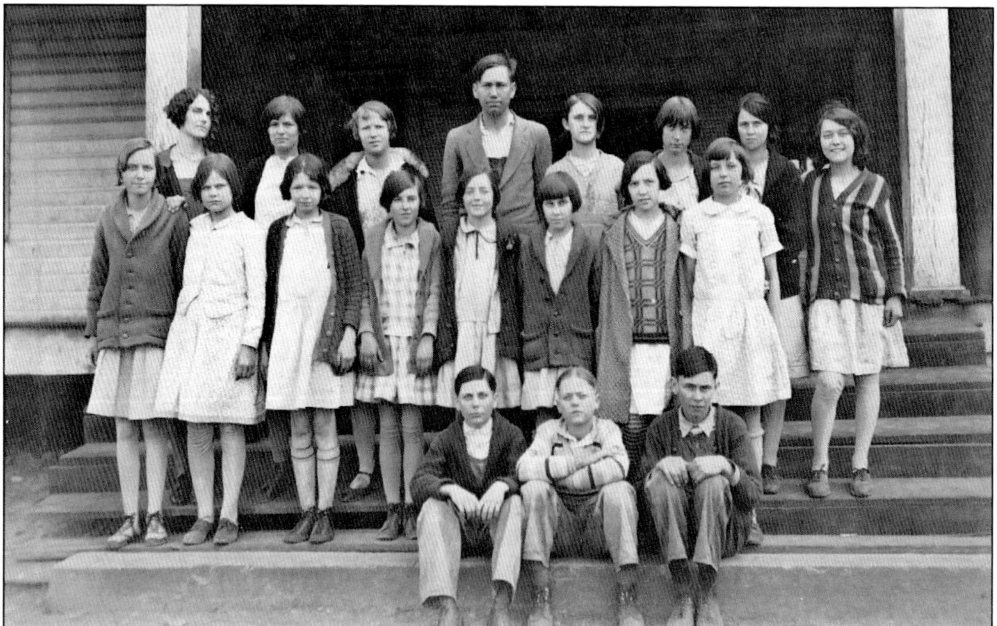

Students attending Gore School in 1922 include, from left to right, (first row) Will Owens, Thomas McKinney, and Fay Grigsby; (second row) Elsie Brown, Helen Mills, Mattie Scott, Margaret Palmour, Marion Baker, Sara Brown, Vivian Dempsey, and Margaret Cordle, (third row) Dixie Lee Robinson (teacher), Inez Anderson, Clara Carr, Tom Lee Neal, Dorothy Allen, unidentified, Maxine Phillips, and Mattie Sue Allen. (Courtesy of Phyllis Grigsby Howell.)

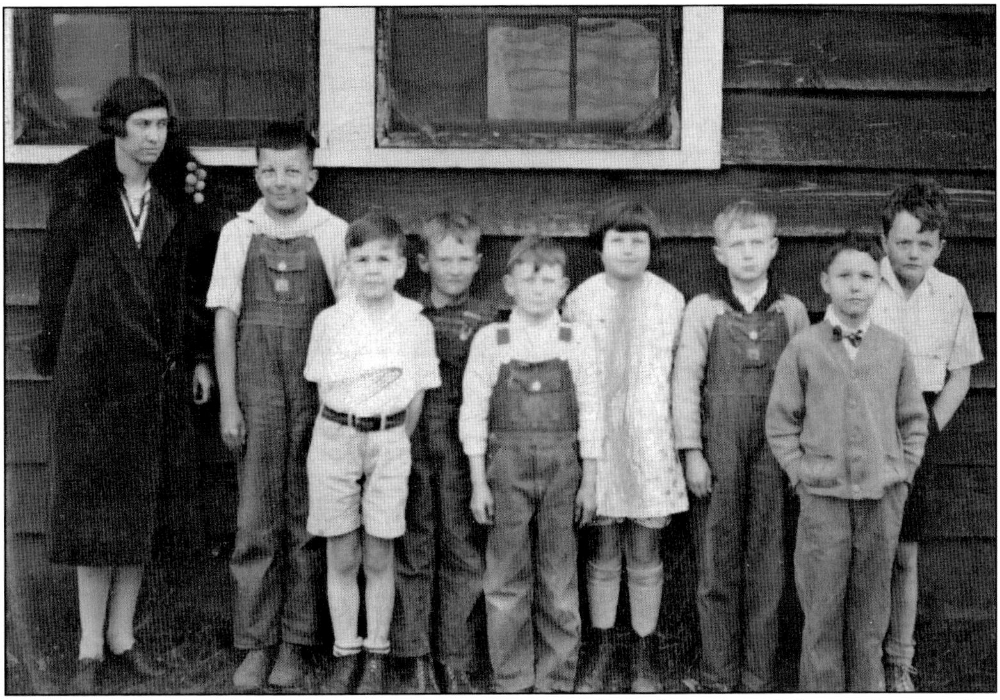

Jessie Hunt (left) operated a private school in Summerville and stands with her students in this photograph made around 1928. Her charges include, from left to right, D.P. Henley Jr., Charles Turner, Arch Farrar, Ira Henderson, Ida Lois Crawford, Charles Trimble, Earl Beatty, and John Black Whisnant Jr. (Courtesy of Janet Farrar Byington.)

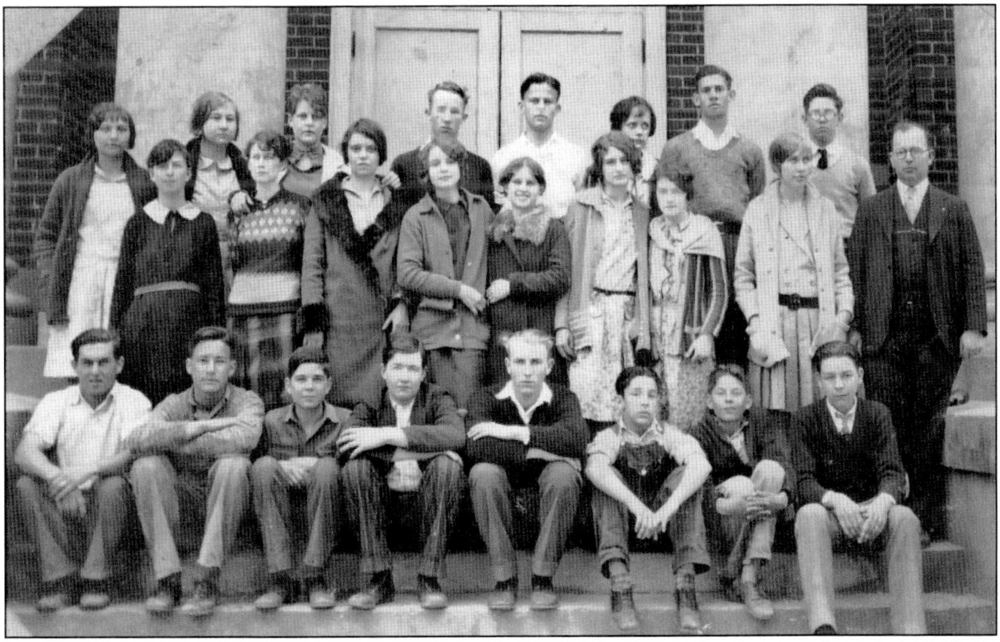

Tenth-grade students from Summerville High School are pictured in 1929. They include L.C. Turner (first row, third from left) and Joe Pullen (first row, third from right). (Courtesy of John Turner.)

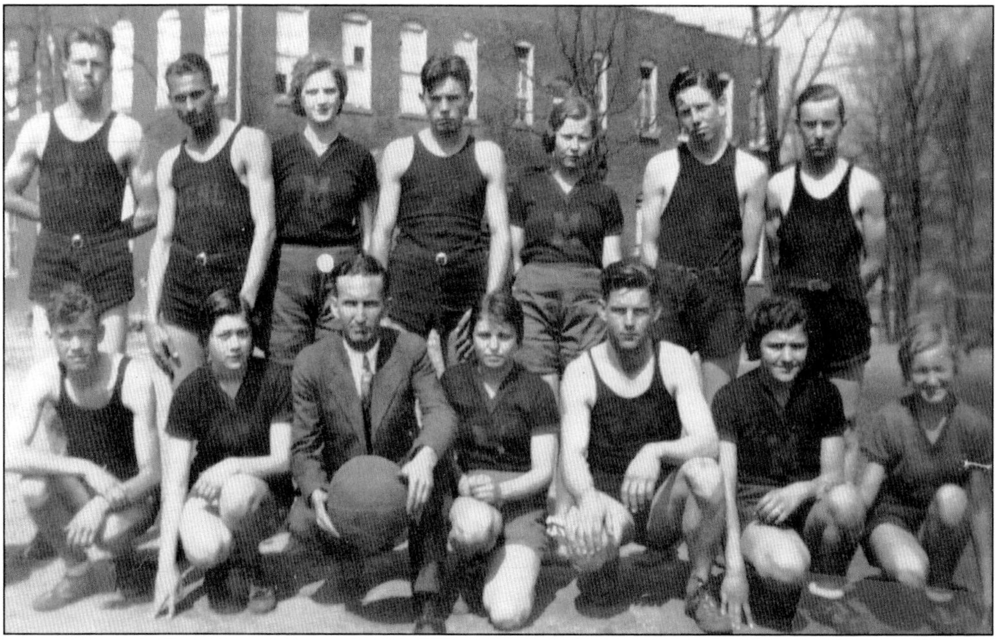

The Menlo School's boys' and girls' basketball teams are shown in front of the school around 1931. Pictured are, from left to right, (first row) John Knox Kennedy, Ruth Clarkson, Principal J.C. Young, Jewel White, Harry Dodd, Martha J. Baker, and Mamie L. Ballard; (second row) Emory Bobo, Carl Webster, Kathleen Graham, Doyle Toles, Pauline Hardwick, John Knox Wyatt, and J.D. Majors. (Courtesy of Chattooga County Library.)

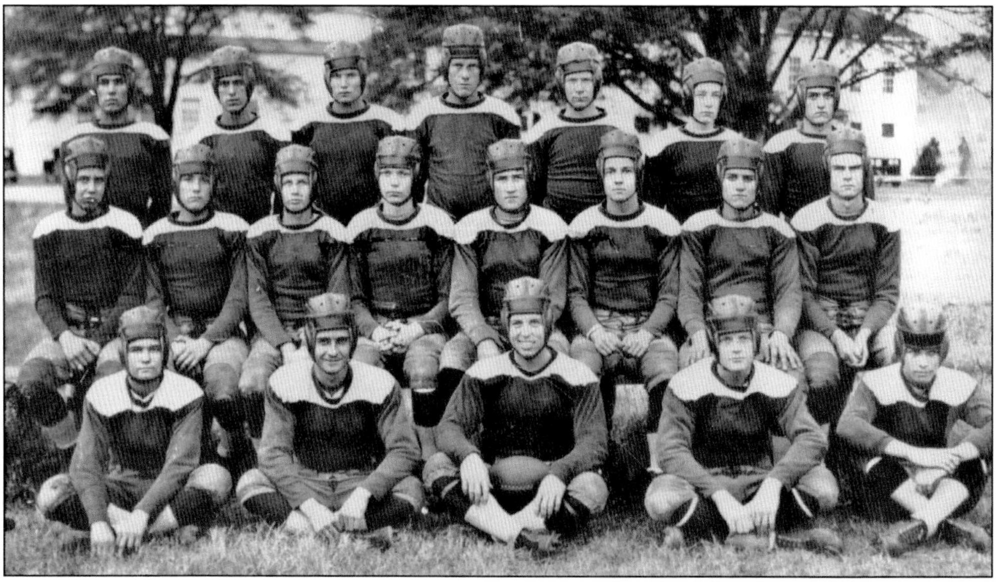

The Trion High School football team is shown in this 1933 photograph. The Bulldogs include, from left to right, (first row) D.F. Lancaster, Lee Broome, Howard McAbee, Ray Woods, and Jim McKenzie; (second row) Harlan Giles, Ted Bean, Joe Henderson, Bobby Bell, Elgin Logan, Leroy Johnson, Hoyt Tinney, and R.W. Williams; (third row) Aaron Buckalew, "Dutchie" Parris, Roland Wardlaw, Morris Rice, "Red" Bulman, Joe Bell Jr., and Max Williams. (Courtesy of the *Summerville News*.)

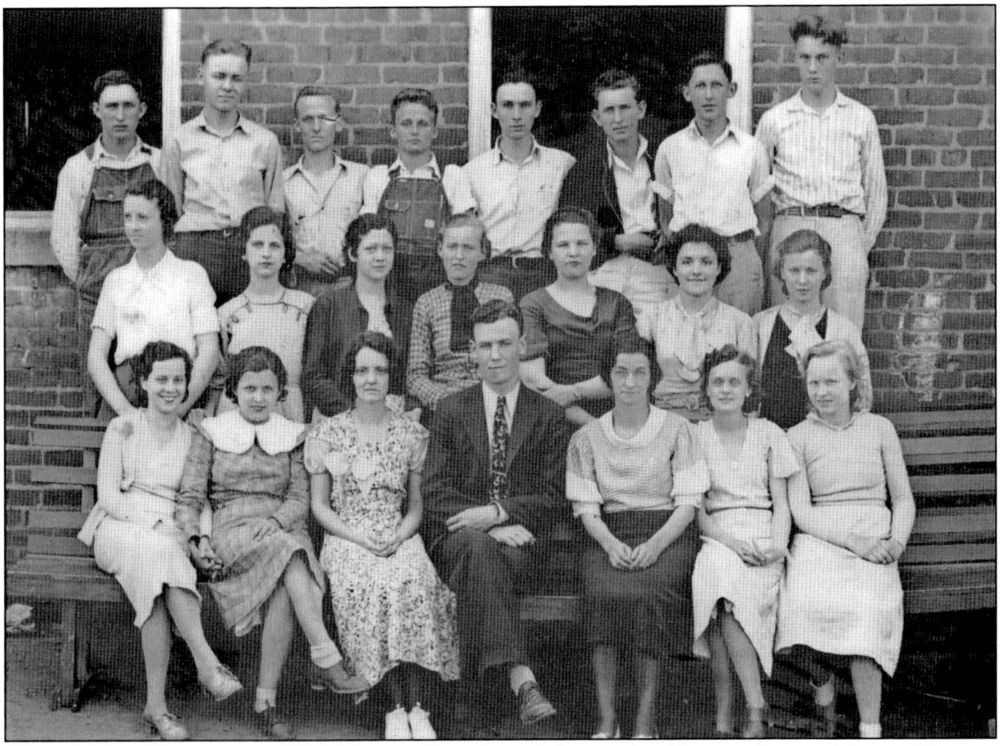

Menlo students and teachers in 1934 include, from left to right, (first row) Irene Murray, Frances Willingham, Virginia Bull, Knox Wyatt, Edna Perry, Helen Webster, and Nellie Stephenson; (second row) Blanche Toles, Mildred Hall, Ruth Clarkson, Mamie Lou Bullard, Elizabeth Baker, Martha Baker, and Pauline Hardwick; (third row) Roy White, Billy Stephenson, Paul Murray, Baker Willingham, J.C. Cavin, Gene Ballard, James King, and Warner Wilson. (Courtesy of Chattooga County Library.)

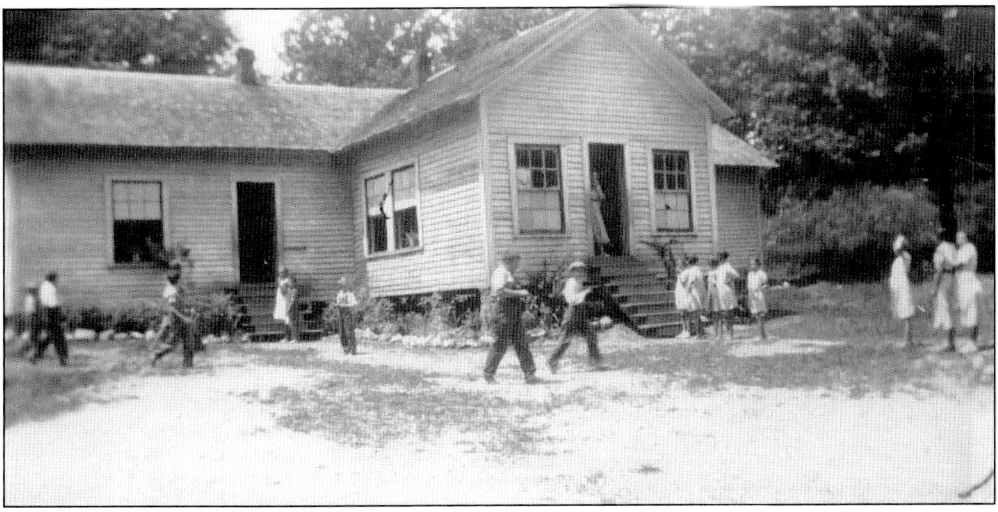

The Pine Grove School was located south of Menlo, between Alpine and Oak Hill. Mrs. Horace Simmons, a teacher and the school's principal, is shown standing in the doorway. Approximately 100 students were enrolled at the Pine Grove School when this photograph was taken in 1937. (Courtesy of Chattooga County Library.)

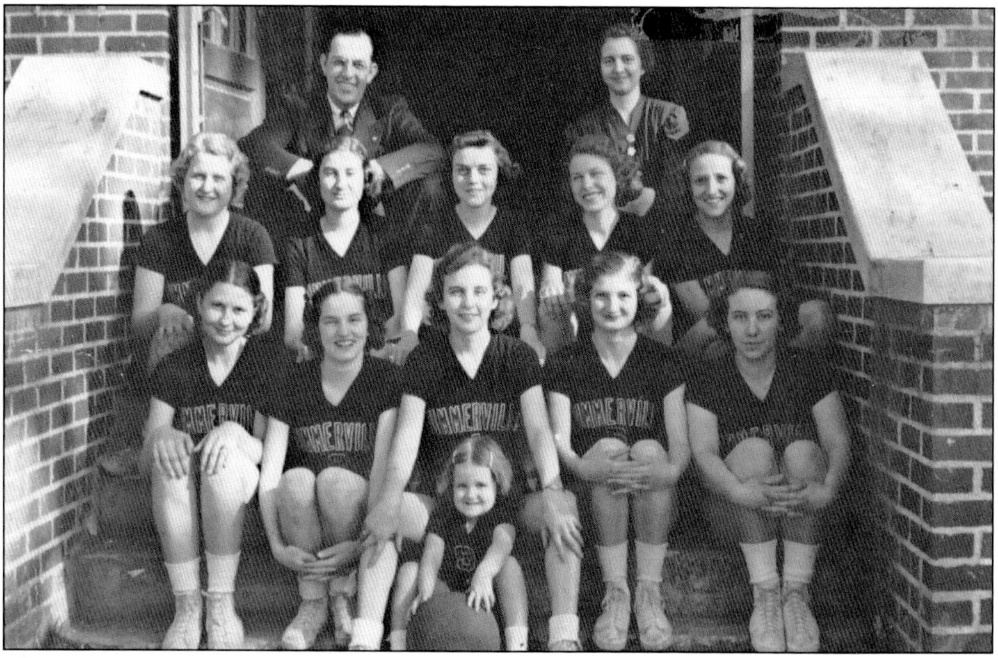

The 1938 Summerville High School girls' basketball team includes mascot Dawn Dillard (with ball) and, from left to right, (first row) Willie Mae Thomas, Betty Broome, Dot McConkey, Arbelle Dodd, and Valerie Dalton; (second row) Essie Brown, Eleanor Thomas, Betty Beavers, Louise Brown, and Geraldine Hill; (third row) school superintendent Frank Dillard and Drucilla Sizemore. (Courtesy of Phyllis Grigsby Howell.)

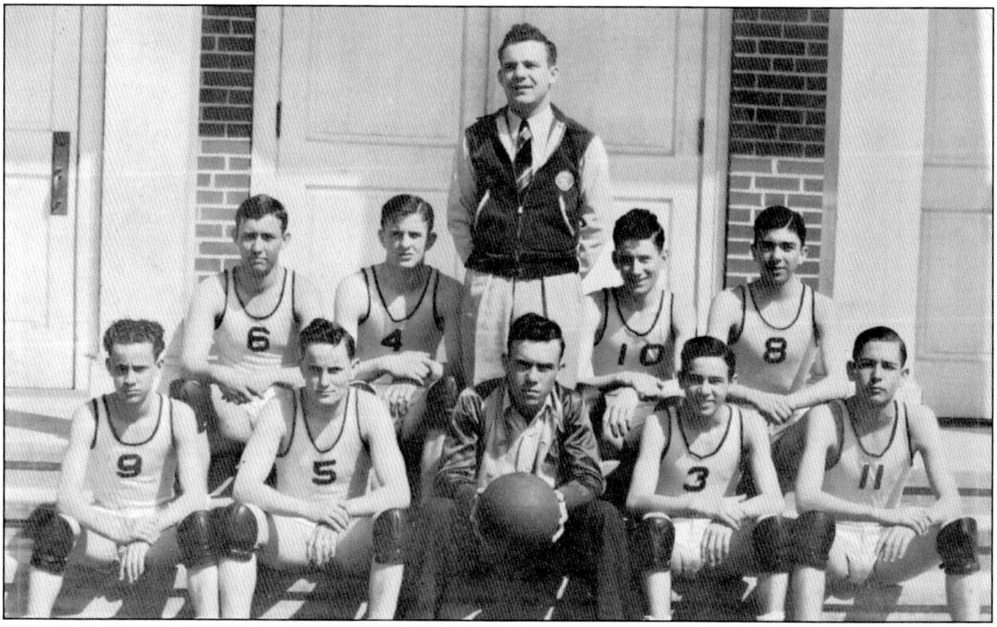

The 1938 Trion High School basketball team is shown on the steps of the school with coach F.H. "Pete" Boney. The names listed on the photograph include, from left to right, (first row) Major, Sloppy, Hill (manager), Merle, and Bud; (second row) Nunn, Calvin, Coach Boney, Parker, and Glee. (Courtesy of Lanny Thomas.)

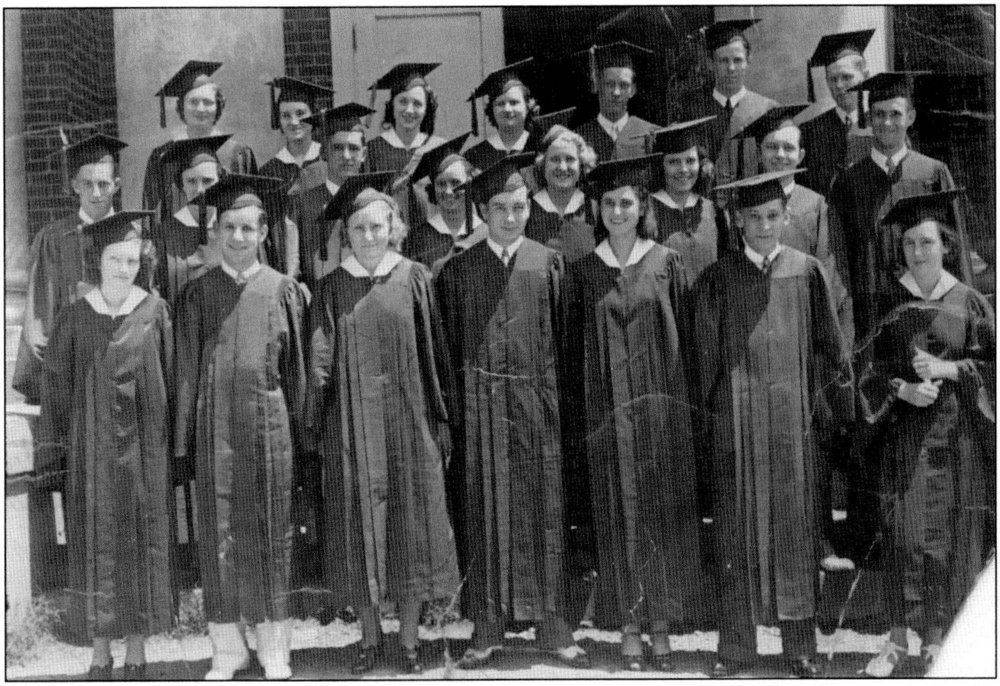

The 1939 Summerville High School graduates include, from left to right, (first row) Ovelle Brown, William Cleghorn, Martha Parker, Sam Cordle, Martha Hayes, Joe Favor, and Edna Rae Dobbs; (second row) Holland Martin, Frances Housch, Bobby Sims, Ann Fletcher, Essie Brown, Eloyes Johnson, Claude Bagley, and Joe Hammonds; (third row) Madelyn Parker, Annie Fay, Helen Hammonds, Ovelle Tallent, G.B. Lambert, Grady Ramey, and Harold Wilson. (Courtesy of Phyllis Grigsby Howell.)

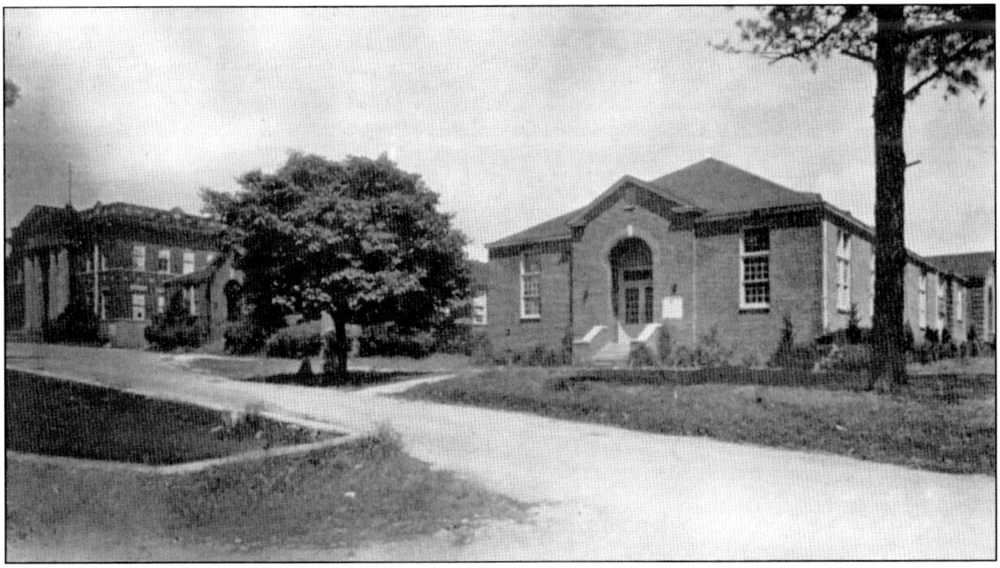

A fire in 1943 destroyed Summerville High School and its auditorium but spared the two-story grammar school (left). The high school was rebuilt the next year and opened in early 1945. A new auditorium was constructed in 1949 and, like the two-story school building, continues to stand. (Courtesy of Chattooga County Library.)

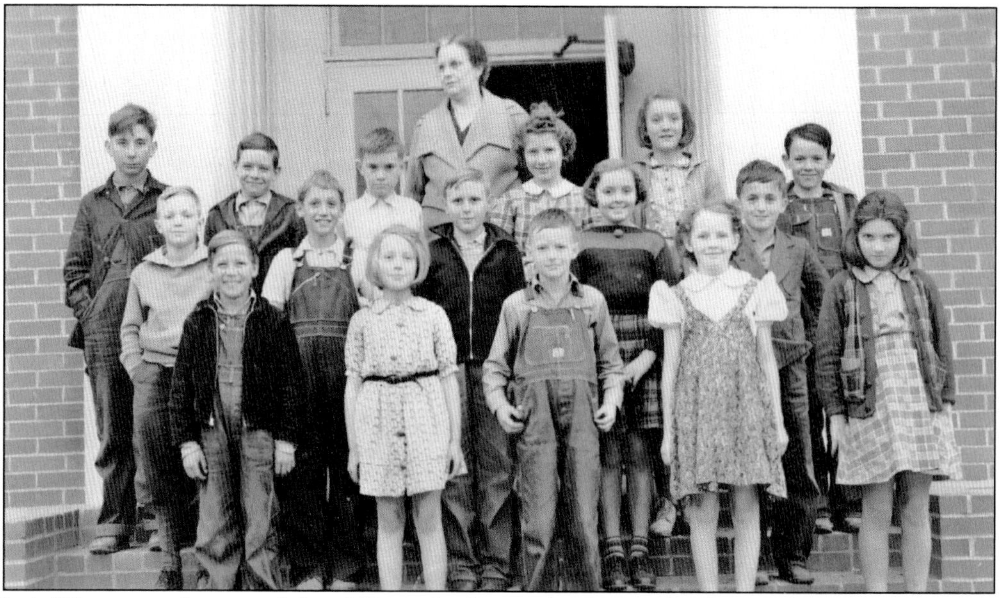

Lula Weesner is shown with her fifth grade class at the Gore School around 1941. Her students pictured here include Max Willingham, Nelda Padgett, Howard Owings, Delores Geise, Harvey Morgan, Smith Willingham, Marion Carpenter, Frances Geise, Louella McEntire, and (second row from left to right) Van Hancock, Stanley Cummings, Dallas Baggett, Madeline Hawkins, and Jack McCallie. (Courtesy of Darlene Norton Mallonee.)

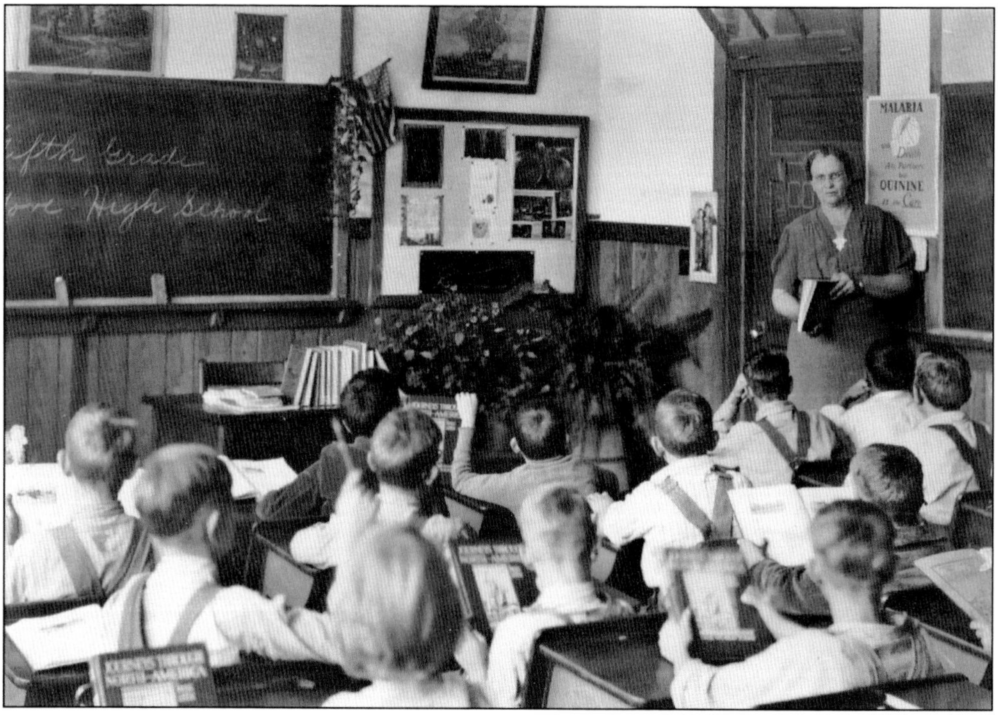

Lula Weesner spent much of her 51-year career teaching at the Gore School. Both the high school and elementary school eventually consolidated with schools in Summerville due to increased costs and declining enrollment. (Courtesy of Brenda Hogg Lanier.)

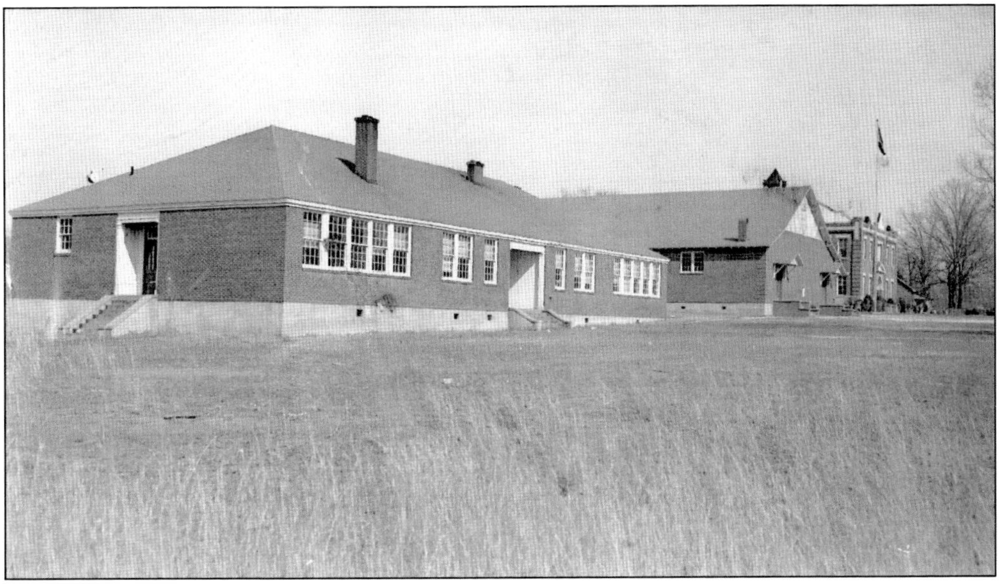

A photograph of the Lyerly schools shows, from left to right, the high school, gymnasium, and elementary school. The gym was a WPA project built in the late 1930s. The high school was constructed around the same time. (Courtesy of Branson and Margaret Gayler.)

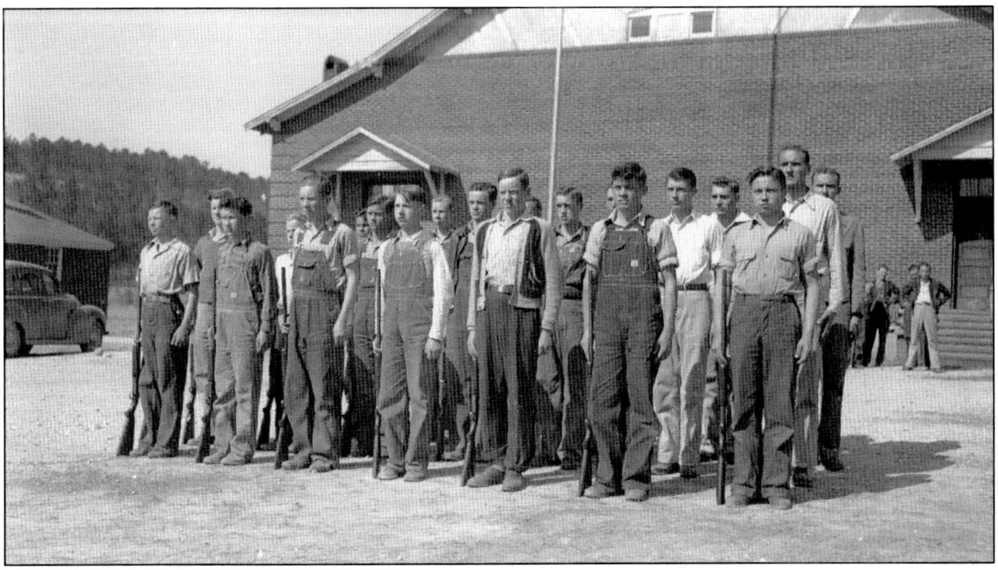

The Lyerly High School Home Guard was organized during World War II by Bob Crawford, a local merchant and veteran of World War I. As shown in this 1944 picture, the group was allowed to bring firearms to school to participate in close-order drills. Branson Gayler stands at attention on the far left side. (Courtesy of Branson and Margaret Gayler.)

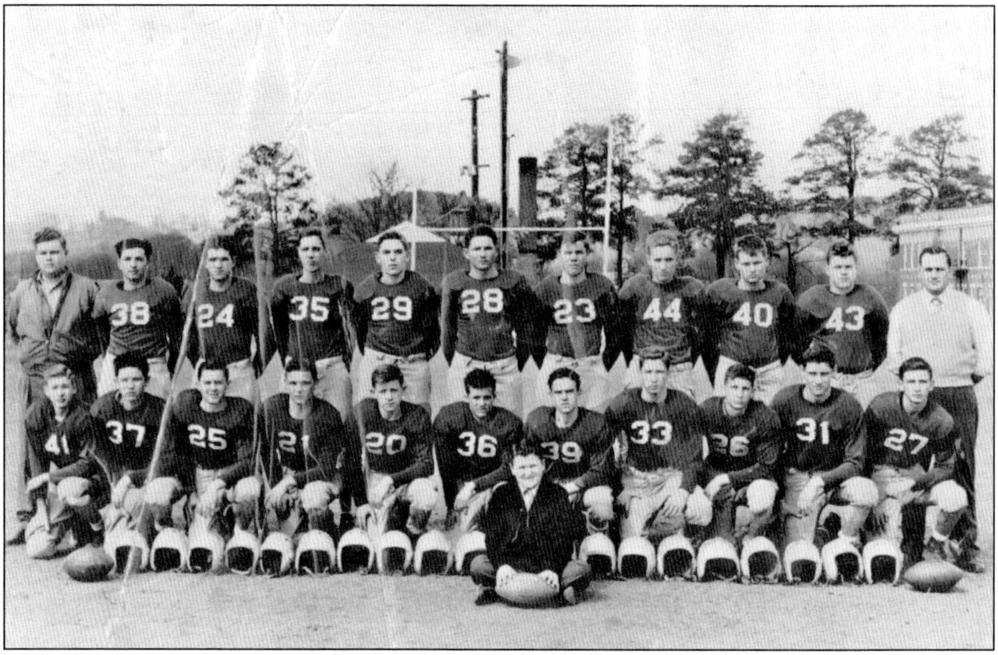

The 1947 Summerville High School football team includes, from left to right, (first row) Newsome, Bagley, Cox, Stanley, B. Bush, Williams, B. Nix, Moore, Dacus, J. Bush, Parker, and (front center) Williams (manager); (second row) Espy, Davison, G. Nix, Morehead, Flanagan, Fletcher, Johnson, Pettyjohn, Donovits, Reece, and Coach Pierce. (Courtesy of Joe and Jan Pullen.)

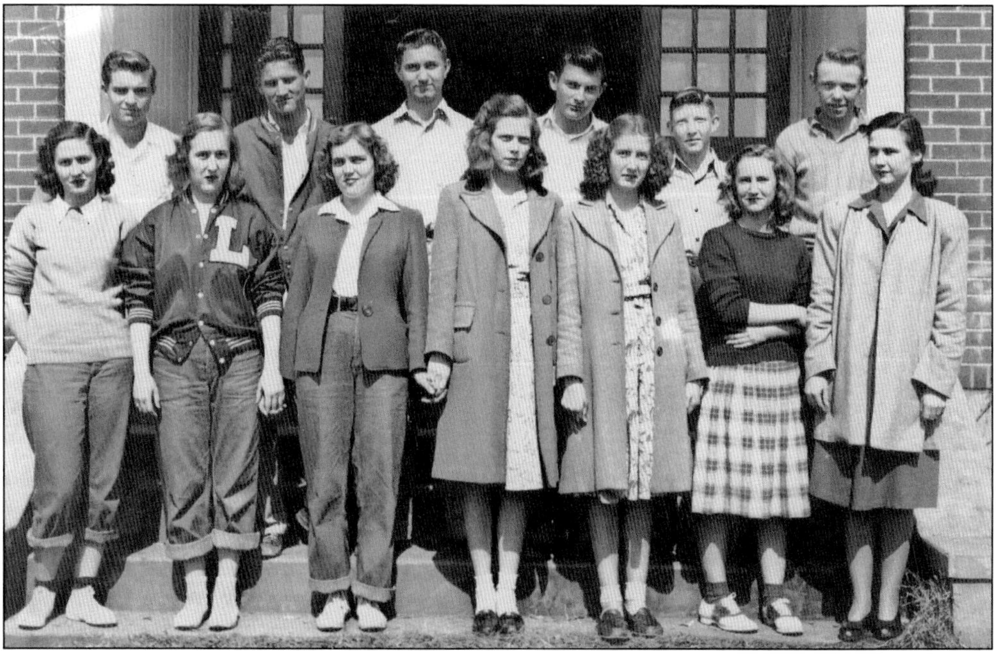

Lyerly High School students pose for a photograph around 1948. They are, from left to right, (first row) Mary Cook, Jo Kirby, Janie Little, Betty Jean Gravley, Nona Kendrick, Willie Sue Abernathy, and Margaret Brewer; (second row) Hayden Mitchell, Kyle Lindsey, Bob Bryson, James Henry Kendrick, John Robert Kendrick, and ? Ratliff. (Courtesy of Branson and Margaret Gayler.)

A Trion native, Brooke Pierce graduated from Trion High School and entered the University of Georgia, where he played football. He graduated in 1943, joined the Marine Corps, and was injured at Iwo Jima. After World War II, he was a teacher, principal, and coach at Summerville High School from 1946 to 1950. The picture is from the 1949 school yearbook dedicated to him. (Courtesy of the *Summerville News*.)

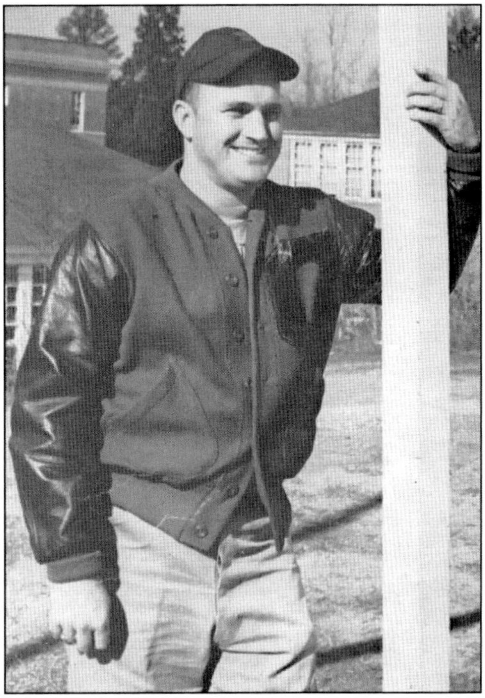

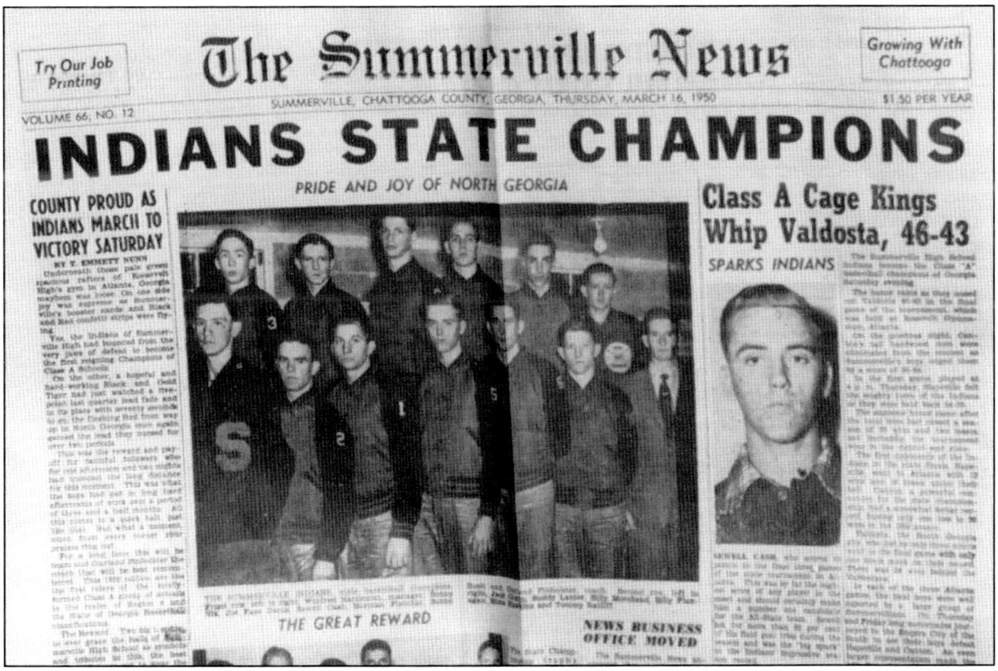

Try Our Job Printing

The Summerville News

Growing With Chattooga

SUMMERVILLE, CHATTOOGA COUNTY, GEORGIA, THURSDAY, MARCH 16, 1950

VOLUME 66, NO. 12

$1.50 PER YEAR

INDIANS STATE CHAMPIONS

PRIDE AND JOY OF NORTH GEORGIA

COUNTY PROUD AS INDIANS MARCH TO VICTORY SATURDAY

Class A Cage Kings Whip Valdosta, 46-43

SPARKS INDIANS

THE GREAT REWARD

NEWS BUSINESS OFFICE MOVED

This 1950 *Summerville News* headline proclaims the "pride and joy of North Georgia." The Summerville High School basketball team won the State Class-A Championship against Valdosta 46-43. Coach Garland Pinholster's team included Bobby Nix, Buddy Lanier, Joe Faye Dacus, Sewell Cash, Billy Morehead, Billy Flanagan, Herman Fletcher, Bobby Bush, Sims Hawkins, Jack Glenn, and Tommy Ratliff, with managers Jimmy Williams and Winfred Hardeman. (Courtesy of Sewell Cash.)

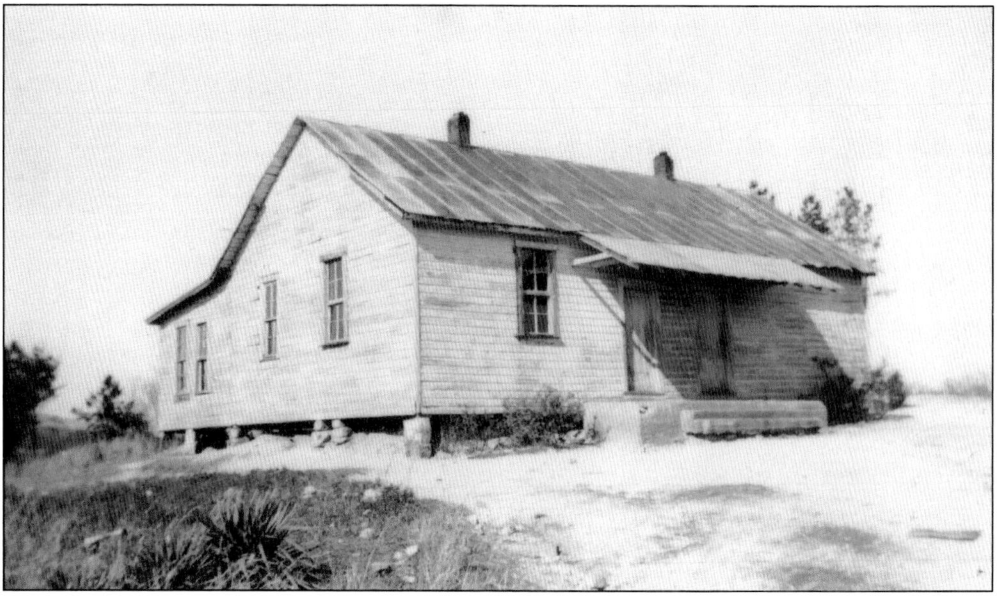

The Menlo Colored School was built in 1922 by the African American citizens of the community on land provided by A.J. Lawrence. The three-room building had two classrooms and a kitchen. (Courtesy of Menlo City Hall.)

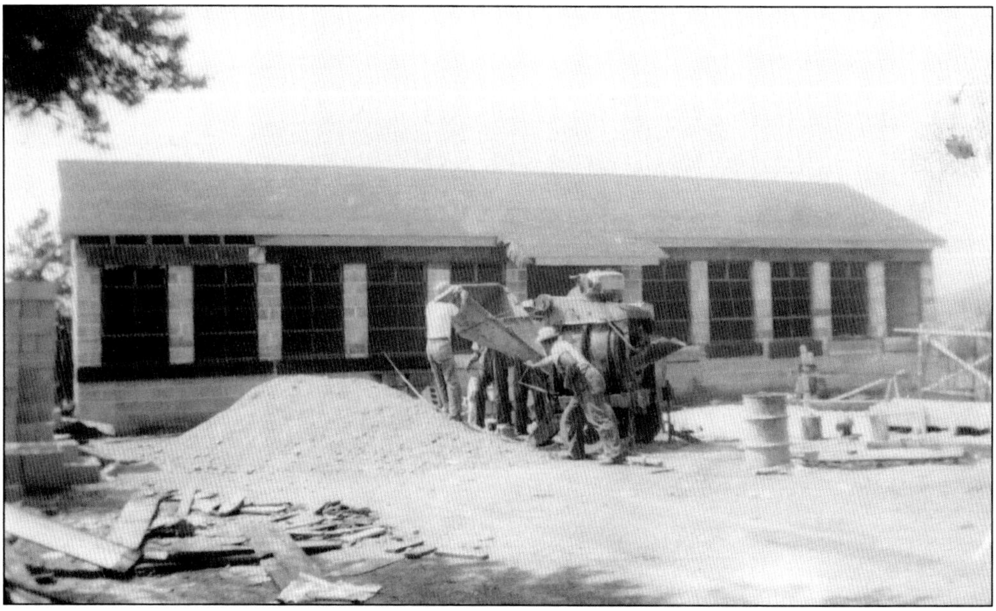

A new building for the Menlo Colored School was constructed in the early 1950s and included two classrooms and restrooms. (Courtesy of Menlo City Hall.)

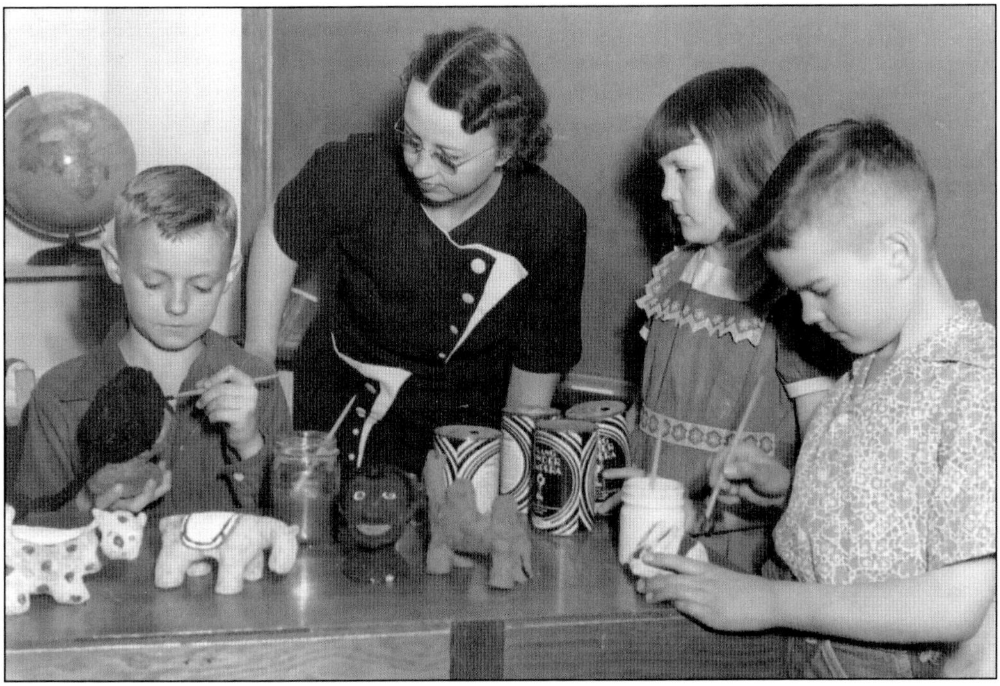

Blanche Toles taught her fourth-grade students at Menlo School how to use backyard clay to create figurines. This 1953 photograph shows, from left to right, Billy Don Gilley, Miss Toles, Judy Langley, and Claude Bullard. (Courtesy of Chattooga County Library.)

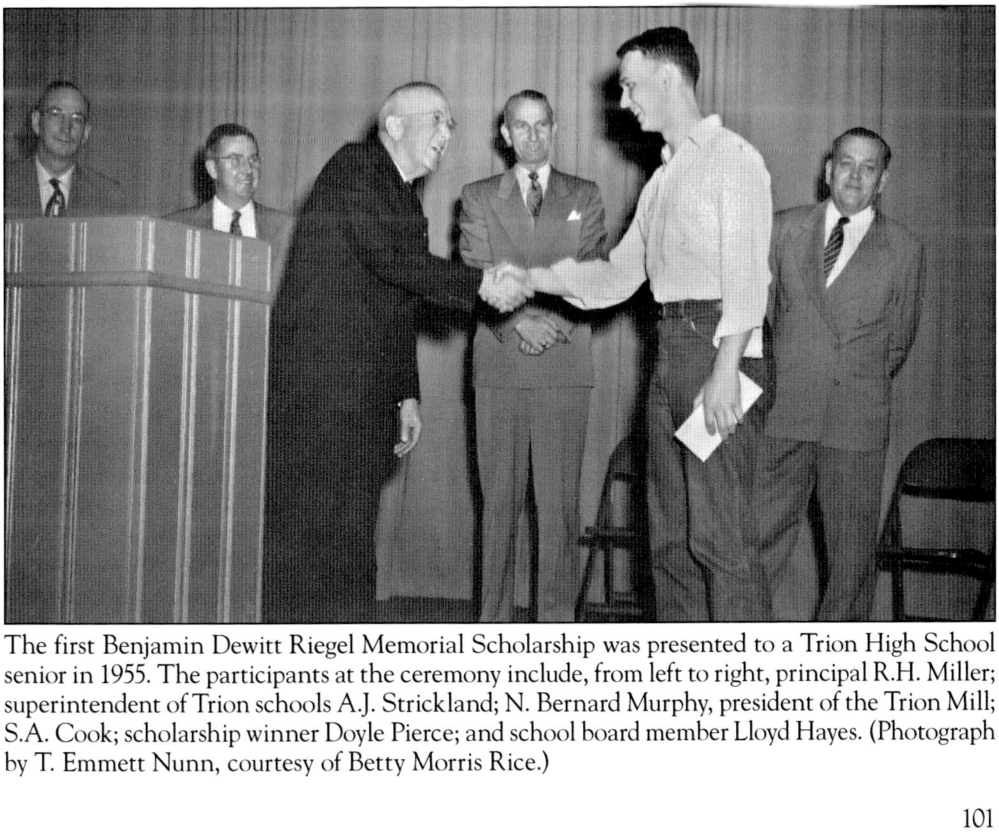

The first Benjamin Dewitt Riegel Memorial Scholarship was presented to a Trion High School senior in 1955. The participants at the ceremony include, from left to right, principal R.H. Miller; superintendent of Trion schools A.J. Strickland; N. Bernard Murphy, president of the Trion Mill; S.A. Cook; scholarship winner Doyle Pierce; and school board member Lloyd Hayes. (Photograph by T. Emmett Nunn, courtesy of Betty Morris Rice.)

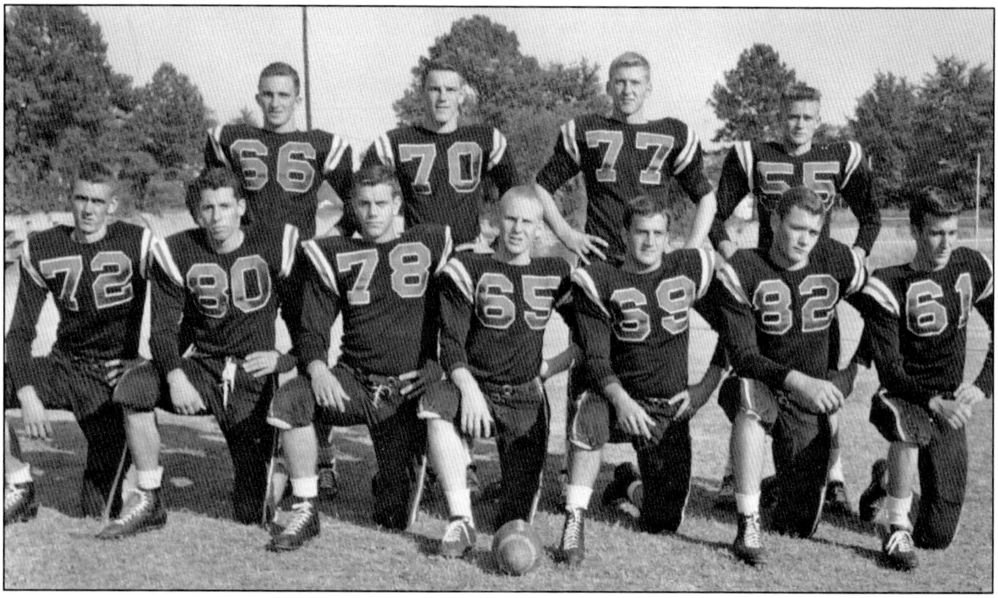

The offense for the 1956 Summerville High School football team includes, from left to right, (first row) William Roach, Billy Murdock, Wayne Hurley, Billy Denson, Frank Elliot, Winston Evett, and Ted Bridges; (second row) Ralph Hall, L.C. Smith, Marnell Ricketts, and Jackie Pierce. (Courtesy of L.C. Smith.)

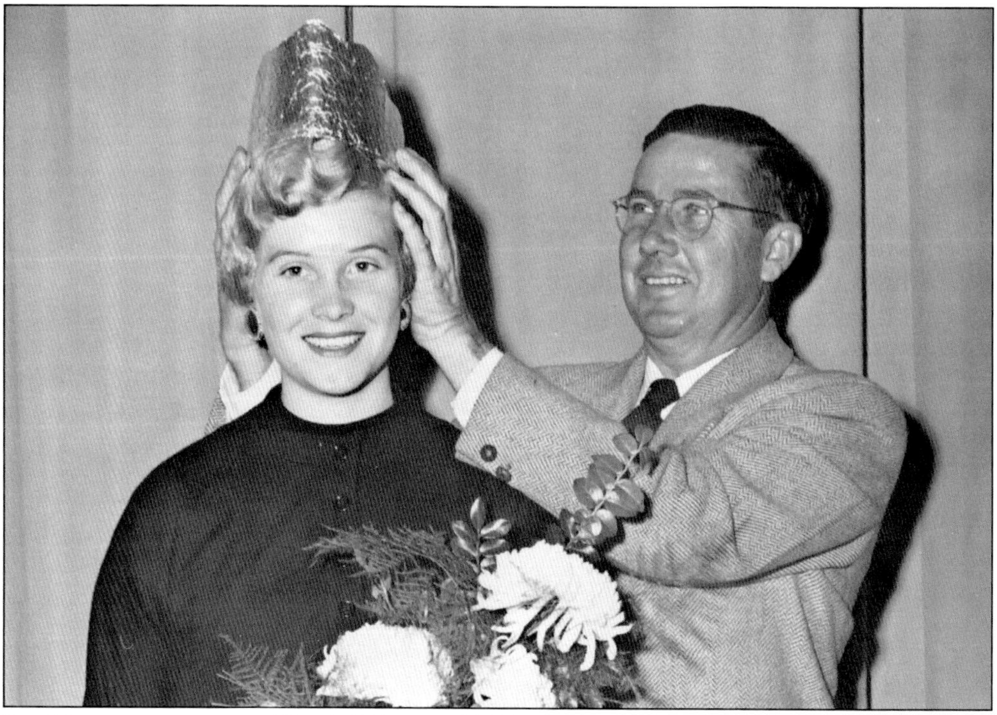

Sara Newsome was crowned Football Queen of 1956 by Trion School superintendent A.J. Strickland. Strickland served as superintendent for 27 years until his retirement in 1975 and was the founding president of the Chattooga County Historical Society. (Photograph by T. Emmett Nunn, courtesy of Betty Morris Rice.)

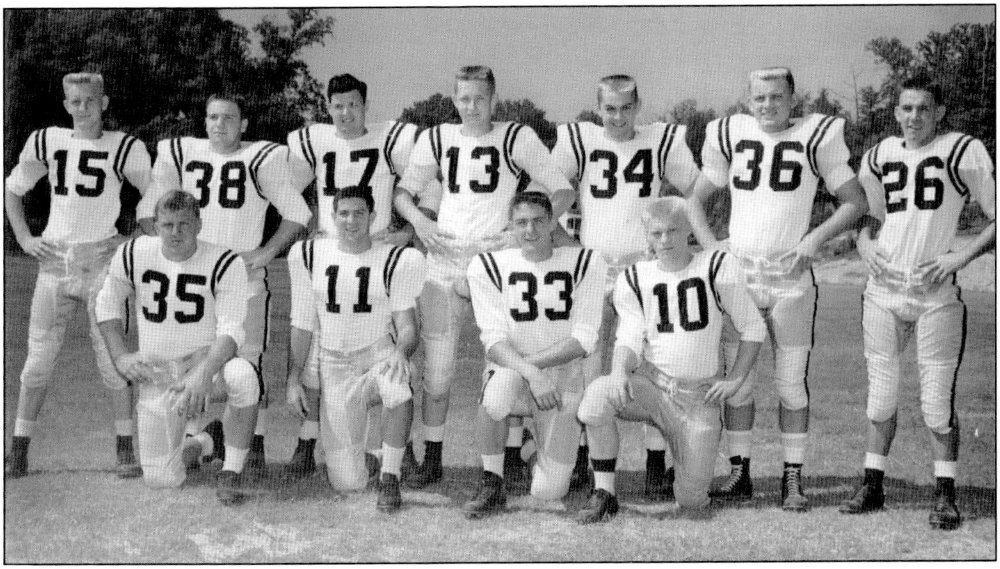

The starting offense for the 1957 Trion Bulldogs includes, from left to right, (first row) Kenneth Day, Bradley Watson, Darriel Broome, and Gary Daniels; (second row) Johnny Ingle, Ritchie Watson, Charles Hensley, Tommy Vines, Jimmy Styles, Kenneth Arden, and Terry Finster. Not shown is the team's eventual quarterback, LaWayne Powell. (Courtesy of Charles Hensley.)

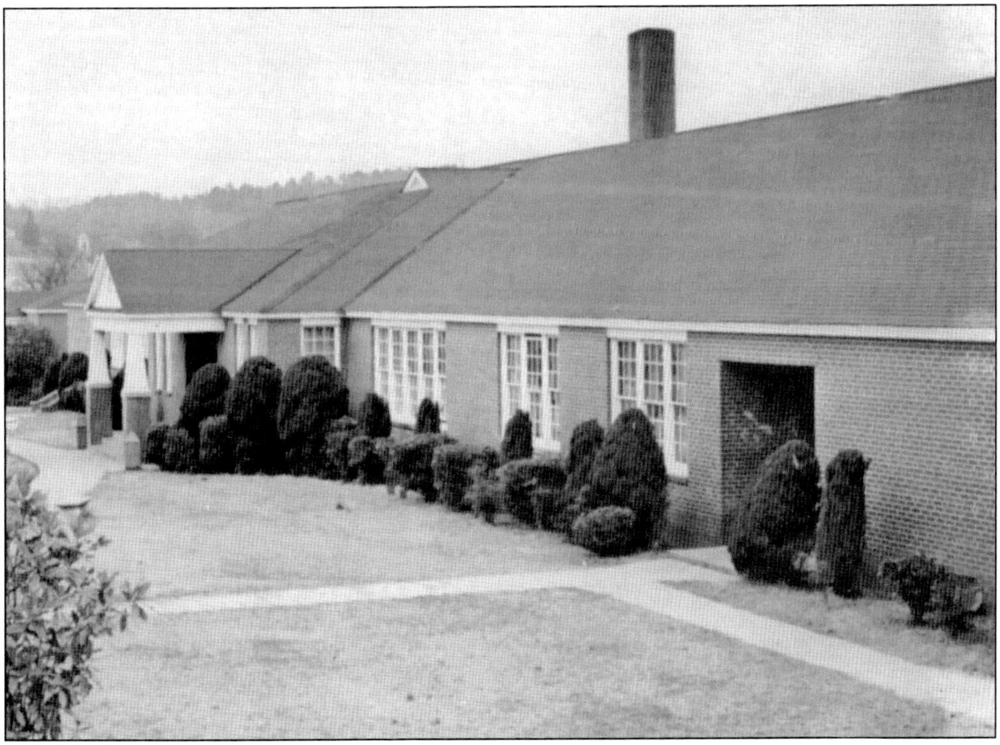

A photograph from Summerville High School's 1959 yearbook shows the building constructed in 1944 after a fire destroyed the previous school a year earlier. This structure was open for classes in January 1945 and remained in use as a middle school following the construction of a new high school in 1965. The 1944 high school was later demolished. (Courtesy of Steve Edwards.)

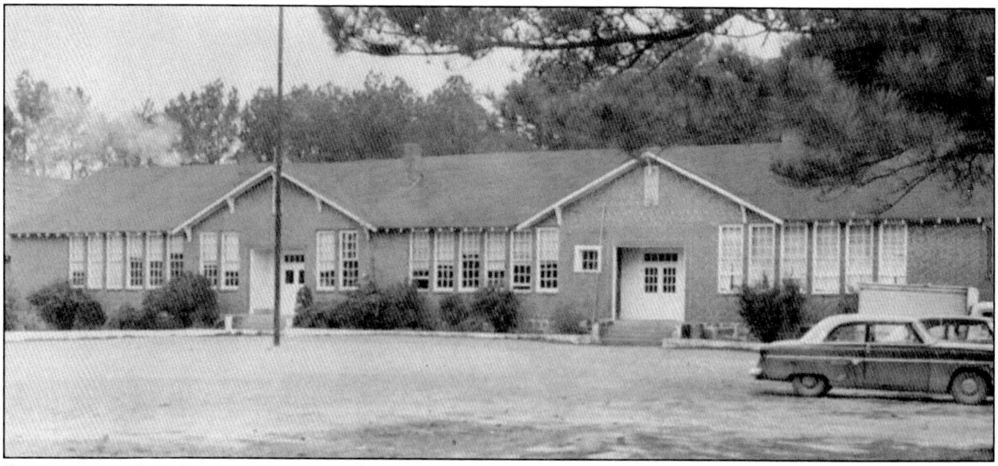

Subligna High School is shown in this 1958 yearbook photograph. Billy L. Jones was the principal. A year later, the school was consolidated with Summerville High School. (Courtesy of Brenda Hogg Lanier.)

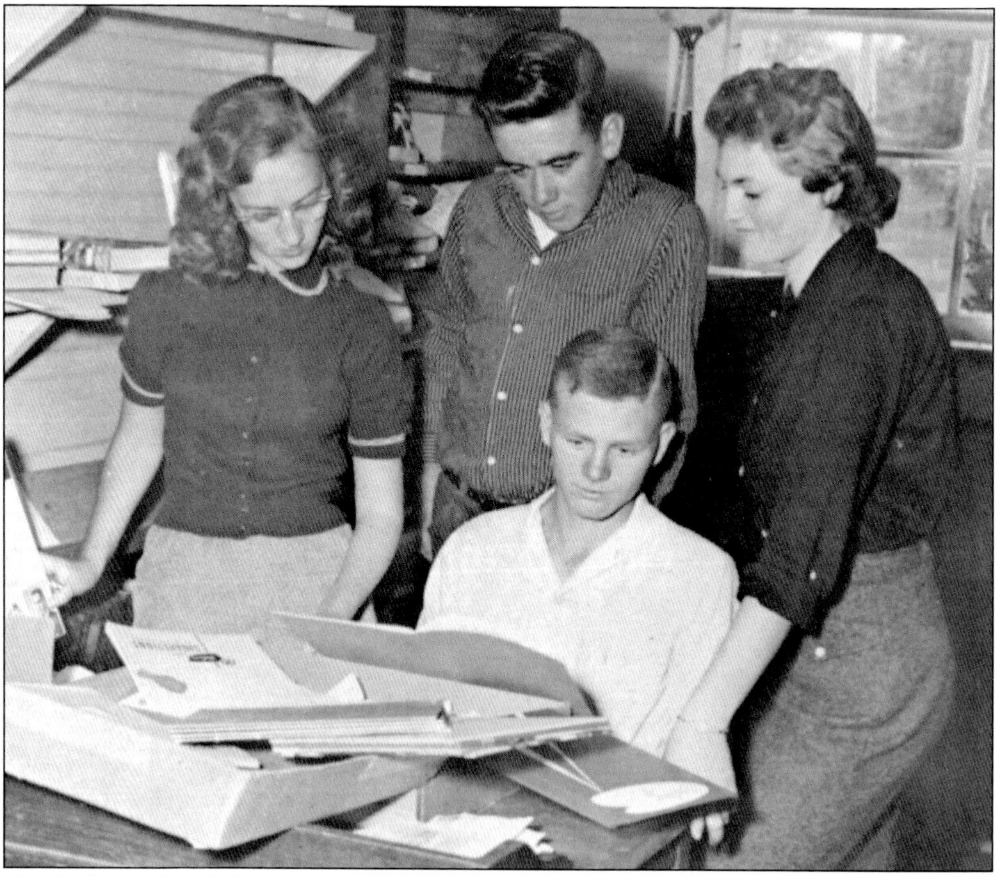

The Subligna High School yearbook, the *Underwood*, was named for one of the first teachers in the area and a community founder. A photograph of the yearbook staff appears in the 1958 edition and includes, from left to right, Winona Hughes, Austin Moore, David Cordle, and Evelyn Hix. (Courtesy of Brenda Hogg Lanier.)

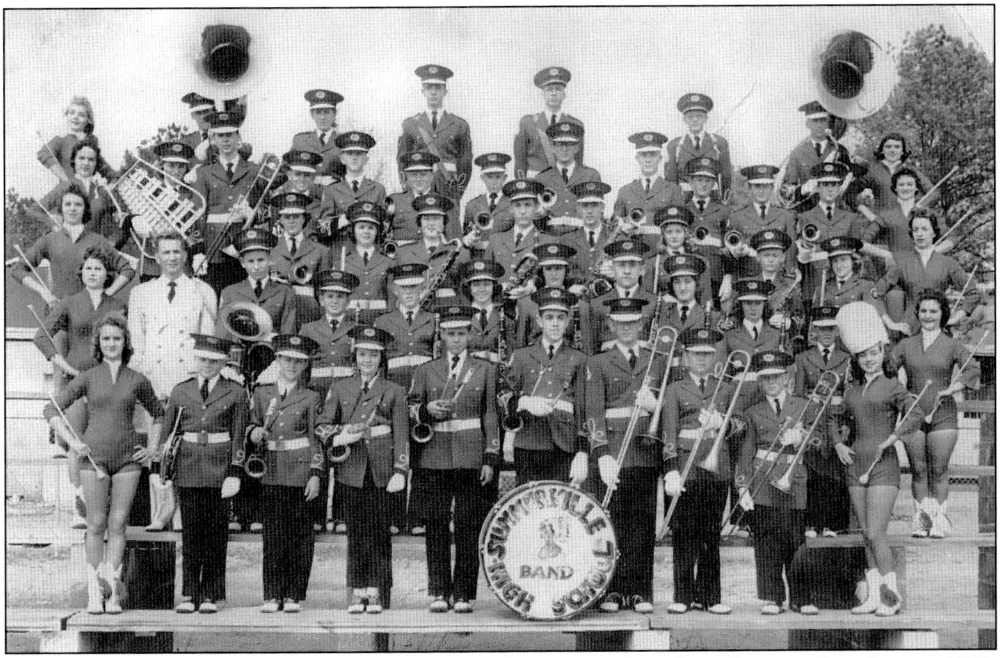

The Summerville High School Marching Band is pictured in this photograph taken in 1959. (Courtesy of the *Summerville News.*)

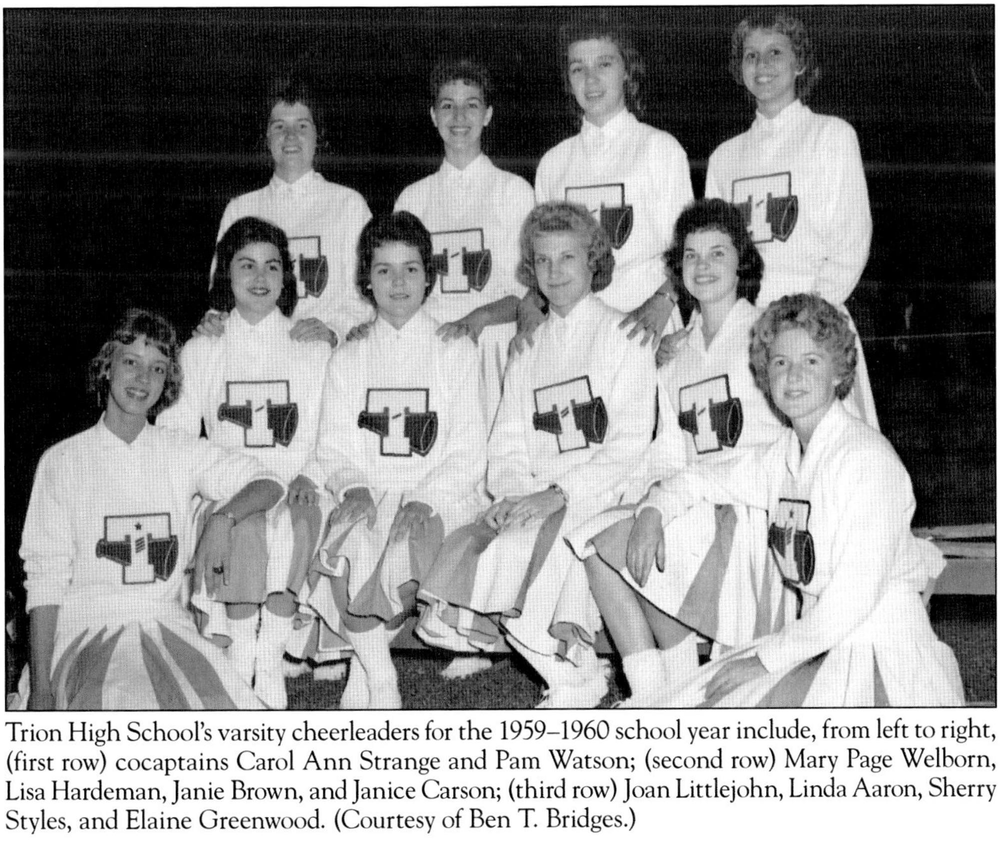

Trion High School's varsity cheerleaders for the 1959–1960 school year include, from left to right, (first row) cocaptains Carol Ann Strange and Pam Watson; (second row) Mary Page Welborn, Lisa Hardeman, Janie Brown, and Janice Carson; (third row) Joan Littlejohn, Linda Aaron, Sherry Styles, and Elaine Greenwood. (Courtesy of Ben T. Bridges.)

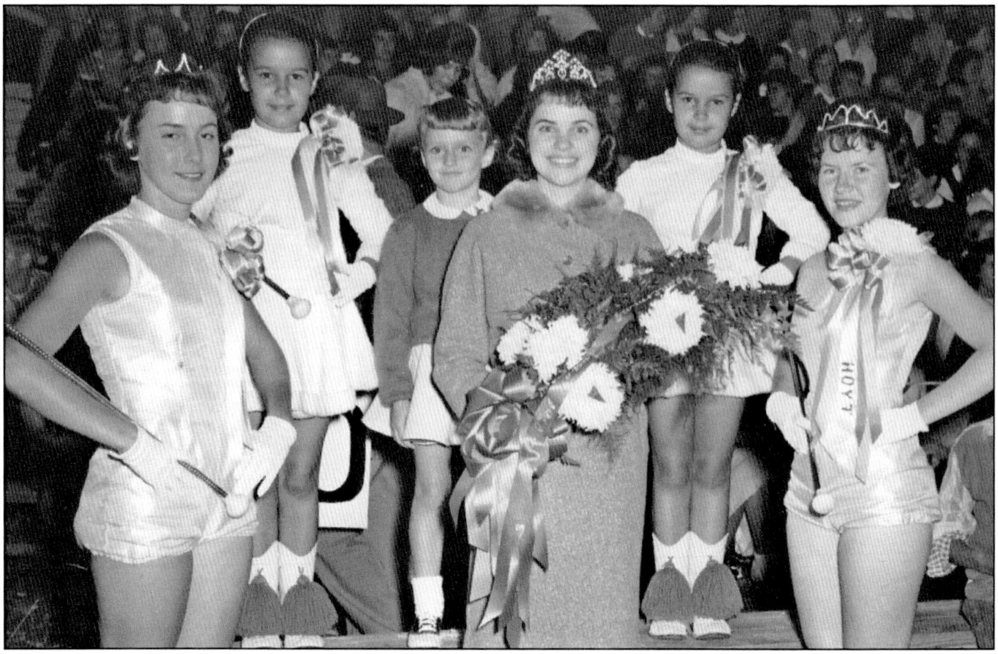

Trion High School's homecoming queen in 1960, Janice Carson, is pictured with the twirlers, mascots, and crown-bearer. Shown are, from left to right, (first row) Nancy Jim Floyd, Janice Carson, and Karen Adams; (second row) unidentified. (Photograph by T. Emmett Nunn, courtesy of Betty Morris Rice.)

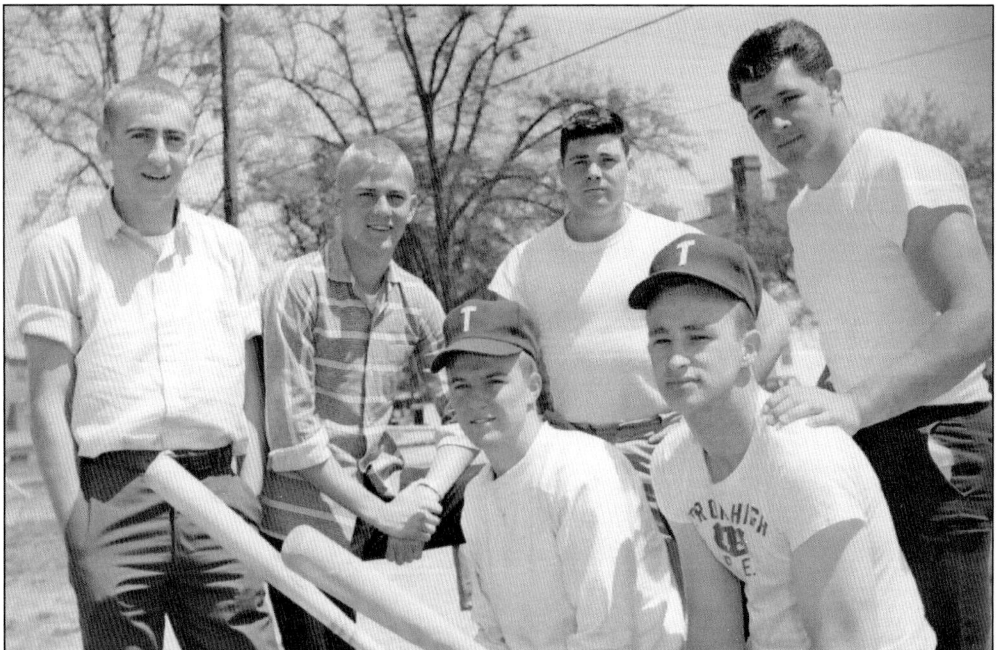

Members of this c. 1963 Trion High School baseball team include, from left to right, (first row) Wayne Parker and Wayne Powell; (second row) Terry Witt, Gary Buice, Ronald Day, and Marshall Dooley. (Photograph by T. Emmett Nunn, courtesy of Betty Morris Rice.)

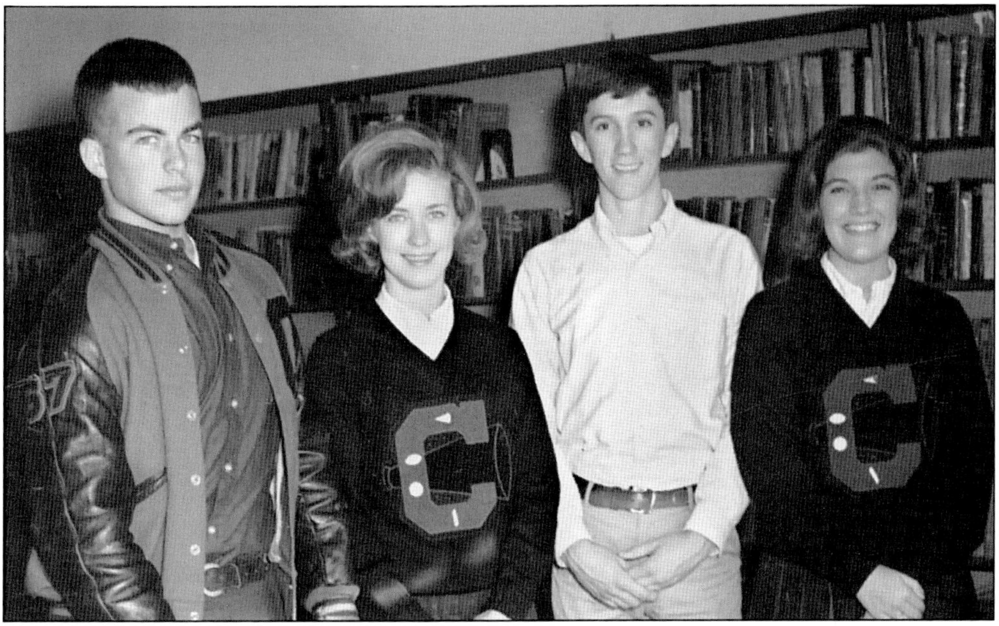

The junior class officers for Chattooga High School in 1965 include, from left to right, Jon Payne, vice president; Kay Baker, treasurer; Van Pullen, president; and Anne Cavin, secretary. (Courtesy of Joe and Jan Pullen.)

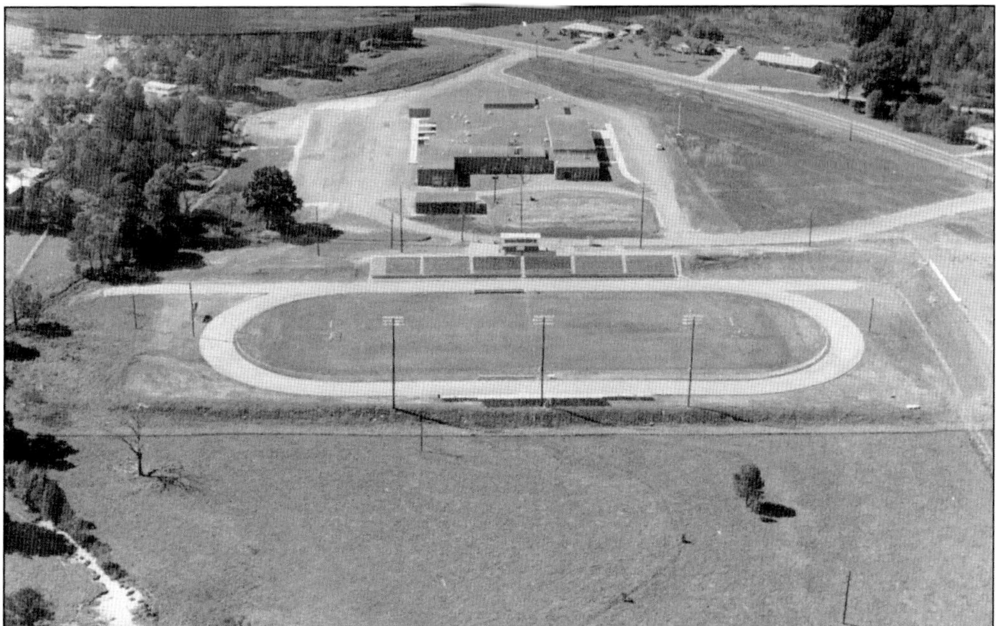

With no government funds available, the citizens of Chattooga County raised $60,000 to build a new Chattooga High School football stadium with donations and the sale of interest-bearing certificates. The new stadium was formally dedicated on October 21, 1966, with Rep. John Davis and Gov. Carl Sanders participating in the program. (Courtesy of the *Summerville News*.)

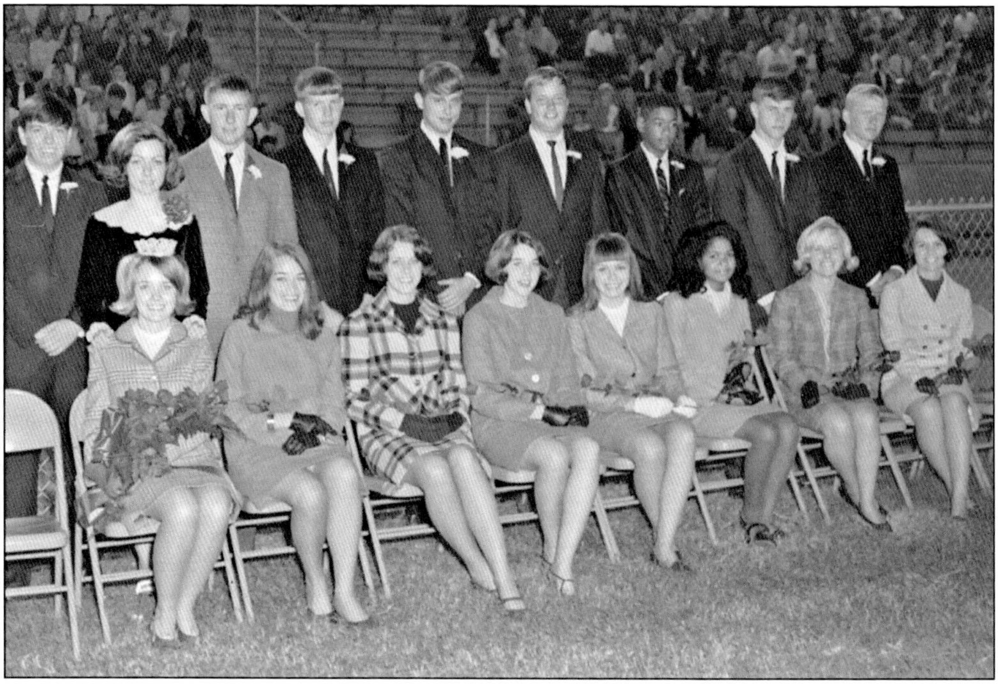

The 1967 Chattooga High School Homecoming Court candidates and escorts include, from left to right, (first row) homecoming queen Yvonne McCollum, Marla Payne, Nancy Hale, Jenette Ponder, Cindy Warren, Denise Sharp, Nancy Marks, and Susan Brooks; (second row) Zane Ham, 1966 queen Claudette Ponder, Bob Farrar, Gary Duke, Ken Kinsey, Jimmy Bagley, James Underwood, Randy James, and Eddie Morrison. (Courtesy of Yvonne McCollum Norton.)

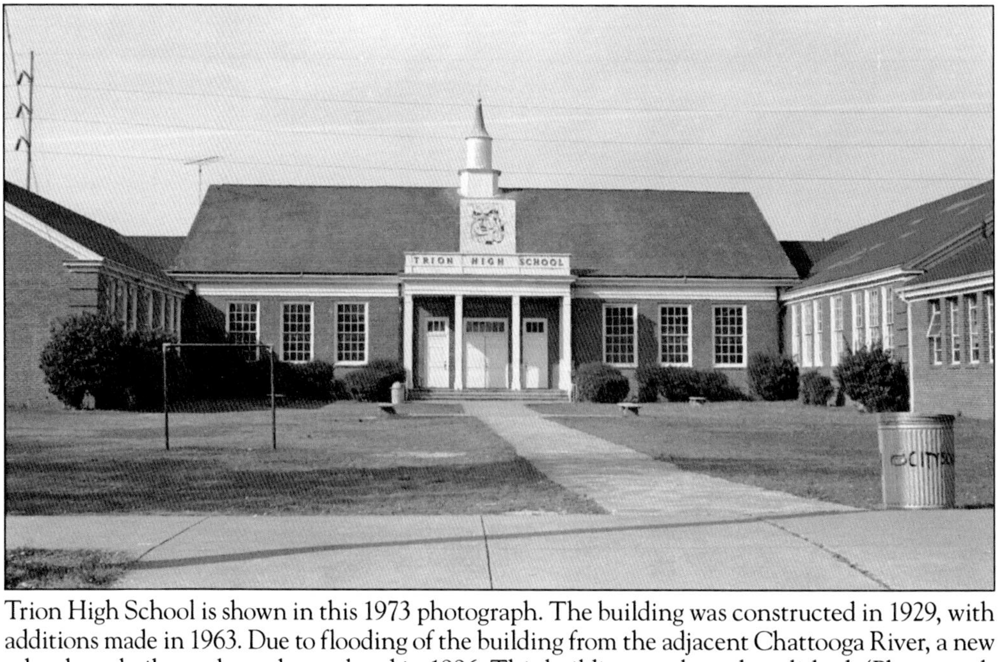

Trion High School is shown in this 1973 photograph. The building was constructed in 1929, with additions made in 1963. Due to flooding of the building from the adjacent Chattooga River, a new school was built nearby and completed in 1996. This building was later demolished. (Photograph by the author.)

Seven

HAVING FUN

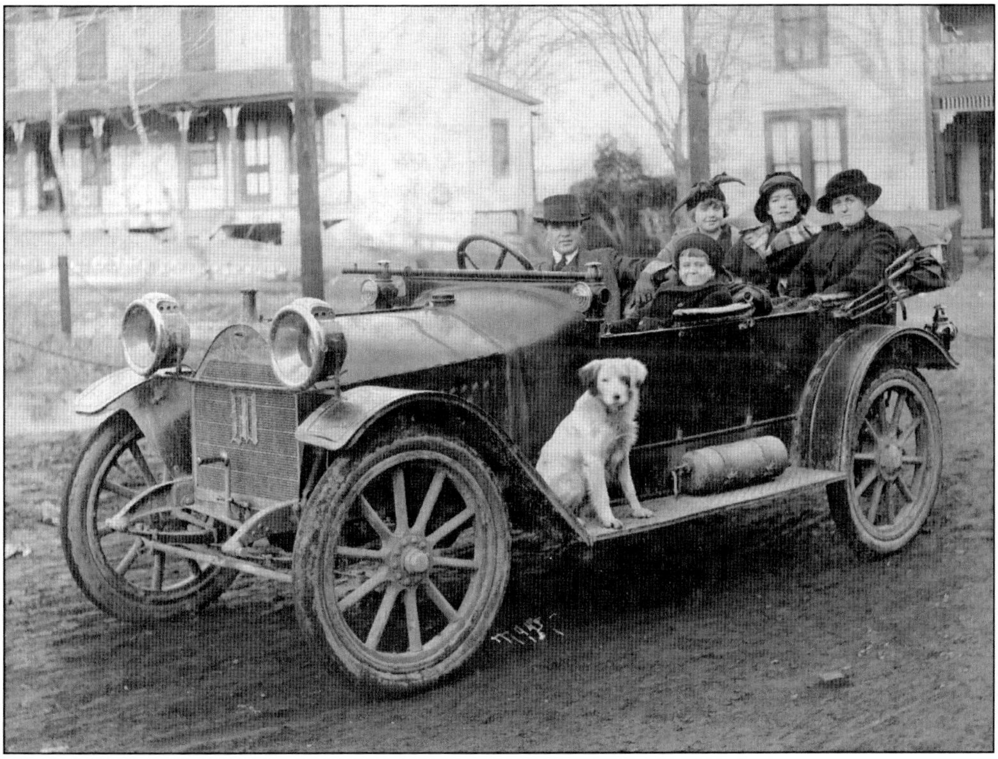

Alexander McMillan Myers Jr. enjoyed riding around Trion in his father's Hupmobile. This photograph shows young Myers with his father, Alexander McMillan Myers Sr., at the wheel. His mother, Hattie, and sister Helen sit behind them. Whenever the vehicle was cranked, his dog, Sport, would jump onto the running board. Right-hand drive automobiles were common in 1914. (Courtesy of the family collection of Alexander McMillan Myers Jr.)

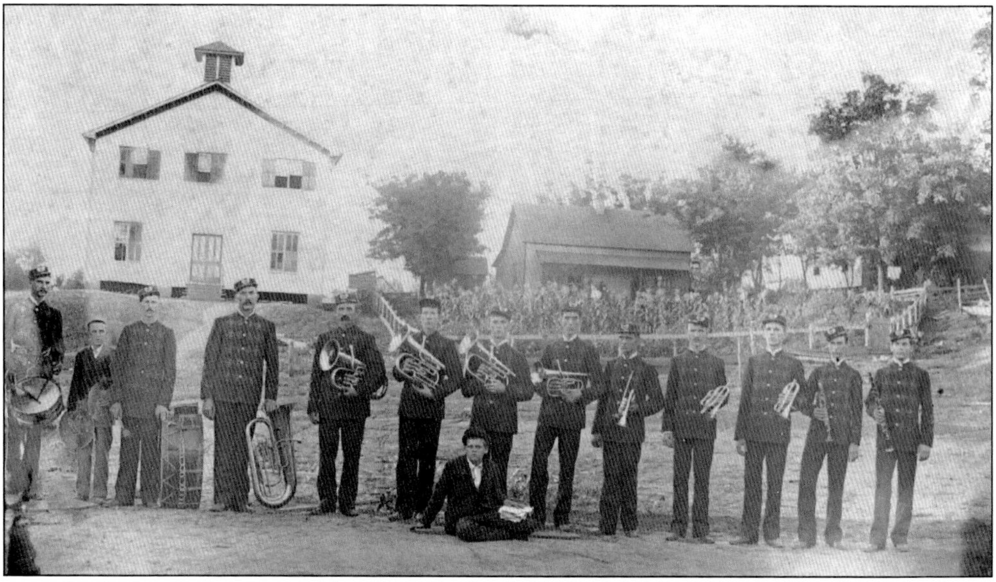

In 1897, the Trion Cornet Band includes, from left to right, Sam Strange, Tom Scoggins, Jeff Fallis, Milledge Green, Cal Green, Sandy Wooten, (sitting) "Prop" Eubanks, Russ Fallis, Walker Bryant, Henry Clark, Will Green, Jim Hogue, Lon Shamblin, and Barney Shamblin. (Photograph by Emmanuel Griffitt, courtesy of Ben T. Bridges.)

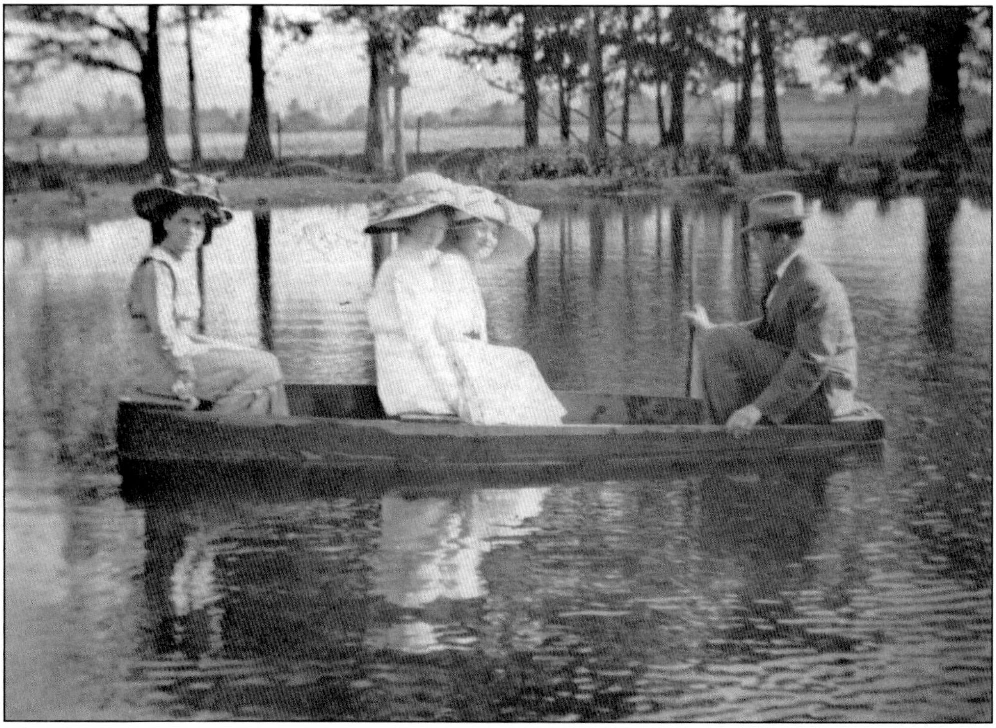

This c. 1908 photograph was taken on Raccoon Creek and shows Bessie Maxey, on the left, and Lucian Claude "L.C." Turner, on the right. Turner was born in 1883, came to Chattooga County in 1903, and later married Maxey. He was the general manager of the Summerville Cotton Mill during the 1920s and 1930s. The women in the middle are unidentified. (Courtesy of John Turner.)

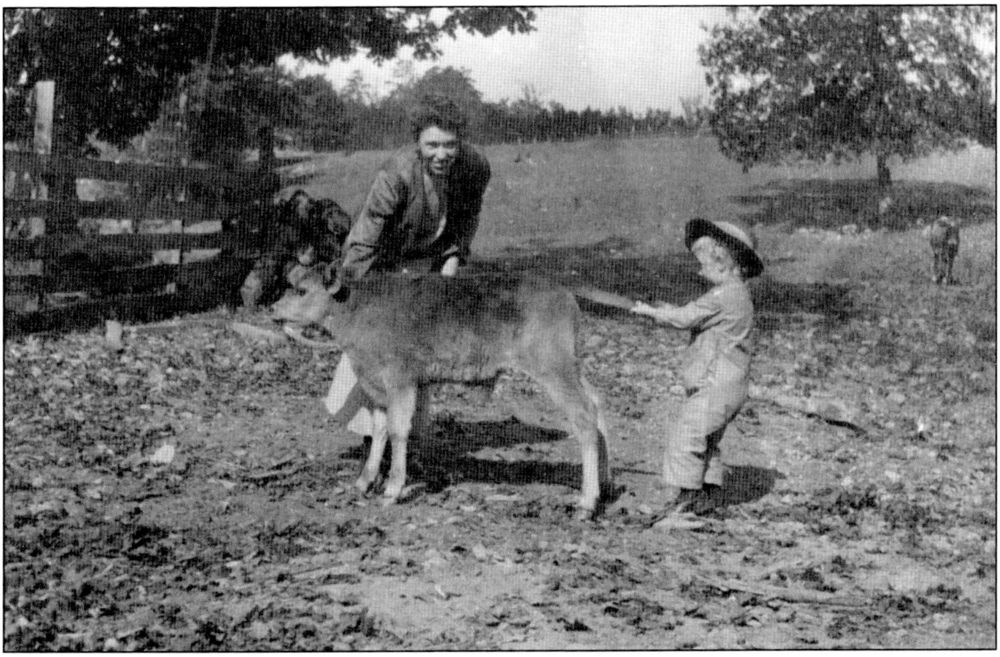

In 1891, Benjamin Franklin Weesner bought a 395-acre farm in Dirt Town and moved his family from Walker County. This photograph, taken in 1916, shows his daughter Margaret helping her nephew E.P. Scott corral a calf. The boy was born in 1913 and was the 13th grandchild of Ben Weesner. Margaret, known as "Mag," was born in 1885. (Courtesy of Thomas W. Weesner.)

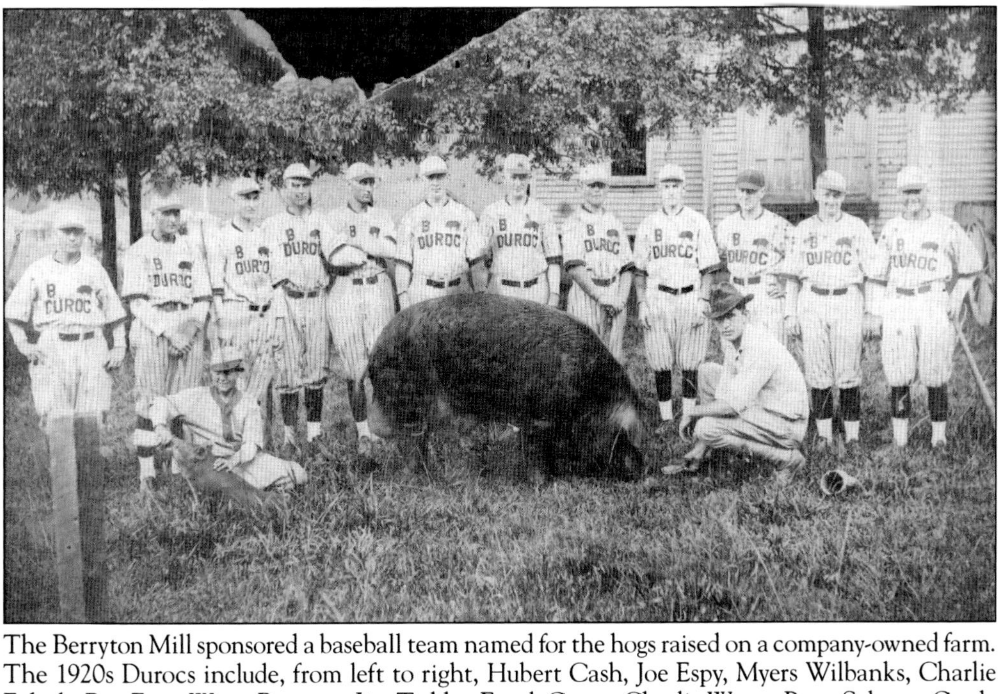

The Berryton Mill sponsored a baseball team named for the hogs raised on a company-owned farm. The 1920s Durocs include, from left to right, Hubert Cash, Joe Espy, Myers Wilbanks, Charlie Echols, Roy Espy, Wyatt Ransom, Jim Tedder, Frank Groce, Charlie Wyatt, Penn Selman, Grady Newsome, and Alfred "Shorty" Cash. Sewell Dendy seated is on the left, and "Hogg" Giles is to the right. (Courtesy of Katherine Echols Camp.)

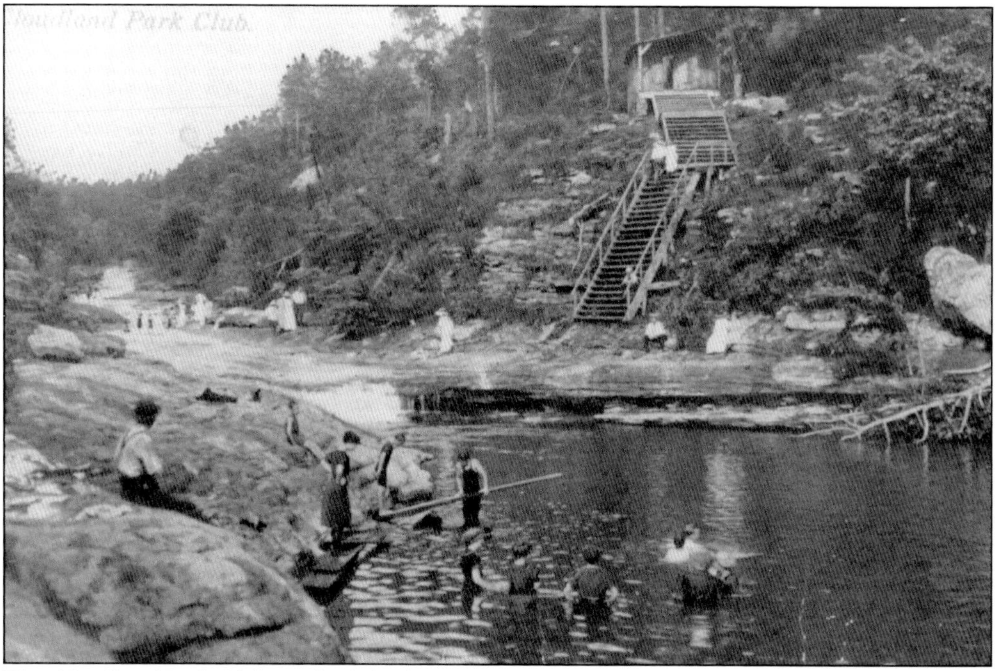

The Cloudland Park Club was built by the Ledbetter brothers of Rome in 1912 and was a popular resort, drawing visitors from surrounding states. The club expanded during the 1920s to include 50 cottages, tennis courts, a playground, and a section along Little River, pictured here, used for swimming. (Courtesy of Gene McGinnis.)

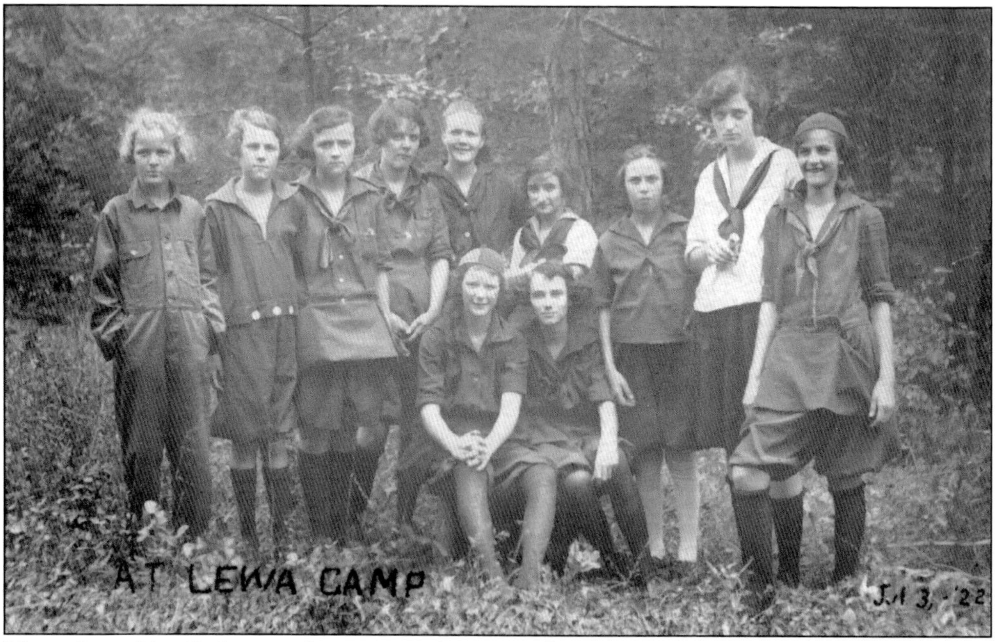

These Camp Fire Girls enjoy the great outdoors in a photograph taken in 1922. The girls include, from left to right, (first row) Jean Pless and Jimmy Cordle; (second row) Annie Marks, Margaret Pullen, Eugenia League, Julia Marks, Lucille Gamble, Katie Lee Fussill, Evelyn Pullen, Mary Meadows, and Cleland Hunt. (Courtesy of Norris Gamble.)

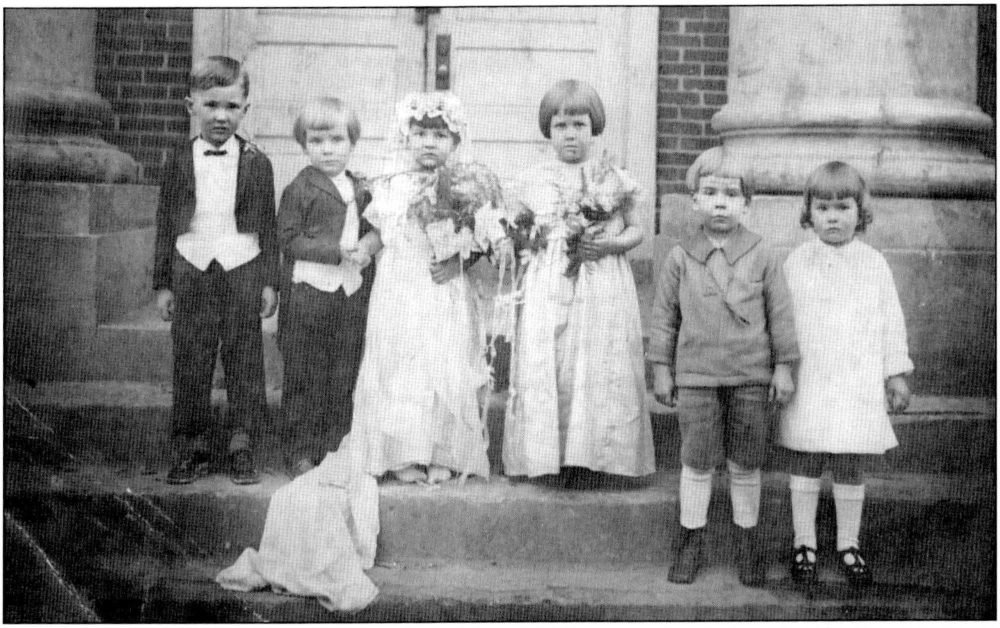

This photograph of a "Tom Thumb Wedding," taken on the steps of the Summerville School, appeared in the *Atlanta Journal* in 1926. Pictured in the photograph are, from left to right, Arch Farrar, best man; William K. Cleghorn, bridegroom; Vivian Howard, bride; Viola Newsome, maid of honor; Charles Turner, ring-bearer; and Clara Whitlow, train-bearer. Miniature weddings became popular fundraisers for schools and churches. (Courtesy of Janet Farrar Byington.)

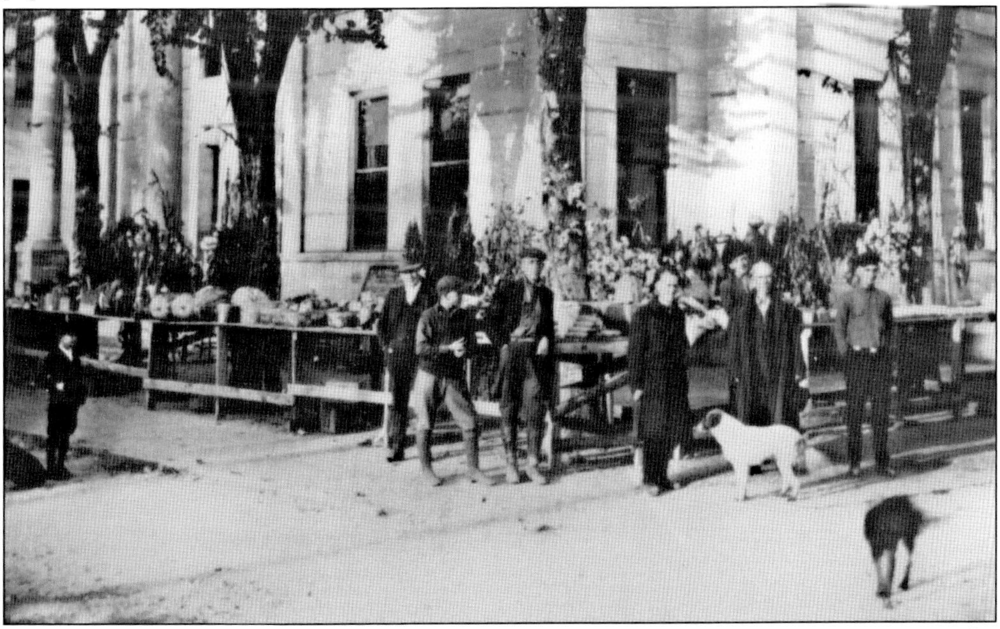

In 1904, the first annual Chattooga County Fair was held on Commerce Street in Summerville. Farmers and their families came from all over Chattooga County to see livestock and farm products, participate in games such as the greased-pig race, and cheer their favorites in foot and bicycle races. This photograph shows some of the exhibit tables lined up around the courthouse. (Courtesy of Gene McGinnis.)

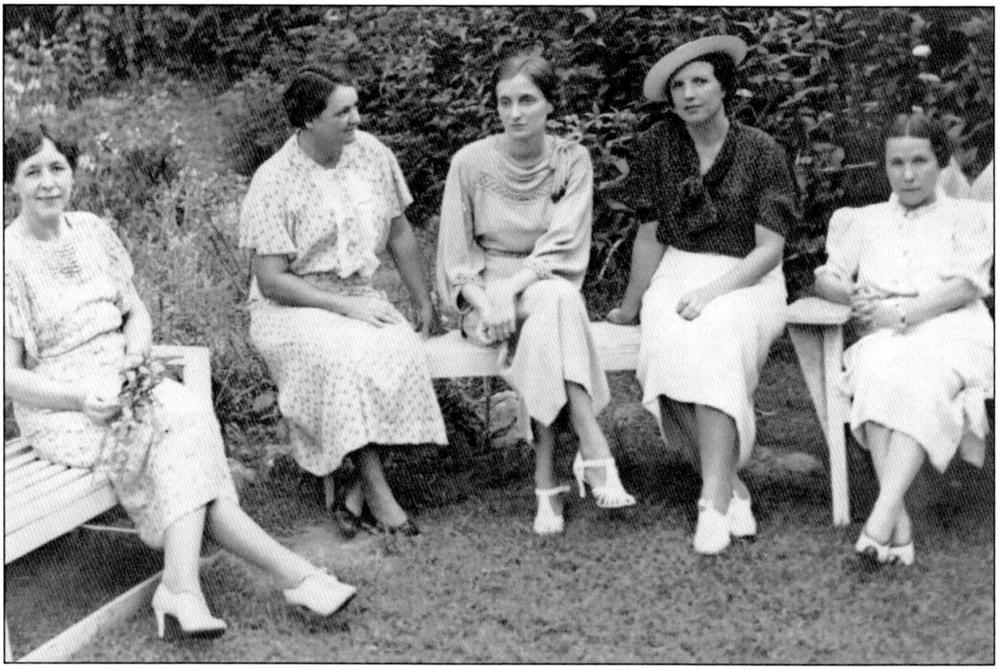

The Chattooga County Garden Club officers in 1936 include, from left to right, Mrs. J.H. Shumate, Mrs. William B. Hair, Mrs. Clarkson, Mrs. Hawkins, and Mrs. E.R. Bufkin. The club started in 1930 with Mrs. Shumate as president. (Courtesy of Will and Judy Hair.)

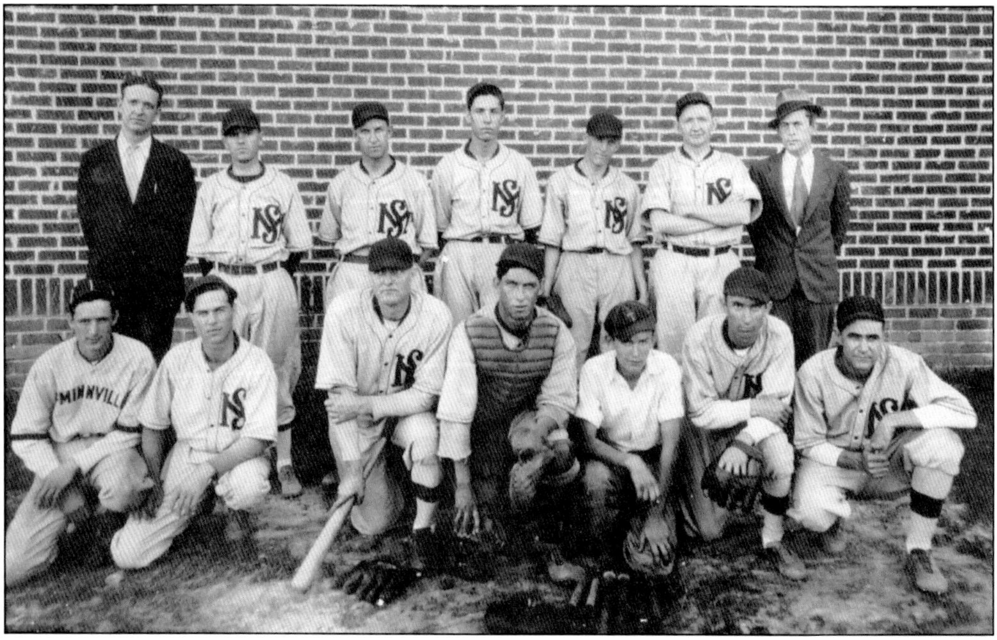

This Summerville Merchants baseball team includes, from left to right, (first row) Fred Stewart, Jim Mosley, Leon Gamble Sr., Ralph Alexander, unidentified, Luther Smith Jr., and unidentified; (second row) unidentified, Marvin "Punk" Pullen, two unidentified, Joe Pullen, J.R. Burgess, and sponsor Walter C. Sturdivant. At the time this photograph was made, around 1939, Sturdivant was the manager of Montgomery Knitting Mill. (Courtesy of L.C. Smith.)

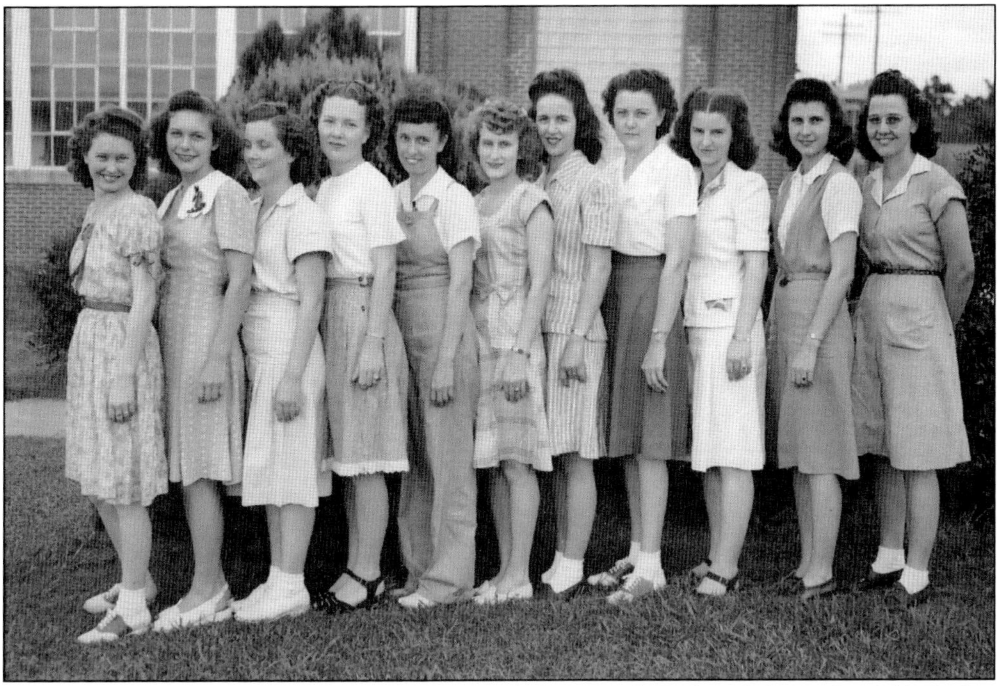

These contestants for the title of Trion Centennial Queen include, from left to right, Syble Butler, Annette Lankford, Mildred Speer, Margaret Wardlaw, Grace Leigh, Bessie Lou Taylor, Thelma Stoker, Frances Mullen, Lorene Lanier, Faye Gilliland, and Evelyn Cook. Each young woman represents one of the departments of the textile mill. Wardlaw won the 1945 title based on votes cast by the Trion Company employees. (Courtesy of Charles Logan.)

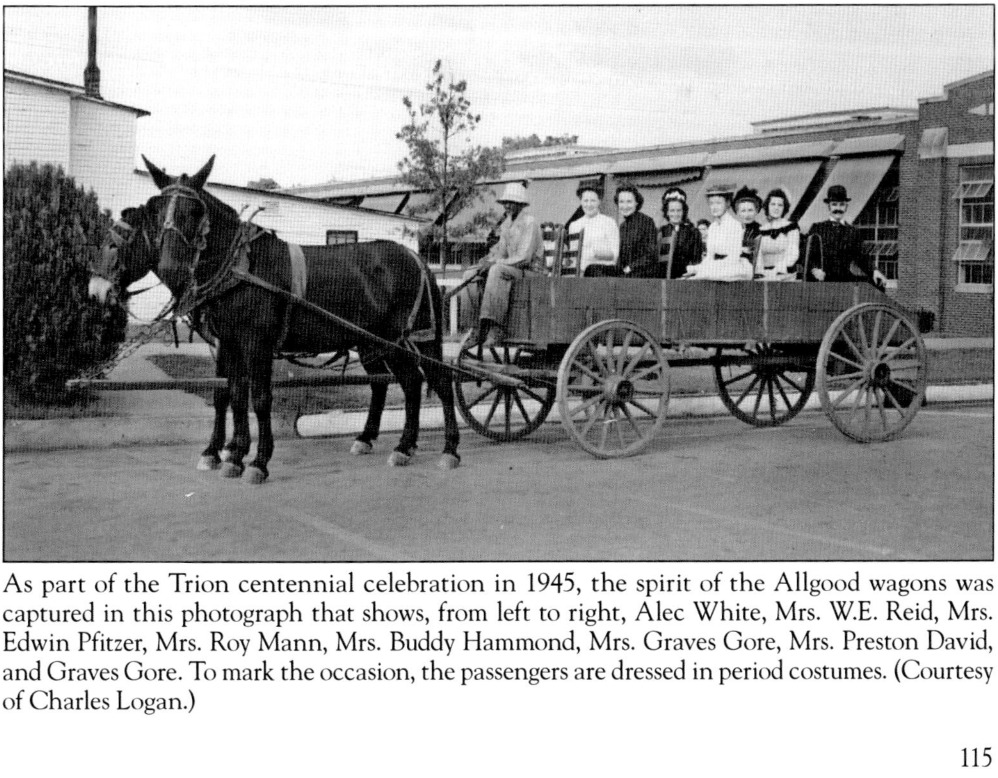

As part of the Trion centennial celebration in 1945, the spirit of the Allgood wagons was captured in this photograph that shows, from left to right, Alec White, Mrs. W.E. Reid, Mrs. Edwin Pfitzer, Mrs. Roy Mann, Mrs. Buddy Hammond, Mrs. Graves Gore, Mrs. Preston David, and Graves Gore. To mark the occasion, the passengers are dressed in period costumes. (Courtesy of Charles Logan.)

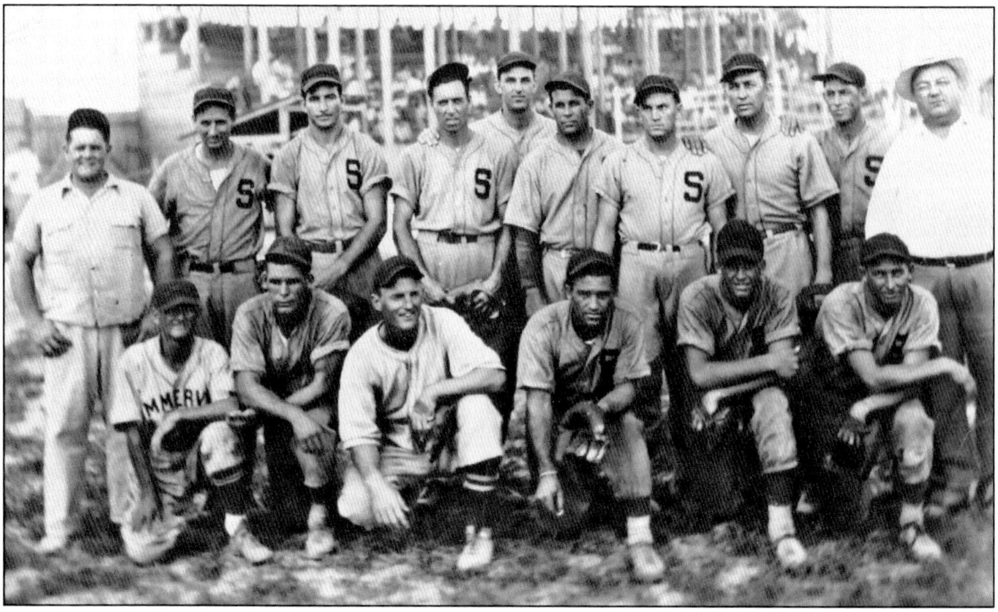

This textile league baseball team, pictured around 1946, includes, from left to right, (first row) Shorty Cash, Bill Young, Bill Cavin, Johnny Nelson, Jack Cash, and A.L. Alexander; (second row) David Koonce, Fred Stewart, Lefty Broome, Buck Rich, Clebow Jackson, Paul Silvers, Joe Pullen, George Baker, and Ralph Alexander. J.A. Wilson (second row, far right) is the team's business manager. (Courtesy of Rex Evans.)

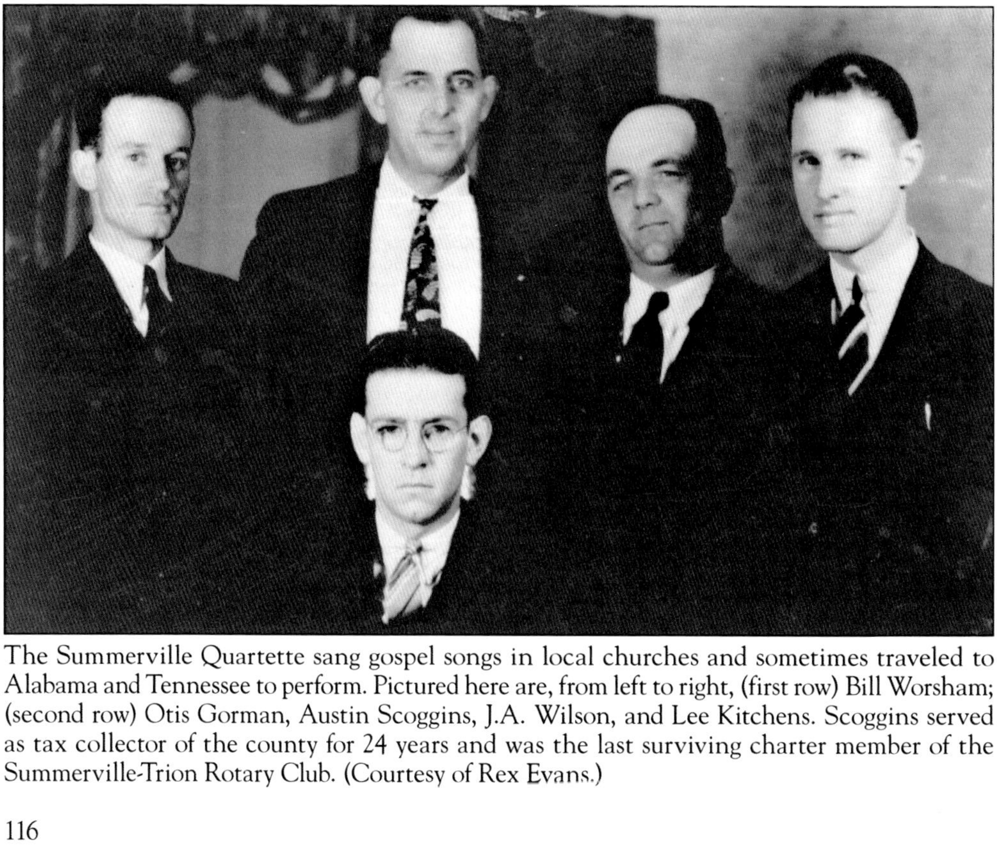

The Summerville Quartette sang gospel songs in local churches and sometimes traveled to Alabama and Tennessee to perform. Pictured here are, from left to right, (first row) Bill Worsham; (second row) Otis Gorman, Austin Scoggins, J.A. Wilson, and Lee Kitchens. Scoggins served as tax collector of the county for 24 years and was the last surviving charter member of the Summerville-Trion Rotary Club. (Courtesy of Rex Evans.)

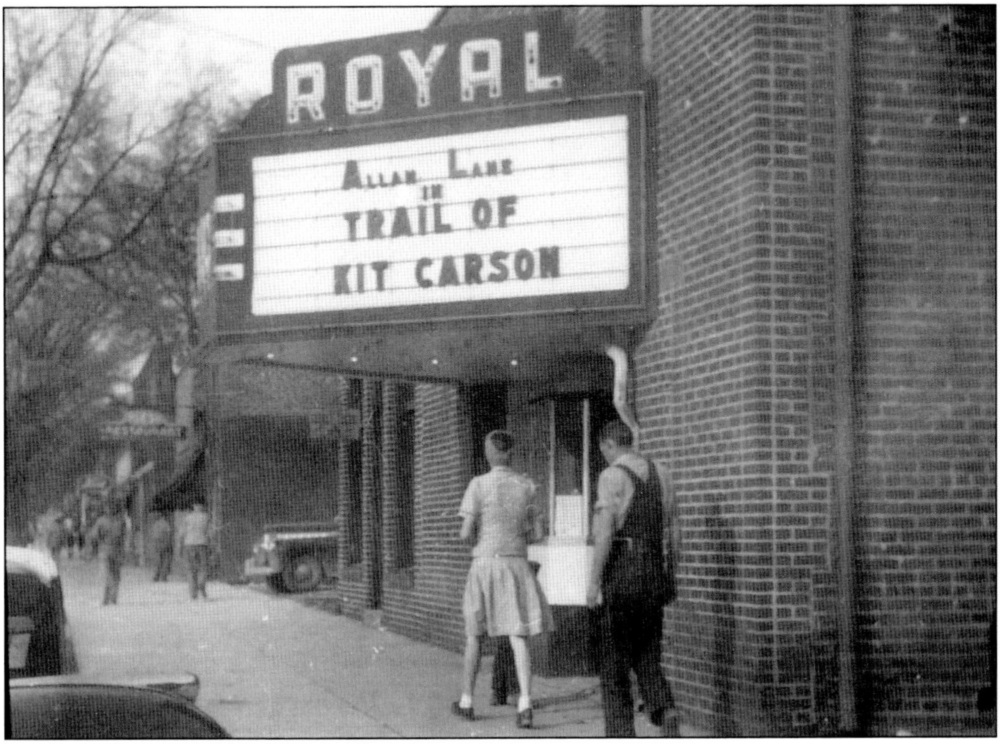

The Royal Theater was built in 1927 at the northeast corner of Commerce Street and Georgia Avenue in Summerville. C.W. Maxey and his sister, Mrs. L.C. Turner (Bessie), were the owners. This photograph was taken in 1946. (Courtesy of L.C. Smith.)

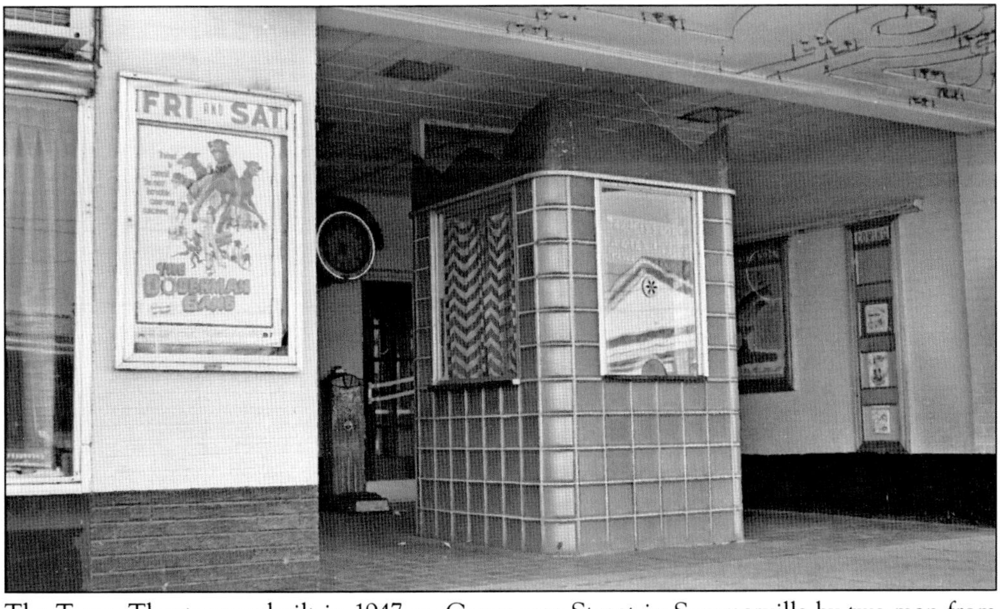

The Tooga Theater was built in 1947 on Commerce Street in Summerville by two men from Ellijay, Georgia. Shortly afterward, the Royal Theater closed, and its manager, Luther C. Smith Jr., transferred to the new Tooga. Smith later purchased the theater and operated it until it closed in the late 1970s. (Photograph by the author.)

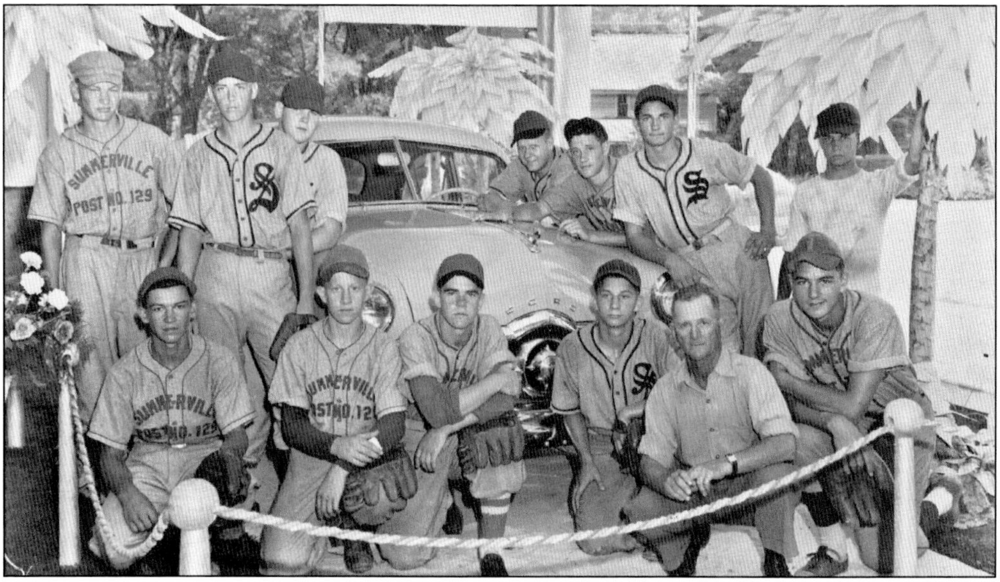

Hair Motor Company was one of the sponsors of this American Legion baseball team. Shown in this 1948 photograph are, from left to right, (first row) Johnny Brady, Bobby Bush, Bobby Nix, Joe Fay Dacus, manager Alfred "Shorty" Cash, and Bennie Perry; (second row) Ski Donovitch, Sewell Cash, Billy Joe Gilmer, Lee Gilbert, Jimmy Bush, Herman Fletcher, and Ralph Stanley. (Courtesy of the *Summerville News*.)

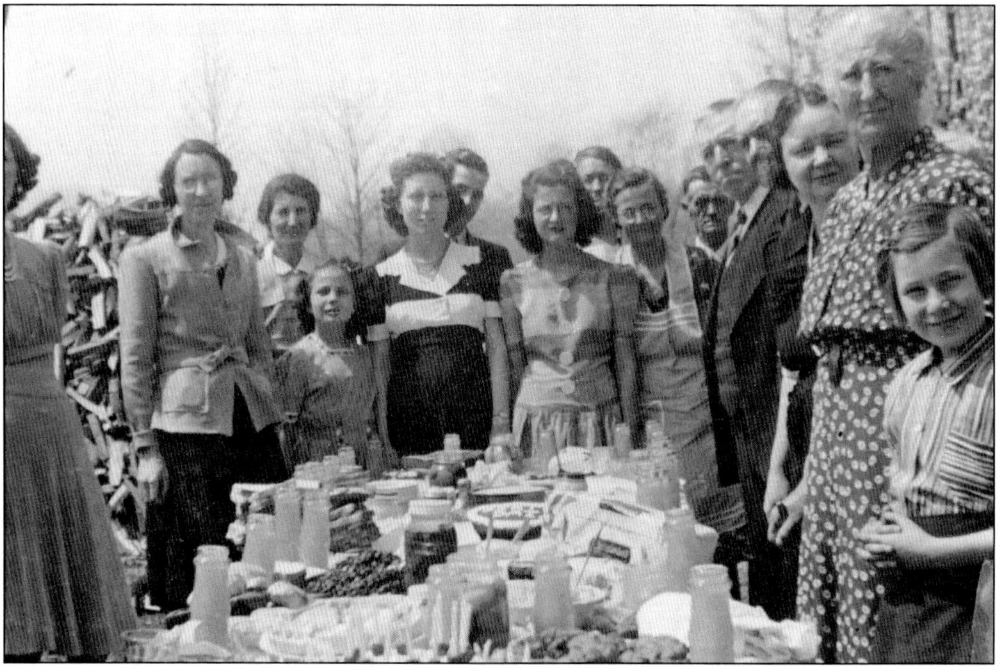

Ella Pettyjohn (on right, behind a granddaughter) celebrates a birthday in the early 1950s with family and friends at her home east of Trion. She was born Ella Queen Hendrix in 1879. Standing at the far end of the table are, from left to right, niece Louise Hendrix Logan, granddaughter Joyce Wooten Brown, daughter Minnie Pettyjohn Wardlaw, and granddaughter Doris Wooten Stowe. (Courtesy of Beth Wardlaw Romine.)

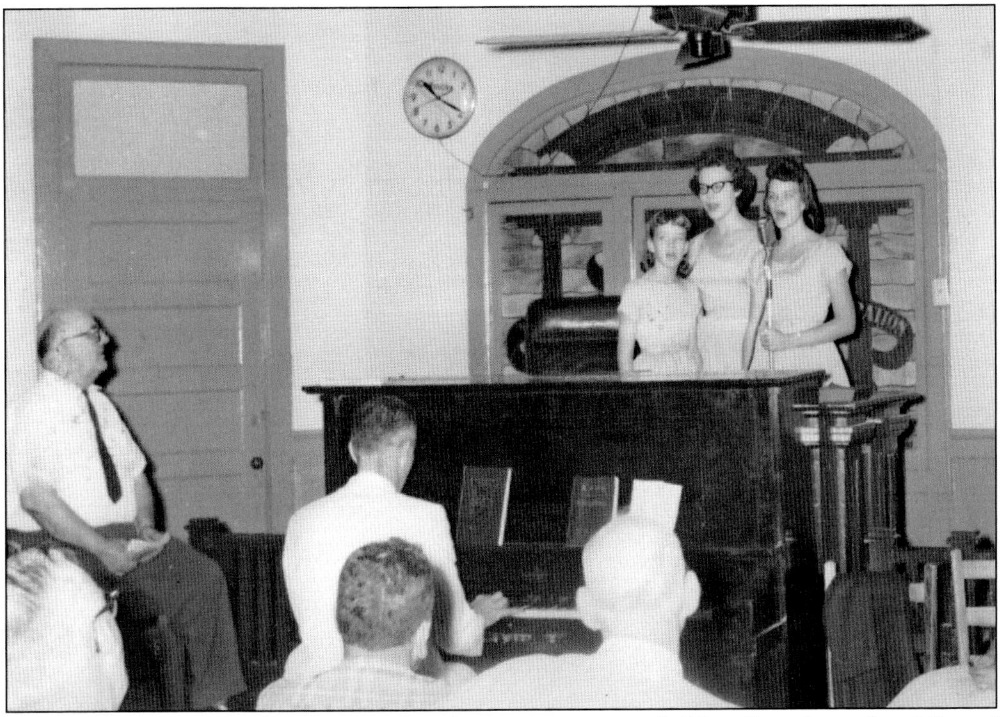

During the late 1940s and early 1950s, courthouse concerts were held on Saturday nights, followed by all-day singings on Sunday. J.A. Wilson, seated on the left, was instrumental in arranging the concerts. The ladies standing behind the piano were known as the Kentucky Singers. (Courtesy of Rex Evans.)

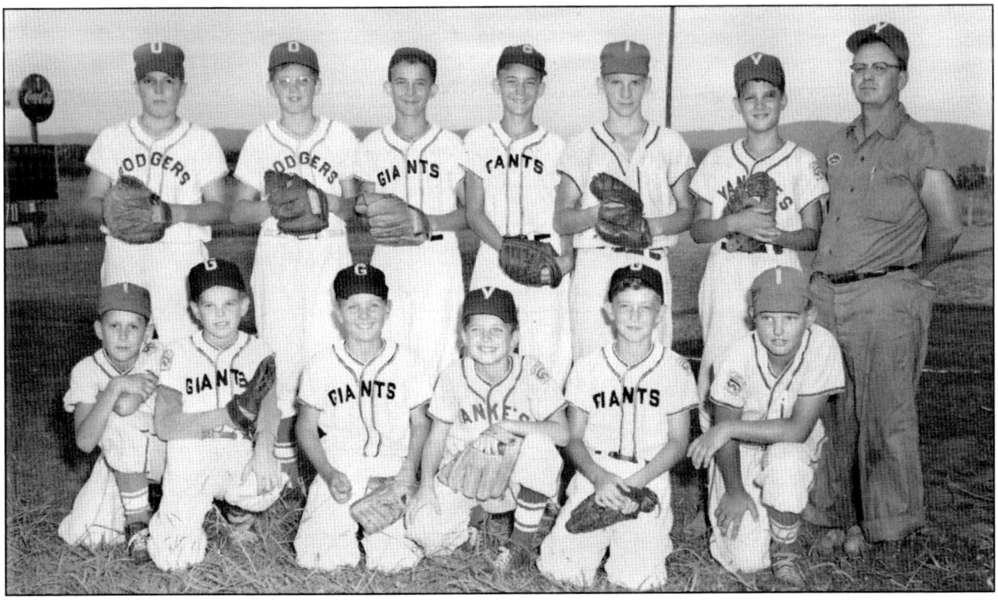

The 1957 Summerville Little League All-Star team includes, from left to right, (first row) Billy Ash, Freddie Edwards, Larry Holbrook, Mike Ash, Mike Baker, and David Mitchell; (second row) Peter Boney, Chip Barnes, Jerry Taylor, Terry Taylor, Billy Hawkins, Ronnie McGill, and coach Harper Edwards. (Courtesy of Steve Edwards.)

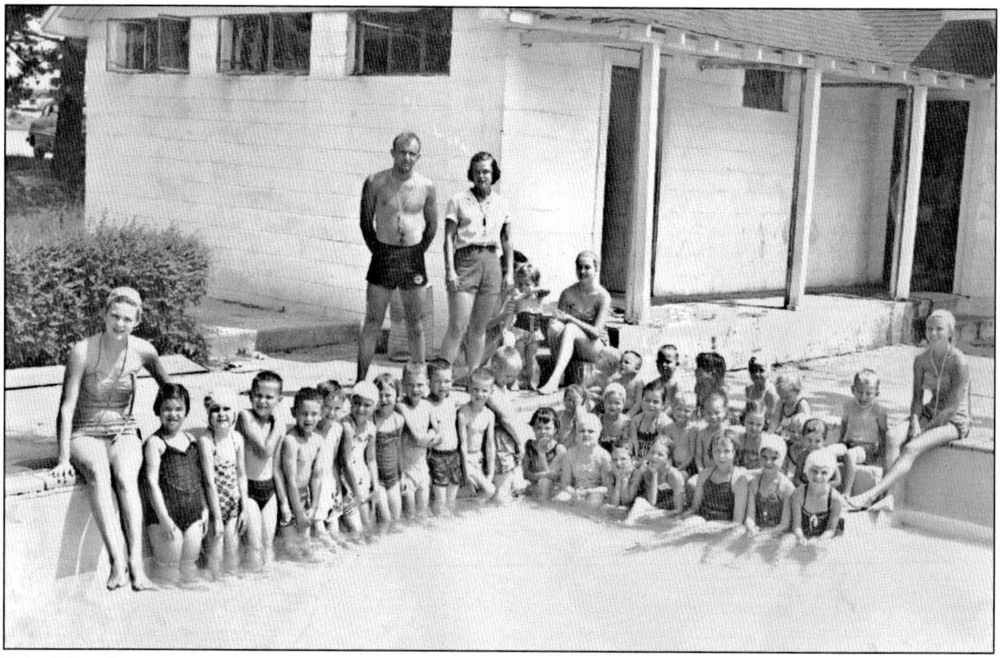

John's Pool was opened in 1946 by Trion resident John Allen Justice. Located in the Dickeyville area south of Trion, it was a popular gathering place for children and teenagers in the 1950s. Many children first learned to swim under the guidance of the pool's instructors, as shown in this 1955 photograph. (Courtesy of Paul Marks.)

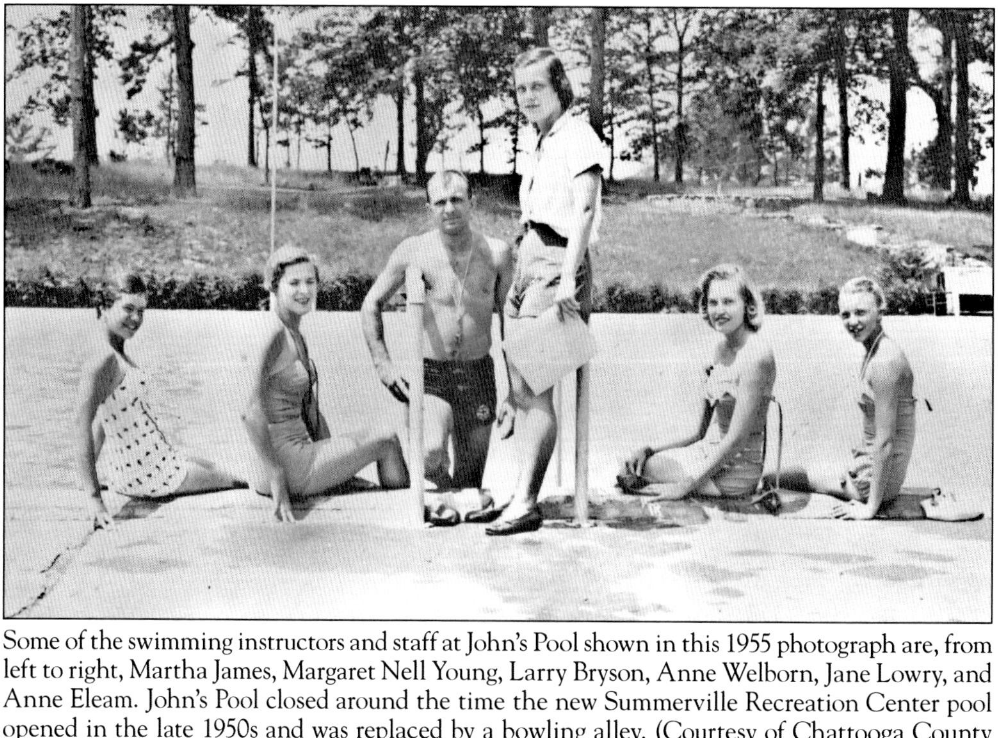

Some of the swimming instructors and staff at John's Pool shown in this 1955 photograph are, from left to right, Martha James, Margaret Nell Young, Larry Bryson, Anne Welborn, Jane Lowry, and Anne Eleam. John's Pool closed around the time the new Summerville Recreation Center pool opened in the late 1950s and was replaced by a bowling alley. (Courtesy of Chattooga County Chamber of Commerce.)

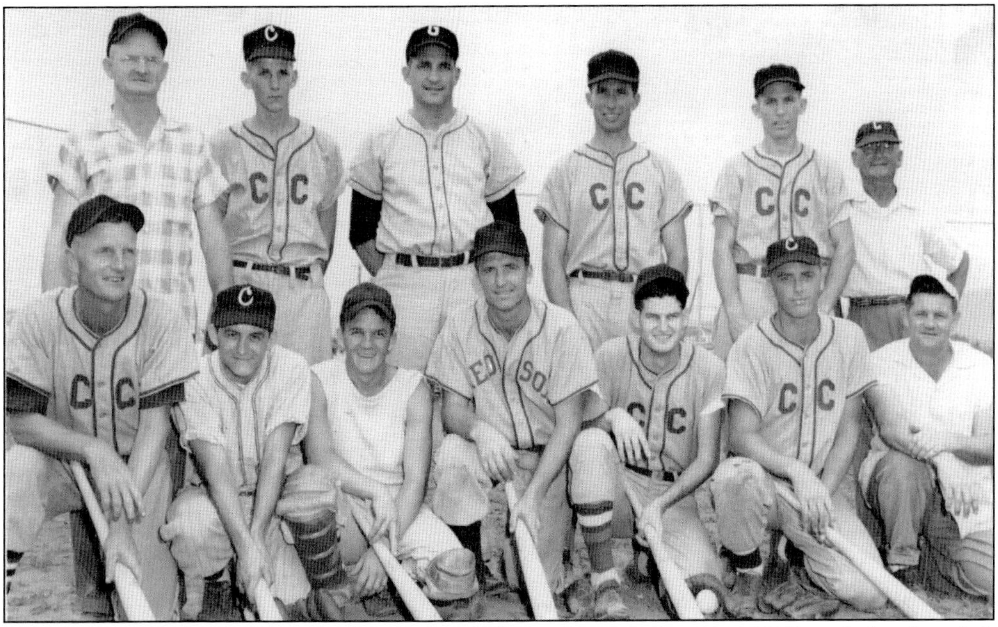

Chattooga County's independent league baseball team, pictured around 1956, includes, from left to right, (first row) Bill Cavin, Roy Cox, David Koonce Jr., Jack Cash, Emory Gilmer, Sewell Cash, and manager David Koonce; (second row) Joe Gilmer, Roy Woods, Herman Fletcher, Wayne Groce, Joe Cash, and Shorty Cash. (Courtesy of Sewell Cash.)

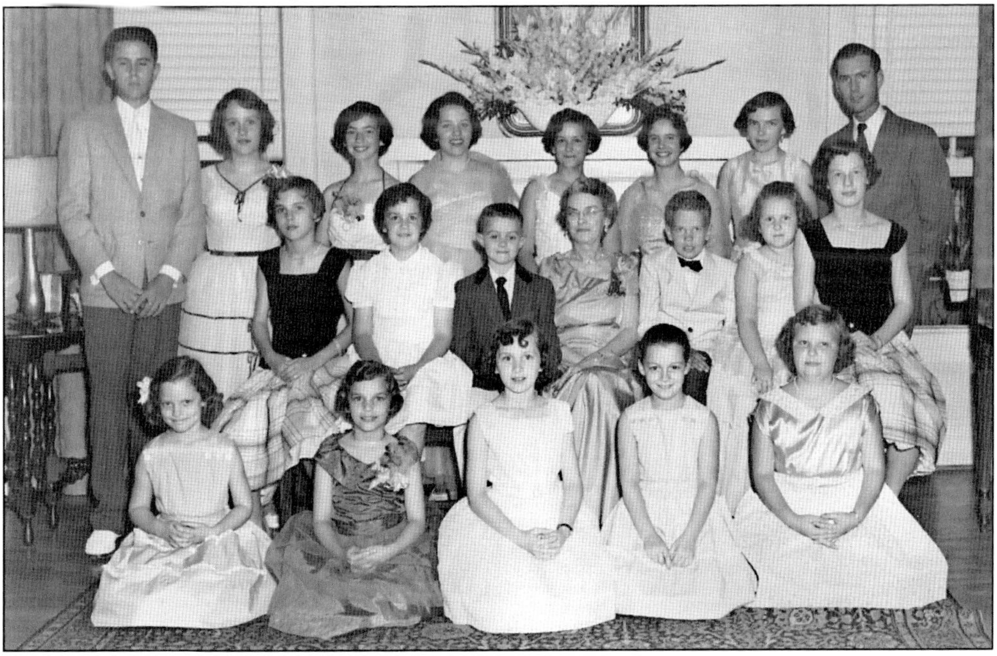

Mrs. Duke Espy is shown with her piano pupils in this 1956 photograph. From left to right are (first row) unidentified, Margaret Wheeler, Jan Packer, unidentified, and Marie Wiley; (second row) Paula Allen, Marcia Boney, Jimmy Hill, Mrs. Espy, Mike Woodard, unidentified, and Jenith Thomas; (third row) Farrell Allen, unidentified, Linda Wheeler, Brenda Wilson, Betty Hamner, Marty James, Mary Fink, and Jimmy Duff. (Courtesy of Gene McGinnis.)

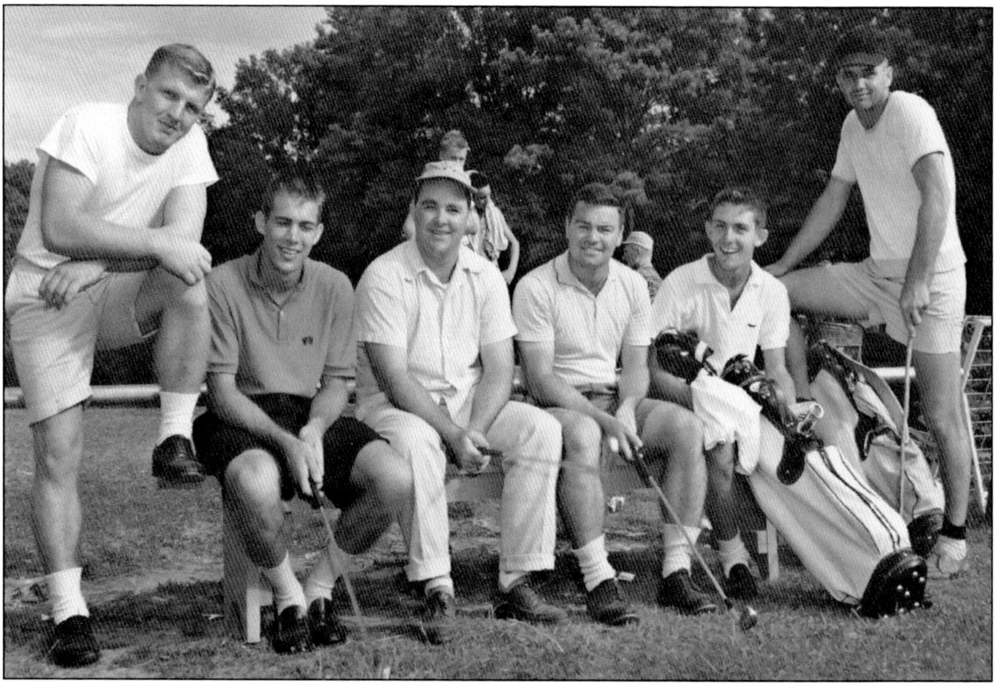

These golfers enjoyed playing in a tournament at the Trion course in August 1958. From left to right are Ken Day, Jack Shamblin, Ralph Tilley, Leon Hardeman, Darriel Broom, and J.W. Greenwood. (Courtesy of Jim Styles.)

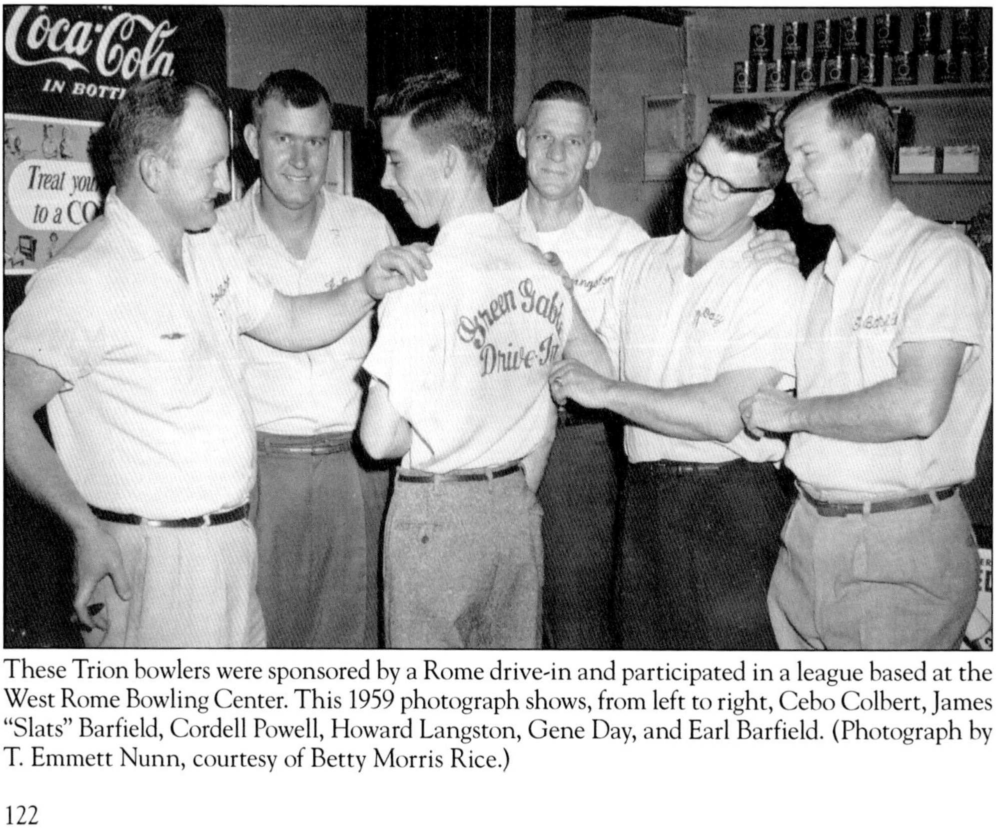

These Trion bowlers were sponsored by a Rome drive-in and participated in a league based at the West Rome Bowling Center. This 1959 photograph shows, from left to right, Cebo Colbert, James "Slats" Barfield, Cordell Powell, Howard Langston, Gene Day, and Earl Barfield. (Photograph by T. Emmett Nunn, courtesy of Betty Morris Rice.)

The Trion Business and Professional Women's Club held a Spring Fashion Show at the school auditorium in 1959. Little Connie Cobb watches as her mother, Bonnie, adjusts her straw hat. (Photograph by T. Emmett Nunn, courtesy of Betty Morris Rice.)

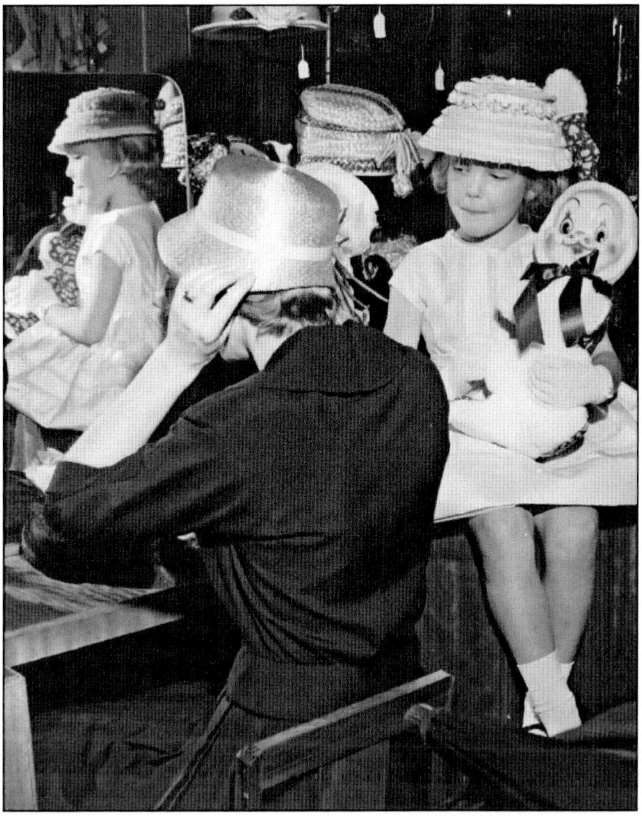

Mary Salley (right) proudly displays her blue ribbon won in the annual Cherokee Rose Garden Club Flower Show in 1959. Standing with her are, from left to right, Kris Cook and Becky Lindsay. The annual flower show was held at the Summerville Recreation Center and was a popular attraction for many years. (Photograph by T. Emmett Nunn, courtesy of Betty Morris Rice.)

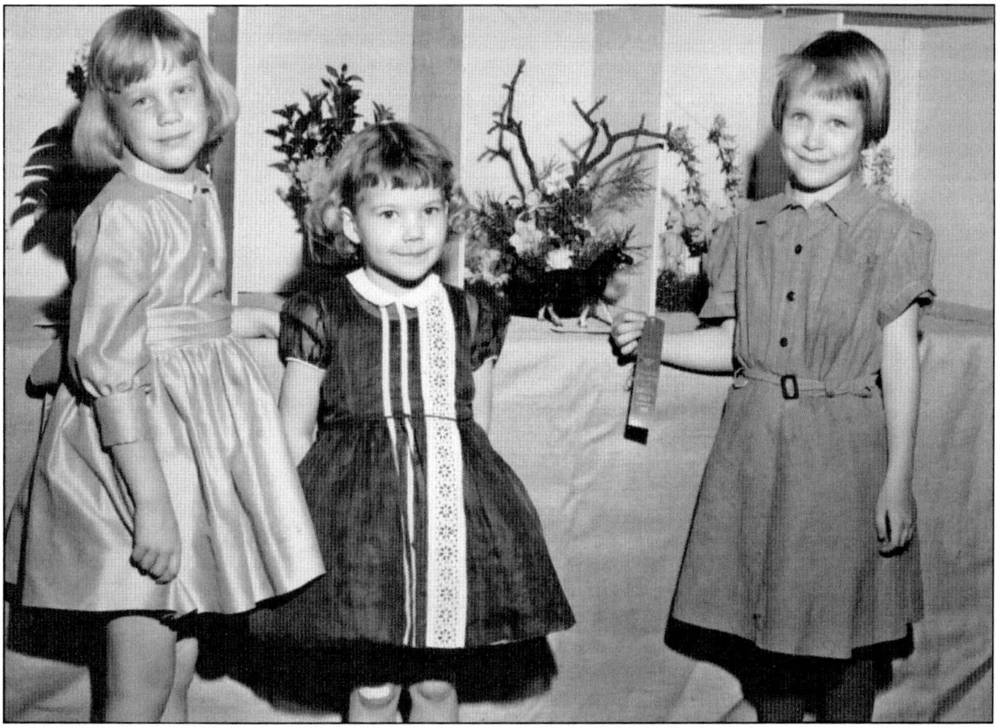

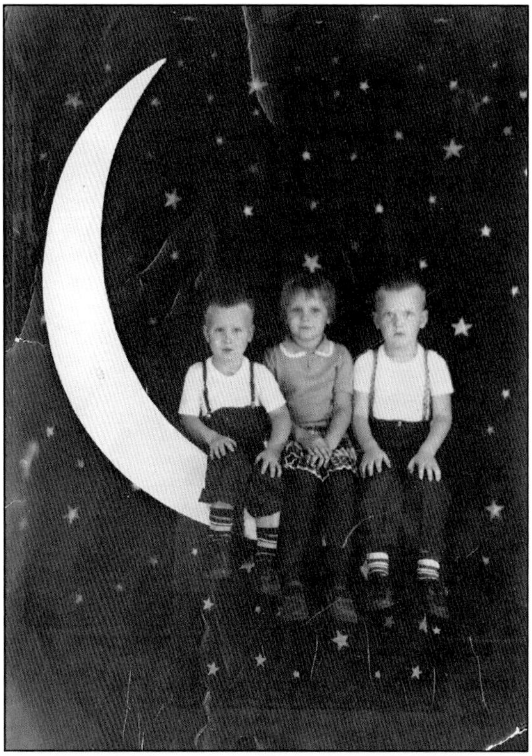

It's only a paper moon for the children of Billy and Doris Norton at the Chattooga County Fair. Shown in this 1959 photograph are, from left to right, Joel, Darlene, and Billy Norton Jr. As agriculture and farming declined in the county and other leisure activities became popular, attendance at the fair declined. After 1977, it was discontinued. (Courtesy of Darlene Norton Mallonee.)

Carolyn Dooley (center) was crowned queen of the First Annual Turkey Bowl in 1962. The youth football event was sponsored by the Summerville Recreation Department and took place at Sturdivant Field on the old Chattooga High School campus. (Photograph by T. Emmett Nunn, courtesy of Betty Morris Rice.)

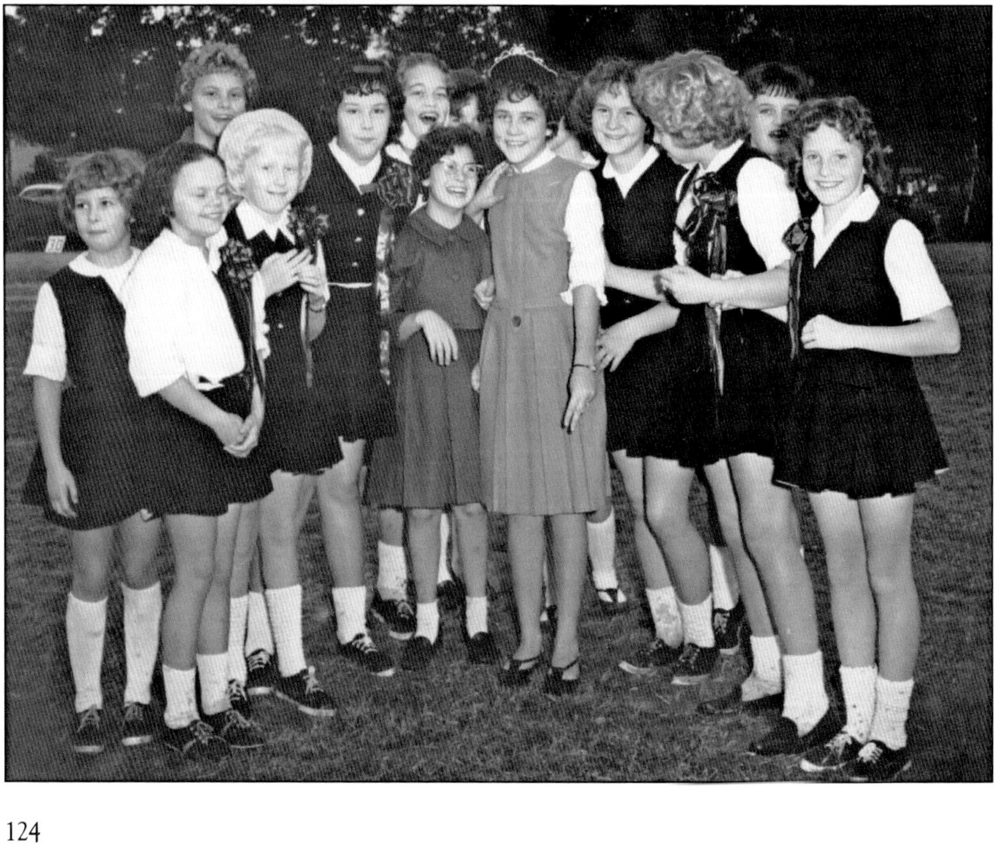

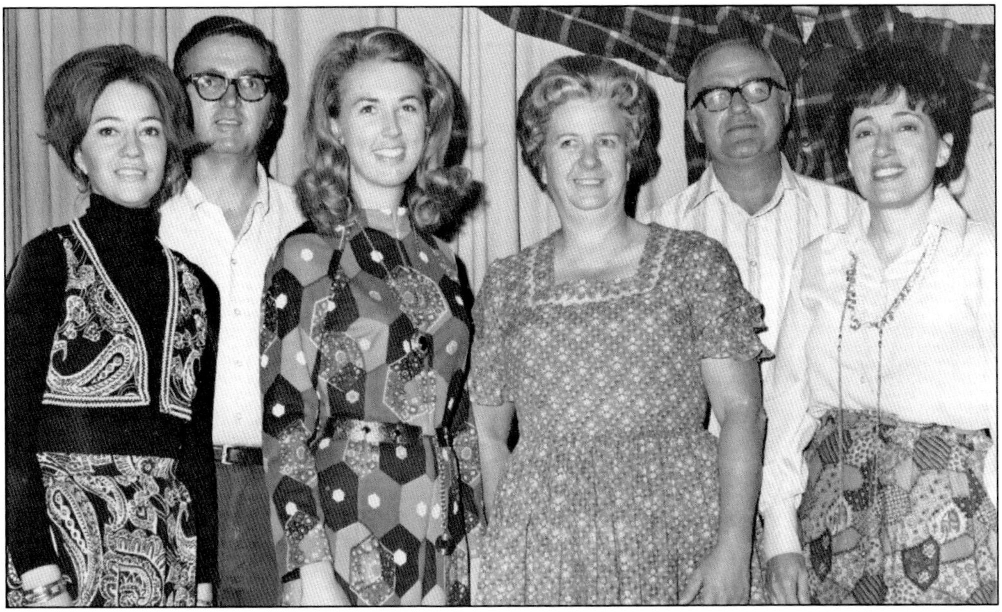

The Follies was a fundraiser for the Chattooga High School Band featuring local singers and dancers. It was performed at the Chattooga Junior High School auditorium in 1978. Some of the people who helped organize the show include, from left to right, Phyllis Payne, Will Hair, Pam Echols, Elliot King, Andrew Williams, and Sue Spivey. (Courtesy of Sue Spivey.)

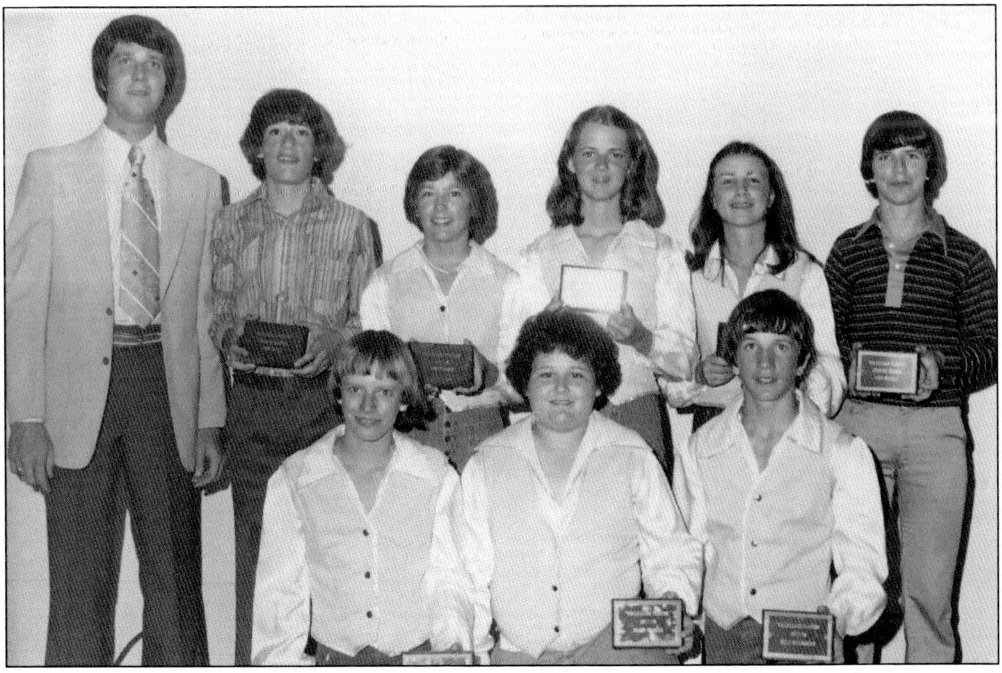

The Hallelujah Players were students from Summerville Junior High School who performed musical variety shows at local schools and throughout the Southeast. This 1978 photograph includes, from left to right, (first row) Alex Brown, Barry Bridges, and Billy Willingham; (second row) teacher and group founder Steve Jones, Peck Spivey, Lori Pledger, Peggy Hair, Molly Thompson, and Lane Sentell. (Courtesy of Sue Spivey.)

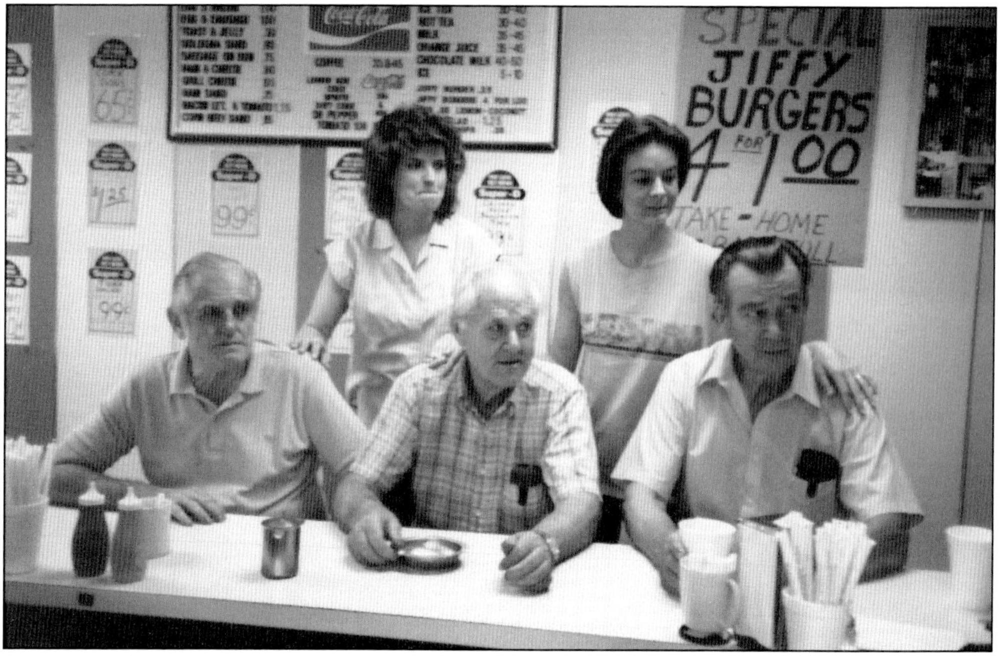

The Super-D Store across from the courthouse on Commerce Street operated a popular lunch counter for many years. This 1986 photograph shows, from left to right, (first row) "Pop" Henderson, Cecil Herod, and Woodrow Greene; (second row) unidentified and Betty Mundy. Longtime manager Robert Floyd recalls having birthday cake for the regulars and caroling at Christmas. The store closed in 1989. (Photograph by Sue Spivey, courtesy of Robert Floyd.)

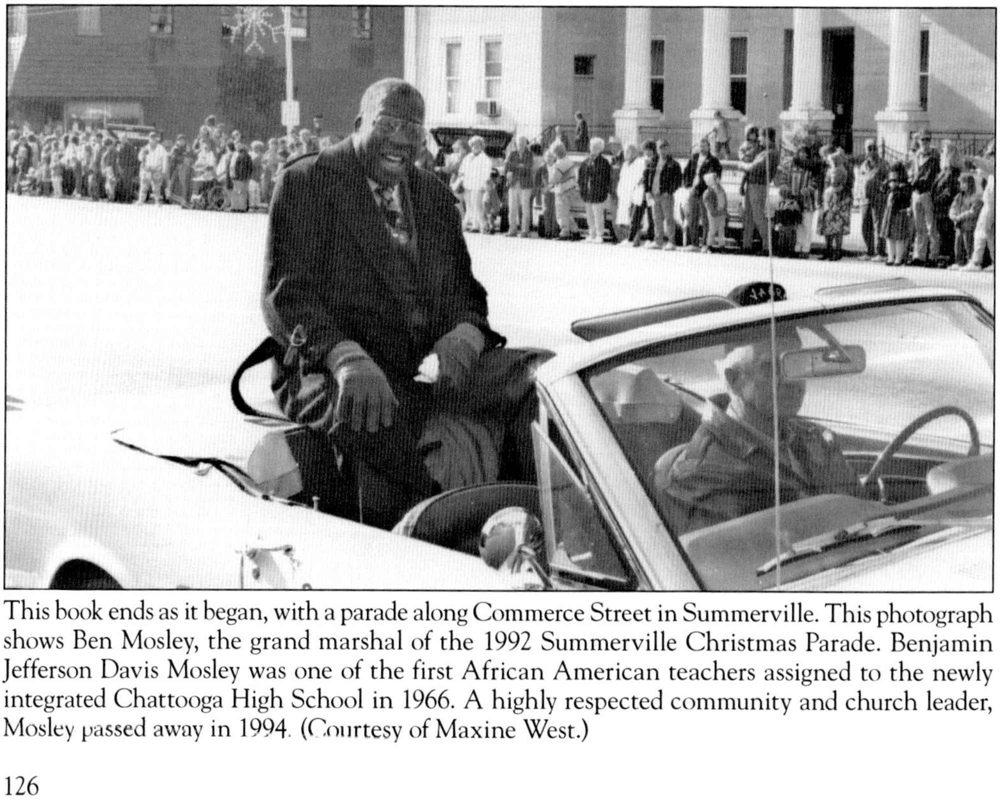

This book ends as it began, with a parade along Commerce Street in Summerville. This photograph shows Ben Mosley, the grand marshal of the 1992 Summerville Christmas Parade. Benjamin Jefferson Davis Mosley was one of the first African American teachers assigned to the newly integrated Chattooga High School in 1966. A highly respected community and church leader, Mosley passed away in 1994. (Courtesy of Maxine West.)

BIBLIOGRAPHY

Baker, Robert S. *Chattooga: The Story of a County and Its People*. Roswell, GA: W.H. Wolfe Associates, 1988.

Chattooga County Heritage Book Committee. *Heritage Book of Chattooga County, Georgia, 1838–2006*. Waynesville, NC: County Heritage, 2006.

Taylor, John D. *Leaves in the Wind*. Summerville, GA: Self-published. 1976.

Watson, Lily Marberry. *The History of Riegeldale Tavern*. Summerville, GA: Espy Publishing, 1976.

Wingfield, Jessie. *Trion: Our Own Favored Land*. Summerville, GA: Espy Publishing, 1976.